Constructing Gendered Bodies

Edited by

Kathryn Backett-Milburn
Senior Research Fellow
Research Unit in Health and Behavioural Change
University of Edinburgh

and

Linda McKie
Research Professor in Sociology
Glasgow Caledonian University

Review Editors

Ellen Annandale
Senior Lecturer
Department of Sociology
University of Leicester

and

Anne Kerr
Research Fellow
Department of Sociology
University of Edinburgh

palgrave

First published 2001 by
PALGRAVE
Houndmills, Basingstoke, Hampshire RG21 6XS and
175 Fifth Avenue, New York, N.Y. 10010
Companies and representatives throughout the world

PALGRAVE is the new global academic imprint of
St. Martin's Press LLC Scholarly and Reference Division and
Palgrave Publishers Ltd (formerly Macmillan Press Ltd).

ISBN 0–333–77461–2 hardback
ISBN 0–333–77462–0 paperback

This book is printed on paper suitable for recycling and
made from fully managed and sustained forest sources.

A catalogue record for this book is available
from the British Library.

Library of Congress Cataloging-in-Publication Data
Constructing gendered bodies / edited by Kathryn Backett-Milburn
and Linda McKie.
        p. cm. — (Explorations in sociology)
    Includes bibliographical references and index.
    ISBN 0–333–77461–2 — ISBN 0–333–77462–0 (pbk.)
    1. Sex role—Congresses. 2. Body, Human (Philosophy)–
–Congresses. 3. Feminist geography—Congresses.
    4. Masculinity—Congresses. 5. Sexism in sociobiology–
–Congresses. I. Backett-Milburn, Kathryn, 1948– II. McKie,
Linda. III. Series.
    HQ1075 .C665 2000
    305.3—dc21
                                                    00–053060

10   9   8   7   6   5   4   3   2   1
10   09   08   07   06   05   04   03   02   01

Printed and bound in Great Britain by
Antony Rowe Ltd, Chippenham, Wiltshire

Explorations in Sociology

10

Contents

Preface and Acknowledgements

This is one of four books comprising chapters originally presented as papers at the annual conference of the British Sociological Association (BSA), held at the University of Edinburgh, 6–9 April 1998. The theme of that conference was 'Making Sense of the Body: Theory, Research and Practice'. This book comprises a representative sample of many high quality papers presented on the theme of the sociology of the body in policy, institutions and work. Companion books to this one comprise chapters on related topics; *Organising Bodies, Institutions and Work*, edited by Linda McKie and Nick Watson, *Exploring the Body*, edited by Sarah Cunningham-Burley and Kathryn Backett-Milburn, and *Reformulating the Body*, edited by Nick Watson and Sarah Cunningham-Burley.

The editors of these books formed the organizing committee for the 1998 BSA conference and our call for papers was rewarded with a conference embracing nearly 300 presentations with over 500 participants. The rich conference programme was organized into 21 streams and these were co-ordinated by members of BSA study groups and interested individuals. Through this process we were able to actively involve many sociologists, at differing stages of their careers, in the process of developing and running the conference. At the end of the conference there were over 180 papers submitted for consideration by the conference organizing committee for inclusion in the four books. The editors of the books have had an extremely difficult task in selecting papers to be revised into the format of chapters. We were greatly assisted in this task by consulting editors who had previously acted as co-ordinators of relevant streams at the conference. We would also like to thank Anna Bobak-Stirrat for her patient administrative support.

It is our hope that this and the companion books reflect the scholarship, energy and enthusiasm of those who gave papers and those who entered into debates during sessions and the many social events. The conference and these books would not have been possible without the input of many people. We would like to thank the staff of the British Sociological Association and University of Edinburgh for their support in the organization of the conference. Many members of the BSA assisted in numerous ways with the academic content of the conference and we would like to thank them for their on-going support. The editors are also grateful to their colleagues at the University of Leicester and

University of Edinburgh. As ever, our family, friends and colleagues helped out in practical and emotional ways; we owe them a personal debt.

We dedicate this book to the stream co-ordinators for the 1998 annual BSA conference. Their enthusiastic support for our goal of running a welcoming, egalitarian and participative conference was much appreciated, and together, we hope we achieved this.

List of Plates

Notes on the Contributors

Paula Black is a lecturer in sociology at the University of Manchester. Her previous research has included work around HIV and sexuality; the disclosure of HIV positive status; and the sexual experiences of British tourists abroad. She is currently researching beauty therapy. Recent publications include; 'Sex and Travel: Making the Links', in S. Carter and S. Clift (eds), *Tourism and Sex: Culture, Commerce and Coercion* (1999).

Ruth Butler is a lecturer in applied social research at the University of Hull. She is co-editor with H. Parr of 'Mind and body spaces: geographies of disability, illness and impairment' (1999). She is currently working with colleagues at Sheffield and Nottingham Trent on 'Living on the edge: understanding the marginalization and resistance of vulnerable youth' funded by the ESRC's Youth, Citizenship and Social Change Research Programme.

Tom Delph-Janiurek is a lecturer in the Department of Geography at the University of Wales, Lampeter. He is the author of a small collection of articles published in Geographical journals that cover various aspects of his work.

Richard Ekins is a psychoanalyst in private practice and reader in sociology at the University of Ulster at Coleraine, where he is Director of the Transgender Research Unit and Archive. His recent books include *Centres and Peripheries of Psychoanalysis* (with Ruth Freeman) (1994); *Blending Genders* (with Dave King) (1996); *Male Femaling* (1997); *Selected Writings by Anna Freud* (with Ruth Freeman) (1998); and *Classical Psychoanalysis: Unconscious Mental Life and Reality* (2000).

Jenz Germon is currently enrolled as a PhD student at the University of Sydney, Australia. Recent publications include J. Germon and M.J. Hird 'Women on the edge of a Dyke-otomy: Confronting subjectivity' in D. Atkins (ed.) *Lesbian Sex Scandals* (1999).

Philip Hancock is a lecturer in sociology and the philosophy of the social sciences at Glasgow Caledonian University. He has recently published in 'Organization' and 'Journal of Management Studies' and in volumes on 'The Body in Sociology' and 'Body and Organization'.

Sheila Henderson is an independent research consultant and a member of research teams based at the Social Science Research Centre at Southbank University and the Health and Social Services Institute, University of Essex. Her recent publications include: D. Teeman, N. South, and S. Henderson 'Multi-impact Drugs Prevention in the Community' in A. Marlow and G. Pearson (eds) *Young People, Drugs and Community Safety* (1999) S. Henderson (1999) 'Drugs and Culture: The Question of Gender' in N. South (ed.) *Drugs: Cultures, Controls and Everyday Life* (1999).

Myra J. Hird is a lecturer in the School of Sociology and Social Policy, The Queen's University of Belfast, Northern Ireland. She is completing *Women, Men and Violence: From Childhood to Adulthood* (forthcoming) and co-editing *Sociology for the Asking* (forthcoming).

Janet Holland is professor of social research and Director of the Social Sciences Research Centre, South Bank University, London, UK. Publications include: *The Male in the Head* (with Caroline Ramazanoglu, Sue Sharpe and Rachel Thomson (1998)) and *Making Spaces: Citizenship and Difference in Schools* (with Tuula Gordon and Elina Lahelma, (2000)).

Stevi Jackson is professor of women's studies and Director of the Centre for Women's Studies at the University of York. Recent publications include *Christine Delphy* in the 'Women of Ideas' series (1996) and *Heterosexuality in Question* (1999). She has also published numerous articles on romance, sexuality and family relationships and is currently working with Sue Scott, Kathryn Milburn and Jennifer Harden completing research on the impact of risk and adult risk anxiety on the everyday world of children.

Dave King is a lecturer in the Department of Sociology, Social Policy and Social Work Studies at the University of Liverpool. He has been researching and writing in the transgender area for a number of years. In addition to several articles, he has written *The Transvestite and the Transsexual: Public Categories and Private Identities* (1993) and is the co-editor (with Richard Ekins) of *Blending Genders: Social Aspects of Cross-dressing and Sex-changing* (1996).

Sheena Mcgrellis is visiting research fellow at the University of Ulster. Her main research interests are in youth, identities, values and traditions.

Terry O'Neill is completing research entitled, 'Managing the Margins: the constitution of the Gay-Disabled Subject'. He is himself both gay and disabled (visual impairment). His research interests are disability studies, gender studies and identity politics, and he is currently the co-ordinator for students and staff with disability at the University of Auckland, New Zealand.

Joanna Phoenix is a lecturer in sociology at the University of Bath in the Department of Social and Political Sciences. Her primary research interests include the sociology of sex and sexuality, prostitution and gender. She has published widely on prostitution, including a recent book entitled *Making Sense of Prostitution* (1999) and is currently engaged in research on the regulation of youth prostitution in Britain.

Sue Scott is professor of sociology at the University of Durham, having worked previously at the Universities of Stirling and Manchester. She has a long-standing interest in the sociology of sexuality, the body and risk. She was a member of the Women Risk and AIDS Project (WRAP) and her current research focuses on children and risk and sex educa-tion. Her publications include *Body Matters: readings in the sociology of the body* with D.H.J. Morgan (1993) and *Feminism and Sexuality: a reader* with Stevi Jackson (1996).

Sue Sharp is a researcher based at the Institute of Education, Univer-sity of London. Her research interests include gender and education, family life, men's health and youth studies. She has recently completed a book on boys and masculinity with Mike O'Donnell entitled *Un-certain Masculinities: Youth, Ethnicity and Class in Contemporary Britain* (2000).

Rachel Thomson is senior research fellow based in the Social Science Research Centre at South Bank University. Recent publications include co-authorship with Janet Holland, Caroline Ramazanoglu and Sue Sharpe of the book *The Male in the Head: Young people, heterosexuality and power* and *Dream on: the logic of sexual practice* to be published in the Journal of Youth Studies series.

Melissa Tyler is a lecturer in sociology at Glasgow Caledonian University. She has published recently on issues of gender, aesthetics, organization and the body in 'Sociology' and 'Gender, Work and Organization'.

Dana Wilson-Kovacs is a researcher at the University of Exeter. She is currently carrying out ethnographic research on intimacy and female sexual consumption. Her research interests are in sexuality, pornography, material culture and patterns of consumption. She has also published a chapter on 'The Fall and Rise of Erotic Lingerie' in the forthcoming collection *Dress, Book, Identity: Looking the (P)art* Will Keenan (ed.).

Carol Wolkowitz is a lecturer in the Department of Sociology, University of Warwick. Her publications include the *Concise Glossary of Feminist Theory*, two books on women and homeworking and recent articles on the history of the Manhattan Project communities in the US. She is currently writing a book on gender, embodiment and the labour process.

Constructing Gendered Bodies

Background

From being under-researched and under-theorized, the body has now become central to the sociological project. We have moved from what Freund (1988: 839) described as a 'curiously disembodied view of human beings' to one in which '[b]odies are in, in academic as well as in popular culture' (Frank 1990: 131). This interest in the body as a site of sociological analysis has in part been driven by the influence of feminism (Martin 1987; Grosz 1996), in part by the work of Michael Foucault (Foucault 1981) and developments in social theory especially in post-modernism (Frank 1991). We all have bodies but how we use bodies and what meaning is ascribed to a body are the product of social relations (Hurst and Woolley 1982), the body has provided the focus for situated, historical analysis. In addition, Freund (1988: 840), amongst others notes, there is an increasing recognition amongst sociologists that 'the social actors that populate their theories have bodies that are integral to human existence and thus a central consideration in any theory'.

Bryan Turner (1984) was one of the first theorists to bring the body into the mainstream of sociological theory, although the pioneering work of Goffman (1969) should not be forgotten. Turner noted that in contrast to sociology the 'human body has been accorded a place of importance in anthropology since the nineteenth century' (Turner 1991: 1). The work of a number of anthropologists, for example, Douglas (1970, 1973) and Caplan (1987), has informed the development of a sociological theory of the body. Subsequent work by, for example Freund (1988), Frank (1990), the edited collection by Featherstone *et al.* (1991), Schilling (1993), Falk (1994) and Crossley (1996) all served to ensure that the body remained in the foreground of sociological theory. The launch of the journal *Body and Society* in 1995 signalled the establishment of sociology of the body as an area of sociological work in its own right. Anybody doubting the upsurge of sociological interest in the body and its consequent relevance to modern day social theory should try typing in 'body' as a key word in any social science search index.

There is, however, no single sociology of the body. In the same way that post-modernism rejects the metanarrative, so sociology of the body incorporates a plurality of theories and empirical work. It has synthe-sized a number of developments in sociological theory in the last twenty years (Davis 1997; Schilling 1997). In summary, these include:

- challenges to concerns that some sociology was replicating the mind/body dualism of Cartesian thought (Turner 1991; Frank 1991; Leder 1992);
- Foucault's conceptualization of power through the exploration of surveillance and control of the body and sexuality (Foucault 1981);
- feminist theorists and researchers whose examination of identity and everyday embodied experiences gave renewed impetus to debates on gender, sexuality and identity (Martin 1987; Butler 1990; Grosz 1996; Lindemann 1997);
- the critique of the medical model through sociological explanations of health and illness and social action (Goffman 1969; Fox 1993; Annandale 1998);
- the blurring of boundaries for bodies and identities, focusing upon the body as a site for shifting notions of consumption (Boyne 1991; Schilling 1993; Jagger 1998); and
- the impact of social and economic changes upon the body in global policies to enhance development and to tackle environmental con-cerns (Connell 2000).

Contributors to this book draw upon a range of sociological theories and research to enhance the distinctive development of the sociology of the body. Chapters demonstrate how the sociology of the body pro-vides an opportunity to study the body as integral to social action and social being, and thus further the discipline of sociology.

References

ANNANDALE, E. (1998) *The Sociology of Health and Medicine*. Cambridge: Polity.

BOWLBY, J. (1988) *A Secure Base: Clinical Applications of Attachment Theory*. London: Routledge.

BOYNE, R. (1991) 'The Art of the Body in the Discourse of Postmodernity', pp. 281–296, in M. Featherstone, M. Hepworth and B.S. Turner (eds) *The Body. Social Process and Cultural Theory*. London: Sage.

BUTLER, J. (1990) *Gender Trouble: Feminism and the Subversion of Identity*. New York: Routledge.

CAPLAN, P. (ed.) (1987) *The Cultural Construction of Sexuality*. London: Tavistock.

CONNELL, R.W. (2001) 'Bodies, Intellectuals and World Society'. Forthcoming in N. Watson and S. Cunningham-Burley (eds) *Reframing the Body*. Basingstoke: Macmillan.

CROSSLEY, N. (1996) *Intersubjectivity: The Fabric of Social Becoming*. London: Sage.

DAVIS, K. (ed.) (1997) *Embodied Practices. Feminist Perspectives on the Body*. London: Sage.

DOUGLAS, M. (1970) *Purity and Danger: An Analysis of Concepts of Pollution and Taboo*. Harmondsworth: Penguin Books.

DOUGLAS, M. (1973) *Natural Symbols: Explorations in Cosmology*. Hamondsworth: Penguin Books.

FALK, P. (1994) *The Consuming Body*. London: Sage.

FEATHERSTONE, M., M. HEPWORTH and B.S. TURNER (1991) *The Body. Social Process and Cultural Theory*. London: Sage.

FOUCAULT, M. (1981) *The History of Sexuality. Volume 1: An Introduction*. Harmondsworth: Penguin.

FOX, N. (1993) *Postmodernism, Sociology and Health*. Buckingham: Open University Press.

FRANK, A. (1990) 'Bringing Bodies Back in: A Decade Review'. *Theory, Culture and Society*, 7, 131–62.

FRANK, A. (1991) 'For a Sociology of the Body: an Analytical Review', pp. 36–102, in M. Featherstone, M. Hepworth and B.S. Turner (eds) *The Body. Social Process and Cultural Theory*. London: Sage.

FREUND, P. (1988) 'Bringing Society into the Body'. *Theory and Society*, 17, 839–64.

GOFFMAN, I. (1969) *The Presentation of Self in Everyday Life*. Harmondsworth: Penguin.

GROSZ, E. (1996) *Space, Time and Perversion. Essays on the Politics of the Body*. New York: Routledge.

HURST, P. and P. WOOLLEY (1982) *Social Relations and Human Attributes*. London: Tavistock.

JAGGER, E. (1988) 'Marketing the Self, Buying An Other: Dating in a Post Modern, Consumer Society.' *Sociology*, 32, 4, 795–814.

LEDER, D. (1992) 'A Take of Two Bodies: the Cartesian Corpse and the Lived Body', in D. Welton (ed.) *Body and Flesh: A Philosophical Reader*. Oxford: Blackwell.

LINDEMANN, G. (1997) 'The Body of Difference' pp. 73–92, in K. Davis (ed.) *Embodied Practices. Feminist Perspectives on the Body*. London: Sage.

MARTIN, E. (1987) *The Woman in the Body*. Milton Keynes: Open University Press.

SCHILLING, C. (1993) *The Body and Social Theory*. London: Sage.

SCHILLING, C. (1997) 'The Undersocialised Conception of the (Embodied) Agent in Modern Sociology'. *Sociology*, 31, 4, 737–54.

TURNER, B.S. (1984) *The Body and Society: Explorations in Social Theory*. Oxford: Basil Blackwell.

TURNER, B.S. (1991) 'Recent Developments in the Theory of the Body', pp. 1–35, *The Body. Social Process and Cultural Theory*. London: Sage.

1
Introduction

This book is specifically concerned with the social organization and expression of the body, self and identity in the arenas of gender and sexualities. As Jackson and Scott argue in Chapter 1, much attention has been paid to these issues in feminist theory and the sociology of sexualities. However, it is only in recent years that theorists and researchers have begun to examine the lived experience of embodiment and, in particular, the social and cultural processes included in the construction of gendered bodies and sexual practices. This book brings together exciting and stimulating research which examines these issues in a variety of settings ranging from the workplace and leisure industry to social arenas of moral and medical regulation.

Part I: Sex, gender and performing bodies

The theoretical chapter by Jackson and Scott opens this volume with a strong argument to pay attention to 'bodies in interaction and as socially located to material social relations and practices'. For them, a central dilemma is how to focus on the body while retaining an engagement with context, action and practice, and vice versa. They argue that sexuality provides an arena where this theoretical and empirical dilemma might usefully be addressed analytically. After re-visiting the work of key theorists and researchers and reconsidering feminist analyses of the sex/gender distinction, Jackson and Scott turn their attention to the theorizing of bodily pleasures. They argue that in these aspects, as elsewhere, the body cannot be separated from the totality of the self and, indeed, to do so might lead to the obscuring of forms of power. Through their discussion of sexuality, Jackson and Scott highlight a key recurrent theme in this volume: that gendered and sexual bodies cannot, and should not, be separated from gendered, sexual and social selves.

Tyler and Hancock take up the challenge of understanding the construction of the 'organizational body' in the context of the gendered organization of work. They draw on theoretical arguments and an empirical study of flight attendants. Their focus is particularly on how female flight attendants carry out 'body work' as demanded by a contemporary service organization, the airline industry. Tyler and Hancock show the ways in which female flight attendants must achieve, and sustain, an imposed concept of the feminine body in the face of a job which is not only physically demanding but also involves emotional and sexual labour. Much of this 'bodywork' involves deploying the 'tacit skills' which, as women, they are deemed to possess. However, flight attendants management of the lived body is also achieved through a variety of practices entailing constraint, containment and concealment. Interestingly, the authors link the bodily and the social when they claim, in conclusion that, as soon as 'somatic surveillance' becomes integral to 'self surveillance', then the lived body has been successfully transformed into the organizational body.

Delph-Janiurek continues this theme of the construction of gendered bodies in the workplace with an analysis of 'sex, talk and making bodies in the science lab'. Delph-Janiurek retains a theoretical interest in the operation of power interactionally and how gender is routinely and physically performed. However, his particular focus is on language as social practice and in understanding the part this plays in the dynamic processes involved in the everyday constitution and reconstitution of gendered and sexualized identities in the workplace. Delph-Janiurek draws on an in-depth analysis of everyday talk among students and researchers in 'hard' science departments. He shows how the negotiation of gendered social embodiment; patterns of social closeness and distance; and notions of sameness and difference were all created and reinforced in everyday talk, despite an overall claim that such issues were erased by the donning of white laboratory coats.

The meanings attached to the gendered self, sexuality and the performing body are addressed in Phoenix's chapter about prostitution. Here the focus returns to issues around the commodification of bodies, how this relates to issues of self and identity and financial gain, and the ambivalences, paradoxes and contradictions which this entails for prostitute women. Through an analysis of their stories, Phoenix argues that prostitute women constitute themselves and their bodies as both like *and* unlike other non-prostitute women. She shows how the women in her sample felt their particular experiences had enabled them to see through all sexual relationships between men and women identifying their essentially financial nexus and potential for male violence.

Part II: The social construction of the gendered bodies: signs and symbols

In Part II the attention shifts to three papers which, in different ways, examine images and representations of gendered bodies. Wolkowitz's chapter presents an historical case study analysis of how the labouring body was represented in photographs and pictures in Victorian times and the early decades of the twentieth century. She examines how such photographs of bodies at work signify gendered differences in the nature and the meaning of work and may be seen as representations of broader societal issues and concerns. The reproduction of some of Wolowitz's case study material allows the reader to see how labouring bodies were represented in class, race and gender-specific terms. These images powerfully support her case for counteracting the influence of late-twentieth-century interpretations of bodies as malleable, consumption-oriented, ontological products with a more historically situated perspective which highlights the relationship between work and the social construction of bodies.

Black, however, has chosen the leisure industry, in the shape of travel and tourism, as the focus of her analysis of the gendered and sexualized body. Echoing issues raised by Jackson and Scott in Chapter 1, the chapter is concerned with the construction of the sentient and sensual body in the liminal arena of travel. Black draws on qualitative and quantitative research with travellers and tourists and argues that the distinctions made by those who self-identified with one or other grouping continually referred to the role of the body. Bodily representations, signs and displays expressed through travel were also, implicitly, class based. For instance, mass tourism is associated (somewhat exaggeratedly, Black argues) with images of working-class ribaldry and extensive sexual encounters. Travellers, however, tended to make claims to greater authenticity of their experience, choosing not to use bodily display simply as a route to sexual encounters but rather to immerse themselves (and their bodies) in intimate and commensual contact with local people and communities.

Wilson-Kovacs is also concerned with sexual symbolism and the cultural representation of the body. Her chapter focuses on the artefacts which have been used in the display and ornamentation of the female body and what these signify. Wilson-Kovacs analyzes the processes involved in the development of erotic female underwear, notably the suspender belt. However, she takes her arguments further to show how the influences of notions of cleanliness, sexuality and the body parallel developments in technology and advertising. These cultural and consumerist changes all contribute to the development of Western concepts of femininity by creating new forms of desire and bodily disciplines.

Part III: The moral and medical regulation of sex, sexualities and gender

Chapters in Part III share a common theme of exploring the moral and medical regulation of sex, sexualities and gender. Thomson and colleagues examine data from young people aged 11–16 who participated in the ESRC study of 'Youth Values: Identity, diversity and social change'. Using material from focus groups and field notes, they concentrate on the place of the body in young people's moral discourses. Thomson *et al.* stress the importance of gender in this embodiment of morality. They show how, in the process of maturation, moral and physical competence are intertwined as masculine and feminine identities are created and reaffirmed. Importantly, they argue that these young people collude with each other and controlling institutions, such as schools, in the construction of gender through the deployment of the body. During the teenage years, young bodies are subject to constant change and also to changing socio-cultural and institutional interpretations of these developments. Thomson *et al.* show how young people interpret these challenges in the process of forging their identities using a moral discourse which works with oppositional narratives of natural and unnatural, choice and authenticity.

Issues of control, regulation and authenticity feature prominently in the chapter by Hird and Germon about the intersexual body. They show how intersexuality has long been a topic in medical and psychiatric discourses, but one that has changed with shifting social responses and medical technologies over the centuries. Hird and Germon argue that intersexuality offers a disruption of gender categories leading to attempts at moral and physical regulation which illuminates the associations between body and gender identity prevailing at any point in time. In modern times the medical regulation of intersexuals has shifted from finding the 'true' sex to a conceptualization of what may be the 'best' sex for an individual; that is, the sex deemed most appropriate, not just physically but in terms of the psychological, and social environment. However, a counter-discourse has developed which challenges this construction of 'pseudo' male and female bodies and argues for a conceptualization of the body which acknowledges the existence of an intersexual subjectivity. Having examined these shifting and contested conceptualizations, Hird and Germon conclude that 'the intersexual body itself may yet prove a site to explore the power-knowledge *truth* of gender'.

Intersexuality is one of the modes of 'transgendering' discussed and illuminated in Ekins and King's chapter, 'Telling body transgendering stories'. In their broad-ranging discussion they give voice to those who both transfer from one pre-existing gender to another (temporarily or permanently) and who wish to transcend gender altogether. For these groups the gendered nature of their bodies cannot be taken for granted and the binary gender divide into male and female bodies may not be seen as mutually exclusive. Through personal narratives Ekins and King illustrate four modes of body transgendering: migrating, oscillating, erasing and transcending and analyze and explore their physical manifestations, and social, political and moral construction.

Moral and political critiques from groups who are marginalized by bodily and sexual difference constitute the dominant theme of the final two chapters. O'Neill and Hird use the term 'double dominated' to encapsulate the position of gay disabled men as they negotiate their masculinity. They argue that, for marginalized males and those who study their experience, it is by no means news that there is a plurality of differentially empowered masculinities. Indeed, for the men themselves, such theoretical developments may be seen both as an validation of a long struggle and a recognition of their own daily self projects to establish their own masculinities. Working with the narratives of thirteen gay disabled men O'Neill and Hird analyze how they develop their own counter-subjectivities in the space which exists between hegemonic masculinity and their own lived experience. This space is noteworthy for a lack of discourse in the face of a largely heterosexist historical national identity in New Zealand, in which a key marker of masculinity is physical prowess. The counter-discourse formulated by gay disabled men includes accommodating both external and universal diversity and almost all of the respondents prefer a gay identity over a disabled identity. O'Neill and Hird conclude that in this respect gay disabled men are reflecting and reconstructing the existing hierarchies within hegemonic masculinity and being unwittingly complicit in the perpetuation of their own disempowerment.

Butler's chapter continues the exploration of how disability issues are marginalized in a gay culture which is predominantly able-bodied. She argues that the 'norms' at the societal level, whether they derive from essentialism or social constructionism, pressure individuals to conform, or at least to develop and evaluate embodied identities within recognized normative structures. However, like O'Neill and Hird, Butler is particularly interested in how an individual experiences and negotiates membership of more than one marginalized category. She notes that 'ableist' views persist in the gay community resulting in continuing pressures on disabled people to conform to a stereotyped asexual role. Moreover, such perceptions may be perpetuated if disabled people are physically unable to respond to another's body language and sexual communication. Butler points out that knowledge of, and communication in, the gay 'scene' and venues involve subtleties of visual symbolism, body language and control which may be difficult for impaired individuals to achieve. Butler shows some positive developments in strategies of resistance of 'queer crips' but concludes with a strong argument for the recognition of difference so that their needs may be met and marginalization challenged.

The diversity of the contributions in this book testify to the heuristic value of embodiment in the area of gender and sexuality. Moreover, it is evident that sociology has moved on from its initial theorizing of the body to exploring the body empirically in a range of settings. Challenges remain in theorizing the role of the body in relation to structure, agency and material practice but the work of the contributors to this book show how far we have come and suggest stimulating areas for future development.

Part I

Sex, Gender and Performing Bodies

2
Putting the Body's Feet on the Ground: Towards a Sociological Reconceptualization of Gendered and Sexual Embodiment

Stevi Jackson and Sue Scott

Amid ever more abstract theorizations of 'the body', calls are now frequently made for greater attention to be given to the lived, fleshy experience of embodiment. Where sexuality, and especially hetero-sexuality, is concerned, such calls are currently more easily made than answered. On the one hand we have theories of the body and of the social construction of sexuality which say little about embodied sexual practices and on the other we have statistical data on who does what with whom and how often, but which tells us nothing about the processes involved.

How, as feminist sociologists, can we conceptualize bodies as socially constructed without viewing the body as floating free of the material actualities of lived experience? There is a fear that in giving attention to fleshy, sensate bodies we will fall back into essentialism or even biologism, as if the only language we have to talk about actual, specific bodies is that of anatomy. Yet as sociologists we know, in other contexts, that experience is never simply given, but is interpreted, theorized and mediated through the meanings which are culturally available to us. Moreover 'experiences' happen and are made meaningful through social interactions within particular social locations.

When sociologists began to pay attention to 'the body' this interest was in part motivated by a need to counter disembodied conceptualizations of social actors. There was a realization that social interaction is facilitated by bodily negotiations; that we recognize others through their bodies, that we categorize them by age, gender, ethnicity – even class – through bodily attributes; that this recognition itself requires a set of cultural competencies through which we read the significance of dress, demeanour and deportment. These basic insights are well worth retaining, alongside the immense contribution which feminists have made to theorizing the body and to embodied political action.

Since the 1970s, the body has figured, at least implicitly, in feminist work. Feminists have challenged the reduction of women to their bodies associated with the historical equation of women with the body and men with the mind. We have critiqued and resisted sexual and medical objectification and all modes of thinking which naturalized women's subordination. Central to this has been the theorization of gender and sexual difference which has given rise to recent debates between those seeking to find new ways of exploring women's embodied specificity and those who refuse to contemplate any account which links women's social being to pre-given bodily attributes or experiences. Alongside these theoretical preoccupations there have been activist campaigns calling for women's bodily self-determination, promoting reproductive rights and resisting male violence. Where theorists often seem to discuss bodies without any reference to the women whose bodies they are, activists have always kept actual embodied women in view.

The body has had a chequered history within sociological and feminist theory. An earlier language of social action and social actors made it possible to think of embodied individuals moving through time and space. The language of agency disembodied us; the language of subjects and subjectivity in some senses readmitted the body, but the emphasis on language constituting subjectivity still privileged mind as either cognitive or unconscious; Foucault legitimized the study of the body, but his focus on governance and surveillance de-emphasized individual agency except in so far as it was engaged in resistance. Post-structuralism, postmodernism and much recent feminist and cultural theory have shifted attention away from an engagement with action and practice, indeed away from sociologically grounded theory in general and towards more philosophical conceptualizations of the body. Where context was central to early sociological theorizations of sexuality, now it is often lost sight of in favour of free-floating desire or sexual acts. It seems that the more we focus on the body, the more we lose sight of the context; when the context comes into focus, the body fades from view.

Putting the body's feet on the ground should entail giving attention to bodies in interaction and bodies as socially located, to material social relations and practices. We need to develop a perspective which avoids both theoretical abstraction and abstracted empiricism. Given that 'having sex' is very obviously about socially located bodies in interaction, sexuality might prove a fruitful field in which to develop such an analysis. Here we concentrate primarily, but not exclusively, on hetero-sexual sexuality in order to begin to set an agenda for a more fully social understanding of embodied practice and experience. In so doing we will outline and critique some modes of theorizing the body which we find particularly problematic.[1]

We will begin by surveying some influential sociological work on embodied social action and actors before focusing more specifically on gendered and sexual embodiment. Since, within recent theoretical debates, both gender and sexuality have come to be contested concepts, we will devote some space to explaining our own perspective on their interrelationship and justifying our continued attachment to the concept of gender. Having established these foundations we then go on to explore some ways of theorizing the gendered processes of embodied sexual interaction.

Embodied interaction and the embodied self

There are, and have long been, traditions in sociology which do, implic-itly at least, deal with embodied social actors – particularly those con-cerned with sociologies of action/agency rather than structure. The best known of these is Goffman, whose acutely observed analyses of every-day social practices paid close attention to bodily interaction: the ways in which embodied actors positioned themselves in lifts or on buses, the bodily signals required by civil inattention, the deportment, deploy-ment and adornment of bodies needed for appropriate presentations of self and so on (Goffman 1963; 1969). Yet while embodied actors are ever present on Goffman's social stage, he was always concerned more with bodily action and performance than with the sensual, visceral body (just as he was concerned far more with the performative manifestations of self reflexivity rather than the ongoing inner process of narrative self construction).

Giddens takes up and develops this and his greater emphasis on reflexivity and on bodies in time and space at first sight appears to offer a deeper understanding of embodied sociality. Yet the body still seems somehow separable from the self, it is monitored through reflexive self construction but not fully part of the reflexive self.

> The reflexivity of the self . . . pervasively affects the body as well as psychic processes. The body is less and less an extrinsic 'given', functioning outside the internally referential systems of modernity,

but becomes itself reflexively mobilized. What might appear as a wholesale movement towards the narcissistic cultivation of bodily appearance is in fact an expression of a concern lying much deeper actively to 'construct' and control the body. (Giddens 1991: 7).

Here the body is not so much a part of the reflexive project of the self as an object of that project, something to be worked upon. This conceptualization of embodiment perpetuates mind–body dualism in which the mind, or reflexive self, seeks to '"construct" and control the body'. While rendering the body socially meaningful, Giddens's perspective still implicitly posits a pre-social body, which is constrained and modified by external social factors. Yet, conversely, Giddens also neglects the fleshy and sensual aspects of the body in favour of a more cognitively and reflexively managed body. This is an obstacle to the development of a fully embodied sociology of intimacy and sexuality. As Shilling and Mellor put it, Giddens 'views people as, essentially, minds who happen to occupy bodies' (1996: 7). We do not, however, share Shilling and Mellor's diagnosis of the problem: that Giddens ignores 'embodied dispositions which lie beneath the reach of thought and reflexive control' (1996: 7) nor their view that the sensual can somehow escape the social or lead people to reject it. Not only are we wary of looking to the unconscious every time we encounter something which is difficult to conceptualize within existing social theory, but, as feminists, we are very aware of the dangers of positing sensual urges which prompt people to overturn the traces of social convention: think of the male mythology of uncontrollable desire and how it has been deployed in justifying rape.

Menstruation can be taken as an example of a physical, bodily process which on one level seems to pre-exist the social, but is also something which needs to be socially managed, something which, if not managed properly disrupts social expectation and interaction. A public show of menstrual blood could be seen as the unruly, leaky body intruding on the social – nature' disrupting 'culture' – indeed this is how women's bodies are often viewed (Grosz 1994). But is it this simple? Is menstruation social only insofar as it is managed, kept from public view? Does the reflexive self come into play only after the event to manage a pre-given natural function? We would say not. As Christine Delphy puts it, 'you do not have "a" period . . . [but] *your* period' which depends on material social conditions and the cultural significance given to a physical event itself 'bereft of meaning'. (Delphy 1984: 194) No bodily function can ever be outside the social. The embodied experience of menstruation is not reducible to bleeding, stomach cramps or any other associated phenomena, but occurs in specific contexts, is already imbued with a range of meanings. The strategies used to keep it out of routine social interaction, the conventions circumscribing when, how, by whom and to whom it can be revealed, in themselves mark it *as* social.

Although it is women's bodies which are more often seen as problematic, disruptive and unruly, both men and women are equally embodied. Men may have historically been privileged as rational actors, capable of mastering and transcending their embodied 'animal' natures (Jackson and Scott 1997), but this should not prevent us from recognizing that even this process of denial requires strategies for managing the body through, for example, dress and demeanour (see Reynaud 1983). Moreover, some versions of masculine transcendence, of exerting mind over bodily matter entail work *on* the body, as for example, in the tradition of masculine heroism evinced through feats of physical endurance. Understanding gendered embodiment, then, entails paying attention to both femininity and masculinity and how each is sustained in relation to the other.

Gendered bodies/sexual bodies

Early formulations of gender defined it in relation to biological sex, taking physical bodily differences between women and men as given (see Oakley 1972). While gender was taken to be cultural and social, the assumption of pre-social sex differences persisted. This distinction between sex and gender has proved difficult to sustain and, within feminist theory, has come under attack from two opposing directions. On the one hand there are those who see it as maintaining a dualism between nature and culture and, in the process, denying women's embodied specificity (Gatens 1983; Brodribb 1992; Braidotti 1994). On the other hand there are those who argue that its challenge to essentialism does not go far enough, that it presupposes a biological root (sex) onto which gender is grafted (Kessler and McKenna 1978; Delphy 1984; 1993; Butler 1990; Lindemann 1997). We would locate ourselves within the latter group and are sceptical of leaving any space for 'difference' which is not by definition social or cultural. The categories 'men' and 'women' are social categories and the 'recognition' of biological 'sex differences' on which this distinction seems to rest is itself a social and cultural practice. Indeed it has been suggested that it is gender (as a cultural or social distinction) which creates sex, rather than the other way round, in that 'the hierarchical division of humanity into two transforms an anatomical difference (which is itself devoid of social implications) into a relevant distinction for social practice' (Delphy 1984: 144).

In recent writings the blurring and contesting of the sex gender distinction has often been resolved by abandoning gender and returning to sex (see, for example, Grosz 1995). While we accept that the sex–gender *distinction* may be unsustainable, we would argue strongly for the retention of 'gender' rather than 'sex' to denote the division between men and women. There are two sets of reasons for this.

First, gender is a sociological concept, it focuses attention on men and women as *social* rather than natural categories and emerged out of debates which sought to challenge the 'naturalness' of differences between men and women (Lindemann 1997). While gender is now often used in an unsociological sense, it remains the best analytical tool we have given that it is difficult to divest the term 'sex' of its naturalistic connotations. Moreover, gender is also sociological in that it focuses our attention on the *division* between women and men and the hierarchical relationship between them (Delphy 1993).

A second reason for retaining the word 'gender' is that the term 'sex' is so much more ambiguous. 'Sex' can refer both to differences between women and men and to specifically sexual (erotic) relations and practices. This ambiguity is itself sociologically interesting in that it is part of the naturalistic construction which links our genitals to our social position (as women or men) and to our sexual identities and practices, which defines femininity and masculinity as 'natural' and privileges heterosexuality as the only 'normal' and therefore legitimate form of sexuality. Theoretically we need to challenge these assumptions, to break the chain which binds anatomy into gender and sexuality. Conceptually we need to know what we are talking about and the ambiguity of the term 'sex' often clouds the issue. If we speak of 'gender relations' we know we refer to all aspects of social life; 'sexual relations' is more often understood as specifically physical/erotic interaction. (Indeed it can sometimes be even more specific than that, as in 'I did not have sexual relations with that woman.')

Hence we are maintaining an analytical distinction between gender and sexuality, while arguing that the two are empirically interrelated, that is sexuality is gendered in fundamental ways and gender divisions sustain and are sustained by normative heterosexuality. To conflate the two, however, tends to reduce the entirety of gender to sexuality, to hide from view the myriad aspects of gender which are not about sexuality.

This is what tends to happen when 'sex' is used instead of gender. In declaring gender redundant Grosz defines 'sex' as referring 'to the domain of sexual difference, to questions of the *morphologies of bodies*' (her emphasis) as distinct from sexuality, 'sexual impulses, desires, wishes, hopes, bodies, pleasures, behaviours and practices'. Gender is redundant because 'all its effects, the field that it designates, are covered by the integration of and sometimes the discord between sexuality and sex' (1995: 213). All the differences between women and men are reduced to 'morphologies of bodies', and all relations between them are reduced to the sexual. The entire field of gender, as sociologists would understand it – encompassing paid and unpaid work and so on – is erased. At the same time as removing any term capable of designating male–female social relations, Grosz also does away with the only word we have for sex as an erotic activity: sexuality does not always work. One 'has sex'; one does not 'have sexuality'.

In formulations such as these, moreover, it is almost impossible to avoid the conceptual slippage between 'sex' as differences between men and women and 'sex' as an erotic activity. The conflation of gender and sexuality which results from designating the former as sex is also evident in psychoanalytic thought which explicitly ties our existence as sexed (gendered) subjects to our sexual being. Hence what we are designating gender has often been referred to as sexuality. (For example, Rosalind Coward's *Female Desire* (1982) which purported to be about female sexuality, actually contained very little about sexuality.) Further confusion occurs when the gendered body is read as the sexual body. We need to differentiate between the sexualization of women's bodies and sexuality as identities, desires and practices. For women, a gendered body often means a sexualized body, a body disciplined into a sexually 'attractive' appearance and demeanour. This performance of sexual desirability is often equated with 'female sexuality', which is thus reduced to 'the look'. Sexualized femininity, however, may have little or nothing to do with autonomous desires and the practice of pleasure. There is a great deal of difference between being a sexual subject and a sexual object. The sexualized body is often a passive body; the sexual body implies something more engaged, whether actively or passively, in sexual practices – a body capable of sensual pleasure, a body which, in anticipating and experiencing desire and pleasure cannot be *just* a body abstracted from mind, self and social context.

Here Gesa Lindemann's (1997) distinction between objectified, experiencing and experienced bodies is helpful. The 'objectified body' refers to a visible, concrete entity moving through social space. (The objectified body in this sense is not one reduced to a sexual object, but simply the one we can all see – someone else's living body.) The 'experiencing body' is the sensory body, experiencing the environment through all senses. The 'experienced body' is our sense of our own bodies, the body through which we feel pleasure and pain, but also the body which we sometimes experience unselfconsciously as simply an unobtrusive part of our being. The experiencing and experienced bodies together, for Lindemann, constitute the 'living body'. In the realm of sexuality it is dangerous to read off properties of the living body from the objectified body, to deduce what another woman is feeling from the body we see. Just because that objectified body is read by us as 'sexy' (or sexually attractive) does not mean it is necessarily being experienced as sexual; even a selfconsciously adopted 'come and get it' look is not necessarily evidence of independent autonomous desire.

What we are suggesting, then, is that the gendered body is not always a sexual body, that the body can be sexual as both object and subject and that the connections between the gendered body and the sexual body require further exploration – we cannot reduce one to the other, but need to explore the relationship between them. Probably the single most influential theorization of this relationship to emerge in recent years is that provided by Judith Butler (1990; 1993).

Butler's materializing bodies

Butler's (1990; 1993) discussion of the practices through which bodies are gendered centres on the 'heterosexual matrix' which links the binary divide of gender with normative heterosexuality. In *Gender Trouble* (1990) gender is seen as performative, in the sense that bodies become gendered through the continual performance of gender. (This is nothing new in sociological terms: see Garfinkel 1967; Goffman 1969; Kessler and McKenna 1978.) Butler is not saying that gender is something you 'put on' in the morning and discard at will (see Butler 1993). She makes it clear that we are constrained into gender, arguing that sexed bodies are forcibly materialized through time. However, her conceptualization of the process whereby gendered bodies are materialized is framed from within philosophical, rather than sociological, preoccupations. As a result, she misses what we would see as crucial elements of the *social* construction of gendered bodies at the level of both social structural power relations and everyday social interaction and practices.

In *Bodies that Matter* (1993) Butler's approach to performativity shifts. Rather than thinking of the 'performative' as a performance, Butler turns to the notion of linguistic performatives – forms of speech which,

by their utterance, bring what they name into being. Hence the pro-
nouncement 'it's a girl', made at an infant's birth, brings a girl into
being, begins the process, as Butler puts it, of 'girling the girl'. The
process works because the phrase 'it's a girl' draws on the authority of
the conventions which establish what a girl is. In naming sex the norms
of sex are being cited. Sex is materialized, according to Butler, through
a complex of such citational practices which are both normative and
regulative – and hence coercive and constraining (if never totally effective). In her emphasis on the normative and regulatory effects of performativity, Butler seems to be reaching towards some notion of a
socially ordered world, but the social eludes her grasp. As Caroline
Ramazanoglu points out, the question of where these norms come from
or why they 'so often produce "heterosexual hegemony"', male dominance, or any other imbalance of power does not appear to be an appropriate question to be asked within the logic of her theory' (1995: 37).

Moreover, there are other, crucial, respects in which Butler's inability
to conceptualize the social limits the utility of her perspective. Clearly
any account of gendered embodiment requires more than an appreciation of the external, coercive force of the gendering process and the
surface appearance of gender effected through performance. Gender
is also incorporated into our inner selves and is integral to our sub-
jetivity. In order to conceptualize this, Butler falls back on a psychoanalytic vocabulary, albeit a radically reinterpreted one, 'guided by the
question of how regulatory norms form a "sexed" subject in terms
which establish the indistinguishability of psychic and bodily formation' (1993: 22).

What can be exteriorized, and thus performed, is limited by the
opacity of the unconscious and can be understood 'by what is barred
from the signifier and the domain of corporeal legibility' (1993: 234).
Here we have the familiar idea that the unknowable, unsayable con-
tents of the unconscious shape conscious thought and bodily action in
mysterious ways. What is missing from Butler's analysis, and what forces
her back on psychoanalysis, is any conception of a reflexive, social,
embodied self in interaction with others. On the one hand we have the
external, coercive constraints of normative gender and heterosexuality
and on the other the inner, largely unconscious psyche. Although Butler
wants to leave space for human agency, for the subversion of normative gender and heterosexuality, she lacks the conceptual tools to enable
her to do this. She is, we think, justly suspicious of the notion of an
autonomous pre-social (or in her words pre-discursive) 'I' (1993: 225);
there is no 'I' which constructs or performs gender since the 'I' is formed

only through gender. This need not, however, exclude the possibility of self-reflexivity. The idea of the reflexive self, in our reading of its Meadian origins, does not assume a pre-social 'I', but an I which is only ever the fleeting mobilization of a socially constituted self (Mead 1934).

In our view, the idea of an embodied social self offers a far better means of conceptualizing the indissolubility of body and mind than psychoanalysis. Even for those less willing to abandon psychoanalysis, there must surely be a space for conscious, reflexive thought and action in the space between unconscious depths and surface appearance, a space which Butler fills through the Derridean notion of the 'undecidability' of the relation between inner psyche and exterior performance. Moreover, not all aspects of gender which are not fully conscious and subject to reflexive monitoring are necessarily 'unconscious' in the psychoanalytic sense. Much of the performance of gender is, in Gesa Lindemann's words, 'realized in absent-minded fashion' (1997: 79). But this absent-mindedness is social, the product of bodily dispositions which are acquired, and have become habitual, through a whole history of interactions within gendered social space (see Young 1990). While we would concur with Butler that 'sex' (in the sense of sex differences) is 'an ideal construct which is forcibly materialized through time' (1993: 1) and that this materialization produces *'the effect of boundary, fixity and surface we call matter'* (1993: 9, Butler's emphasis), this formulation needs some sociological input. It is not enough to conceive of the operation of power in materializing gender in a purely Foucauldian sense, adding on psychoanalysis to deal with our psychic investment in gender and the origins of 'desire'. What is needed is, on the one hand, a sense of the ways in which gender and heterosexuality are institutionalized and, on the other hand, of the ways in which embodied human beings interact with others, and reflexively with themselves, in producing, sustaining and (sometimes) subverting gender.

Bodily pleasures

Although sexuality appears central to Butler's work, she devotes surprisingly little attention to it. Her account of sexuality centres on the normativity of heterosexuality. While she has a great deal to say about bodily practices which can potentially subvert the gendered heteroseual order, she says little about sexual practices: the sexual, erotic body is strangely silent in her work, discussed only in abstract theorizations of 'desire' (as in the 'lesbian phallus' chapter) which seem to us to bear little relation to the experienced and experiencing, living bodies which, in the everyday and everynight world, engage in sexual acts.

Sexuality and sexual activity is very much about living bodies, what we do with them, what we feel through them, but it is not just about bodies. In discussion of the body, especially in relation to sexuality, it is very easy to forget that we are not just bodies, that the 'we' who inhabit these bodies are not reducible to the body. We must be wary of representing the body as uninhabited, of discussing embodied practices as if bodies existed without people. It would be ridiculous to say 'last night my body was in bed with my lover's body'. Sex entails embodied selves engaged in embodied social activity and embodied interaction. Here as elsewhere, the body is inseparable from the totality of the self. If we forget this, foregrounding the body does not challenge body–mind dualism, but actually reinstates it. Moreover, this can be politically dangerous. If, for example, we speak of sexual violence as violence against 'women's bodies', it is as if the women themselves escape the consequences, thus negating their experience of an attack on their person and depoliticizing violence against women (qua women) (see Kappeler 1993).

The body with a life of its own appears in the most unlikely places. Numerous critics of Foucault have noted a residual essentialism of the body in his work, especially in the first volume of *The History of Sexuality*. Although Foucault is committed to the idea that the body is produced through discursive practices, rather than given by nature, he nonetheless sees 'bodies and pleasures' as a site of resistance to power, as if they lie outside the social (Fraser 1989; Grosz 1995). More importantly, however, this emphasis on bodies and pleasures can obscure forms of power other than those operating through the discursive constitution of sexuality. The classic example of this in Foucault's own work is the infamous passage where he characterizes an episode of what would now be seen as child abuse as 'inconsequential bucolic pleasures' (Foucault 1981: 31). In today's world, the problem is manifested in an unwillingness, in some quarters, to acknowledge the pervasiveness and ubiquity of power within consensual heterosexual relations.

Lynne Segal has been a staunch defender of the possibility of pleasure within heterosexual relations (1994; 1997). As heterosexual feminists we have interests in common with Segal: we, too, believe that pleasure is attainable within heterosexual relationships, that equality and mutuality in sexual relations between women and men might be possible. Where we differ from her is that we do not think that this is achievable in the absence of a critique of heterosexuality as both-istitution and practice. Segal is not unaware of inequalities in heterosexual relations, of sexual coercion and violence, but she appears to consider these as incidental to heterosexuality.

She is, in our view, overly optimistic about the potential for changing heterosexual sex and the degree of equality currently existing within (hetero)sexual practice. She believes, for example, that since both men and women experience vulnerability and loss of control when in the throes of sexual passion, that this can undermine masculinity and produce sexual mutuality. Thus through sex, gender is transformed: sex 'easily *threatens* rather than confirms gender polarity' (Segal 1997: 86, her emphasis). In our view it is a mistake to confuse emotional responses during sex (vulnerability, loss of self, loss of control) with the social relations within which sexual acts take place – and to assume, thereby, that sexual passion is capable of transforming, even dissolving gender:

> In consensual sex, when bodies meet, the epiphany of that meeting – its threat and excitement – is surely that all the great dichotomies (activity/passivity, subject/object, heterosexual/homosexual) slide away. (1997: 86)

As well as decontextualizing sexual bodies, this statement is a further instance of the uninhabited body. It is as if bodies have sex with each other leaving the biographies, social locations and social identities of their inhabitants outside the bedroom door. It implies that there is no history of sex between these people, or of sex with others, which they bring to the encounter, no history of any other relationships and no other aspects to the current one. It is also a highly romanticized (Mills and Boon) view of sex as magical, transcendent, raising us above mundane, quotidian realities. There is no room here for boring, routine sex which can be as consensual as passionate, ecstatic sex – or even for pleasant playful sex.

Another writer who makes radical claims for the transformative effects of bodily pleasure, while simultaneously abstracting the body from self and context is Elizabeth Grosz (1995). In her discussion of queer subjectivity, Grosz suggests that there is an 'instability at the heart of bodies and sex', that 'the fact that the body is what it is capable of doing, and what any body is capable of doing is well beyond the tolerance of any given culture.' Her argument concerns the transformative potential of queer sex. According to Grosz, what is specific to the oppression of lesbians and gay men is that it is based on what they do rather than who they are 'on the *activities* of members of a group, and not on any definitive group attributes'. (1995: 225) This, she says 'is precisely why the forces of cultural reaction are so intent on separating a body from

what it can (sexually) do' (225–6), reducing homosexuality to a category of person. '(T)he forces of reaction function by trying to solidify
or congeal a personage, a being through and through laden with
deviancy.' (226)

   It seems that the only way of resisting this is through sexuality, assert-
ing the plasticity of desire. The threat homosexuality poses to heterosexuality is its own contingency and open endedness; its own tenuous
hold over the multiplicity of sexual impulses and possibilities characterizing all human sexuality. '. . . Queer pleasures show that one does
not have to settle for the predictable, formulaic, the respected' (226).
Grosz sees queer sexuality as 'seeping into', 'infiltrating' straight sex,
making it possible for the supposedly 'natural coupling' of male and
female to come 'unstuck'. Queer here is a sort of solvent, ungluing the
heterosexual couple. This is not a vision of sex transforming the world
– what Grosz wants is to transform sex itself, to enhance pleasure, to
free it of the constraints which limit our bodily potential (a goal not
dissimilar to Segal's). Not only does this depoliticize the critique of
heterosexuality, but it brings us back to the essentialism of the body,
the idea of a bodily sexuality beyond the social, a sexuality which can
be freed from the chains which bind it to the predictable: back, indeed,
to the repressive hypothesis.

   Grosz's work is one example among many of overly abstract theorizations which detach the body from its social context and mystify
everyday embodied experience. Grosz's vision of the body is ultimately
of a mindless body – the body is, simply, what the body does. Closely
allied to the (uninhabited) mindless body is the meaningless body, the
body emptied of meaning. Meaningfulness requires that bodies are not
separated off from those who inhabit them. Bodies are more than just
the sum of their anatomical parts or what is done with those parts.
Bodies have no meaning, no significance apart from cultural context,
social situation and interaction with others. It is these cultural and
social practices which render our bodies intelligible to ourselves and
others, as indicative of our gendered and sexual being (Delphy 1984;
1993; Butler 1990).

Composing the sexual self

It is worth returning here to one of the earlier conceptualizations of the
social construction of sexuality – Gagnon and Simon's sexual scripts –
reviving sociological understandings of bodily action and interaction.
The term 'scripts', though, is in some ways unfortunate since it connotes
something fixed – a problem noted by Gagnon and Simon themselves

in that the term 'suggests the conventional dramatic narrative form, which more often than not is inappropriate' (1974: 23). A script in their terms is not a closed text which locks us into predictable plots and roles, but something much more fluid and open, offering opportunities to improvise. Scripts are played with, not simply played out; they are open to renegotiation. Actors in intimate erotic dramas do not necessarily share the same interpretation of what is going on, or the same understanding of how to go on. In sexual encounters we improvise, and extemporize, taking cues from partners as we compose our own sexual drama.

We should remember that this perspective comes from a symbolic interactionist tradition in which the self is provisional and always in process; in which meanings are emergent, negotiated and renegotiable. We are not suggesting that this perspective is without its problems, but it is worth recovering some of its insights. Historically it was overtaken by the influence of Foucault, and discourse became a more fashionable term than scripts. The problems with scripting are two-fold: a lack of attention to social structure, and hence the question of where scripts come from, and the ambiguity of the term scripts.

We would like to suggest an alternative metaphor – composing the sexual body, playing on the double meaning of the verb to compose.[2] We compose narratives of self and hence compose ourselves. To be composed is to be in control and bodily composure suggests control over a potentially unruly body. However, we suggest that though sexual bodies appear to lack what counts as composure in other social locations they are nonetheless composed and adopt a certain sexual composure. The process of playing out sexual encounters is one which we compose as we go along. The elements of the composition come from the cultural resources available to us: these are not infinite but present us with a range of possibilities (such as conventions relating to keys, cords and tempo in music). We need to know these conventions in order to engage actively in sexual encounters.

What Gagnon and Simon called scripting and we are calling composition is not just about acts – what we 'do' – but how we make sense of what we feel and thus what we can make intelligible to ourselves as feeling – both emotion and sensation – and what we can therefore convey to others. All this is absolutely essential to what goes on between the sheets (or wherever else). Our sense of ourselves as sexual and as gendered is an ongoing composition, and both gendered and sexual embodiment require that we compose ourselves bodily, construct an ongoing sense of embodied self within social space.

Where do we go from here?

Gendered bodies and sexual bodies, then, are inseparable from gendered and sexual selves or subjects. While we have suggested that the sexual and gendered self should be viewed as embodied, the body should not be treated as if it were separable from the rest of our social being. What is lacking in the imaginary bodies of much social and feminist theory is the socially located body: we have abstract (disembodied) bodies, bodies materializing outside any social context, uninhabited bodies which exist independently of people – mindless and meaningless bodies. It is perhaps surprising that this has occurred even in discussions of sexuality, which paradigmatically entails socially located bodies in interaction. Even masturbation, after all, is social. As Mead told us long ago, we are social beings even when we are alone; solo sex, like sex with another, involves a process of composition drawing on cultural resources shaped and re-shaped through our past biography, resources which guide both our minds (our fantasies) and our hands.

We know relatively little, sociologically, about embodied sexuality. Film censorship once decreed that when couples were pictured kissing each should keep at least one foot on the ground. While we know that the rules governing the public representation of sexual bodies have changed, we know little about bodily deployment within private sexual negotiations. We are suggesting that one way forward entails resuscitating earlier work on bodily interaction in order to breathe life into an embodied sociology and to animate the abstract bodies of much feminist theory.

Notes

1. We are not attempting an overview of theorizing on the body, nor of theories of sexuality. Hence not all prominent theorists in this field are covered in this paper. Rather, we have chosen the work of particular theorists to represent tendencies within current thinking which we wish to challenge.
2. This idea came to us through reading Tia DeNora's work on music and erotic agency (DeNora 1997).

Bibliography

BRAIDOTTI, R. (1994) 'Feminism by any other name' (interview), *Differences*, 6(2/3):27–61.
BRODRIBB, S. (1992) *Nothing Mat(t)ers: A Feminist Critique of Postmodernism*. Melbourne: Spinifex.
BUTLER, J. (1990) *Gender Trouble: Feminism and the Subversion of Identity*. New York: Routledge.

BUTLER, J. (1993) *Bodies that Matter*. New York: Routledge.

COWARD, R. (1982) *Female Desire*. London: Paladin.

DELPHY, C. (1984) *Close to Home: A Materialist Analysis of Women's Oppression*. London: Hutchinson.

DELPHY, C. (1993) 'Rethinking sex and gender', *Women's Studies International Forum*, 16(1):1–9.

DENORA, T. (1997) 'Music and erotic agency – sonic resources and socio-sexual action', *Body and Society*, 3(2):43–65

FOUCALT, M. (1981) *The History of Sexuality, Volume One*. Harmondsworth: Penguin.

FRASER, N. (1989) *Unruly Practices: Power, Discourse and Gender in Contemporary Social Theory*. Cambridge: Polity.

GAGNON, J. and W. SIMON (1974) *Sexual Conduct*. London: Hutchinson.

GARFINKEL, H. (1967) *Studies in Ethnomethodology*. Englewood Cliffs, NJ: Prentice Hall.

GATENS, M. (1983) 'A critique of the sex/gender distinction', in J. Allen and P. Patton (eds) *Beyond Marxism?* New South Wales: Intervention Publications. Reprinted in her *Imaginary Bodies*. London: Routledge (1996).

GIDDENS, A. (1991) *Modernity and Self-Identity*. Cambridge: Polity.

GOFFMAN, E. (1963) *Behaviour in Public Places*. New York: The Free Press.

GOFFMAN, E. (1969) *The Presentation of Self in Everyday Life*. London: Allen Lane.

GROSZ, E. (1994) *Volatile Bodies*. Bloomington: Indiana University Press.

GROSZ, E. (1995) 'Experimental desire: re-thinking queer subjectivity' in E. Grosz, *Space, Time and Perversion*. New York: Routledge.

KAPPELER, S. (1993) 'From Sexual Politics to Body Politics' *Trouble and Strife* 29/30 pp. 73–9.

KESSLER, S.J. and W. MCKENNA (1978) *Gender: An Ethnomethodological Approach*. New York: Wiley.

LINDEMANN, G. (1997) 'The body of gender difference' in K. Davis (ed.) *Embodied Practices: Feminist perspectives on the Body*. London: Sage.

MEAD, G.H. (1934) *Mind self and Society*. Chicago: University of Chicago Press.

OAKLEY, A. (1972) *Sex, Gender and Society*. Oxford: Martin Robertson.

RAMAZANOGLU, C. (1995) 'Back to basics: heterosexuality, biology and why men stay on top', in M. Maynard and J. Purvis (eds) *(Hetero)sexual Politics*. London: Taylor & Francis.

REYNAUD, E. (1983) *Holy Virility*. London: Pluto Press.

JACKSON, S. and S. SCOTT (1997) 'Gut Reactions to Matters of the Heart: Reflections on Rationality, Irrationality and Sexuality'. *Sociological Review* 45(4):551–75.

SEGAL, L. (1994) *Straight Sex*. London: Virago.

SEGAL, L. (1997) 'Feminist sexual politics and the heterosexual predicament' in L. Segal (ed.) *New Sexual Agendas*. Basingstoke: Macmillan Press – now Palgrave.

SHILLING, C. and P. MELLOR (1996) 'Embodiment, structuration theory and Modernity: mind–body dualism and the repression of sensuality' *Body and Society* 2(4):1–15.

YOUNG, I.M. (1990) 'Throwing like a girl' in *Throwing Like a Girl and Other Essays*. Bloomington: Indiana.

3
Flight Attendants and the Management of Gendered 'Organizational Bodies'

Melissa Tyler and Philip Hancock

Introduction

The management of the 'organizational bodies' of flight attendants is our main focus in this chapter. Building on Witz, Halford and Savage's (1997) concept of temporally and spatially 'organized bodies', we use the term 'organizational body' here to refer to the mode of embodiment, the manipulation of the presentation and performance of the body, which must be maintained in order to become and remain an employee of a particular organization and to 'embody' that organization. In an examination of the gendered organization and regulation of organizational bodies in the context of waged work, the chapter draws on empirical research into the recruitment, training and supervision of female flight attendants as an example of the constitution of 'organizational bodies' as fundamental to the functioning of contemporary service organizations. In the case of a flight attendant, the achievement and maintenance of an 'organizational body' involves being subject not only to organizationally specific management techniques, but also to those occupational discourses which operate in the industry generally and which serve to define the role and identity of a flight attendant (Tyler and Abbott 1998). At least in part, this is as the embodiment of an organizational identity – as the material signifier of an organizational ethos – or as one Qantas executive put it, 'the packaging of a product' (cited in Williams 1988). A female flight attendant must, therefore, learn to practice certain 'body techniques' (Mauss 1973).

This chapter then attempts to highlight the symbolic and material significance of 'body work' (Shilling 1993) and its management to a sociological understanding of the relationship between gendered bodies and the gendered organization of work. Our research indicates the extent to which flight attendants are managed, at least in part, through the supervision of their 'organizational bodies' in a highly gender-differentiated way. In the final section of the chapter, we consider the ways in which 'body work' and in particular, the deployment of 'tacit skills' (Manwaring and Wood 1985) in the presentation and performance of an organizational body, are fundamental to the flight attendant labour process and its gendered organization. We conclude that the essentialized *female* body is required to act as the material signifier of an organizational (service) ethos, and is managed through highly gendered techniques of corporeal management, demanding skilled labour or 'body work', which is effectively naturalized (and therefore not remunerated) because it is performed by women.

Gendered 'organizational bodies'

The regulation and subjugation of bodies, especially women's bodies, has clearly been fundamental to the development of human civilization (Elias 1991, Turner 1992, Shilling 1993). Similarly, the rationalization of labour and hence of the body, has been an essential feature of the development of modern capitalism. The instrumental control of the body can thus be seen as a fundamental part of the 'integration of human being and human doing for production, and a . . . triumph for instrumental rationality' (Casey 1995: 194). This rationalization of labour has been achieved, at least in part, through practices of discipline, diet, training and body regulation (Foucault 1979, Mauss 1973).

   Within both scientific management and human relations thought, management theorists have documented ways in which human performance might be increased through a focus on the body, using organizational structures (Gilbreth 1911) and ergonomic adjustment (Taylor 1911), cultural manipulation and emotional control (Mayo 1933, Roethlisberger and Dickson 1939). Each of these approaches shared in common a concern with the reproduction and regulation of the human body as an instrument of work. More recently, organization theorists have explored how organizational forms and practices have appropriated and diminished the body (Townley 1993, Barry and Hazen 1996). As Barry and Hazen (1996: 146) have put it 'it would seem our bodies have been hopelessly moulded, regimented and made to disappear by managerial and organizational practices, projects that in turn owe their rise to widespread societal and technological movements'.

A similar critique has emerged from recent feminist analyses that have focused on gender differences in the role and management of the body at work. Cockburn (1991) alerts us to a 'politics of bodies in the workplace'. Similarly, Acker (1990, 1992) has argued that the body is very much a part of processes of control in organizations. Hearn and Parkin have argued that the management of the dialectical relationship that is 'organization sexuality' is based largely on 'precision in the control of the body' (Hearn and Parkin 1995: 20). Empirical studies of 'women's work' have identified several examples of occupations in which certain 'properties, qualities and attributes' (De Lauretis 1989) associated with women's bodies come to be commodified – in nursing (James 1989), in clerical work (Davies 1979), in waitressing and bar work (Hall 1993, Adkins 1995), in the betting and gaming industry (Filby 1992) and also in secretarial work (Pringle 1989, 1993). Such studies have focused on the extent to which women's bodies are commodified in the performance of both sexual and emotional labour (Adkins 1995, Hochschild 1983). Recent feminist accounts have, therefore, drawn attention to the control of women's bodies and the gendered organization of work as intimately connected: 'the general trajectory of new theorizing of gender in the workplace, then, would appear to be more and more towards ... the recognition that real workers and real jobs are embodied' (Witz, Halford and Savage 1994: 5).

The body remains relatively undertheorized, however, within both critical organization studies and recent feminist studies of gender, work and organization; the processes through which bodies are 'incorporated' into organizational life and through which organizations are materialized in the bodies of employees, and how these processes relate to gender difference, remain something of a 'present absence', to invert Shilling's phrase (1993). In other words, the body is discussed, referred to and so on, but this discussion remains firmly embedded within the idea that the body exists as a 'pre-social' or rather 'pre-organizational' given. Throughout this chapter, we aim to address various ways in which (certain types of) lived bodies are incorporated into organizations, and vice versa, and how this incorporation relates to gender and to the labour process.

Through a process of 'incorporation', the materiality of an employee's body comes to act as a signifier of their employing organization, having incorporated its aesthetic standards into his/her embodied presentation and performance. We take as our starting point here the idea that as, Witkin (1990) has argued, an organization must continuously revivify and recreate itself as a dynamic 'agency' in order to create and to disseminate a unity of *organizational being* out of the diverse variety of 'interests' that enters into the structure of organizational action. It is only through realizing values common to this diverse variety of interests that the organization, as a dynamic agency (we might even say, as an 'active subject'), can be made 'present' and 'affective'. . . (192, original emphasis).

This broadly phenomenological understanding of organizational ontology enables us to focus on the ways in which it is in and through the cultivation of 'organizational bodies' that 'organizations develop and disseminate a *modus vivendi*, an 'organizational being' or 'presence' (ibid: 192). Understood in this way, organizational bodies can be perceived as constituted in and through organizational interaction, or 'incorporation' as it might be conceived, as the intercorporeal process through which an organizational subjectivity comes into 'being'. 'Incorporation' could therefore be understood as the means through which an organization comes to recognize itself, as organizational bodies interact and recognize each other as embodying the same organization and thus come to assume a collective, corporate (corporeal) identity. Uniformity of dress, for instance, operates as an important signifier and facilitator of the organization in this respect, in so far as it simultaneously conveys identity and asserts control (Pratt and Rafaeli 1997).

In the analysis that follows, we aim to address this relationship between identity and control in relation to the 'body work' of female flight attendants. Our research suggests that, in the case of the female flight attendant, the management of organizational bodies is particularly concerned with the body as the material signifier of the airline as a corporeal manifestation of an organizational ethos, and it is to this symbolic function of the 'organizational bodies' of flight attendants that we now turn.

The management of gendered organizational bodies in the airline industry

The empirical research upon which this chapter is based involved three main phases of fieldwork which were conducted between September 1994 and August 1995 (Tyler 1997). The first phase involved two case studies of the recruitment, training and supervision of flight attendants at two international airlines. The attendants studied during this first phase were largely employed on transatlantic services that were aimed at meeting the demands of a highly segmented and overwhelmingly male dominated market. As such, they were considered to be the 'elite' of their occupation, providing high levels of service to an informed, discerning and culturally powerful client group. A concurrent analysis of company documentation was undertaken at both airlines. Subsequently, observational flights were undertaken in various classes of travel with both organizations – in economy, business class and first class (ten in total, six with one airline and four with the other). During these flights, particular attention was paid to interaction between flight attendants and between flight attendants and passengers.

The second phase of the fieldwork involved three series of semi-structured interviews with a variety of airline personnel and with airline passengers: with applicants to airlines (12 in total, nine women and three men); with trainee and experienced flight attendants, including those who were involved in the recruitment, training and supervision of other flight attendants (25 in total, 19 women and six men) and with passengers (48 in total, 33 men and 15 women).

The third phase of the research entailed a content analysis of a wide variety of airline documentation, ranging from company mission statements, recruitment and training literature to advertising and marketing materials depicting female flight attendants obtained from some 48 airlines (from a total of 64 who were contacted).

This research suggested that the work of female flight attendants requires the deployment of 'tacit skills' (Manwaring and Wood 1985) and abilities which they are deemed to possess simply by virtue of being women. These include, for instance, 'caring' physically, emotionally and even sexually, in anticipating and responding to the needs and expectations of others. As one respondent (who was an experienced, male flight attendant) put it,

> . . . women are best suited to this role because they are much more patient and caring than men . . . of other people's needs . . . they are much more thoughtful by nature . . .

Consequently, these 'skills' are not recognized formally or remunerated by airline management. As Manwaring and Wood (1985: 190) have put it, 'dependence on tacit skills need not necessarily be reflected in . . . wages or . . . status'. But these skills which female flight attendants were expected to deploy as sexually differentiated labourers were nonetheless managed, largely through techniques of somatic supervision, and were implicated in various ways in the recruitment, training and supervision of flight attendants, each of which we will now consider in turn.

In the flight attendant recruitment process, the importance of tacit skills in the presentation and performance of the flight attendant's 'organizational body' is reflected in the quest for workers who can 'fit in' (ibid: 173) corporeally. Applicants to airlines were found to be rejected for some of the following reasons: the applicant was too old, the applicant's skin was blemished, the applicant's hair was too short, too messy or too severe, the applicants nails were too short or bitten, the applicant's posture was poor or the applicant's legs were too chubby. Other applicants were rejected on the basis that their weight was not considered to be in proportion to their height, they were too intro-verted, they lacked 'poise and style'. Others were rejected because, as one of the recruitment interviewers noted, they had a 'common accent'. One applicant was rejected by recruitment personnel on the basis that her teeth were too prominent in relation to her other facial features, others were rejected for being considered slightly 'pear shaped', or out of proportion (Tyler and Abbott 1998).

Drawing on the language of Goffman's dramaturgical sociology (Goffman 1959), we could suggest that in the flight attendant recruit-ment process, the airline industry demands of its employees a presen-tation of self through which the lived body is scripted, staged and performed in accordance with a standardized role, namely the 'organi-zational body', in a highly Procrustean way (Messing and Stevenson 1996), in so far as employees' bodies are required to conform to a predetermined organizational ideal in terms of uniformity of bodily appearance. For instance, in recruitment literature issued to potential applicants by one of the airlines we studied, it is stated that '. . . your grooming must be immaculate at all times – even at the end of a long and tiring flight . . . so that *you* fully complement *our* uniform' (emphasis added).

Applicants were found to be selected on the basis of their being capable of following stage directions, particularly those on how to project an (organizational) image or 'look': how to have 'poise' and 'grooming', as recruitment interviewers put it. In other words, female flight attendants were found to be selected, at least in part, for being able to perform an 'organizational body', without making the end result seem like a performance; that is, without revealing any evidence that the performance itself requires labour. Following Goffman (1963), the 'organizational body' can thus be understood as constituting an 'identity claim', except that it is a 'conditionally spoiled identity' (Tseelon 1995) in so far as it is only through constant labour that this identity claim can be sustained. The female flight attendant's organizational body could perhaps be understood as a kind of 'somatic simulacrum', in this sense – a copy of an original 'body' which does not exist. Her body is no more 'naturally' beautiful than her male colleagues and for her to conform to, or simulate, the embodiment of an organizational ideal therefore takes hard work and concerted effort, skills and resources. Yet, a female flight attendant must conceal her efforts behind an appearance of 'naturalness'. As one particular recruitment interviewer put it,

> . . . female flight attendants should have poise, they should be elegant . . . they should be . . . well sort of feminine . . . they should have a charm that comes naturally to them . . .

Similarly, in flight attendant training, female trainees in particular were found to be instructed to use their 'body language' as much as possible: '. . . above all, use your hips, hands, arms and your voice'. They were given no training or instruction in this use of 'body language', but like providing 'TLC' to passengers who are nervous or require first aid, they were told 'it's just common-sense really' (Tyler and Taylor 1998). Three particular uses of body language were considered to be fundamental to the establishment of a 'rapport' with passengers, and therefore to the efficient and effective provision of a 'more personal service' as training instructors put it. These require flight attendants to

> . . . always *walk softly* through the cabin, always *make eye contact* with each and every passenger, and always *smile* at them. This makes for a much more personal service, and is what First Class travel and [we] as a company are all about. *It's what we're here for* (emphasis added).

The presentation and performance of a lived, female body as a feminine 'organizational body' can thus be seen as a 'skill' which women at work in the airline industry are expected to be capable of deploying, yet they are given no specific training in this presentation or performance but are told to 'just do what comes naturally'.

Flight attendants are required to conform to company specific *formal* Uniform and Grooming Regulations, which stipulate, as well as regulations on clothing, shoes, hair and make-up and height–weight regulations. These *formal* regulations are reinforced throughout the contemporary airline industry by more gender-specific, *informal* peer pressure and self-appraisal, in the norms and values which permeate the occupational culture of flight attendants. These formal and informal elements combine to produce what amounts to a 'colonization of chang-ing room culture' (Tyler and Abbott 1998), forcing female flight attendants into a competition with one another over embodiment. Female flight attendants thus experience their bodies as being 'on stage' (Goffman 1963: 43–4): they must remain selfconscious about the impres-sion they are making, with very few 'back stage' opportunities. The female flight attendant has, therefore, to remain constantly 'body conscious' so as not to make a spectacle of herself, by inadvertently dis-closing or exposing parts of her uncontrolled and undisciplined 'natural' body as failures of diet, grooming or exercise. This results in flight atten-dants being constantly caught up in a 'feminine body paradox' within which they perceive their bodies as 'a hindrance, a prison, weighed down by everything peculiar to it' (De Beauvoir 1988: 15) and simultaneously, as the raw material of their commodified selves providing 'opportunities' for them in highly gender segregated labour markets. Thus, a paradoxi-cal existence is inscribed into the presentation and performance, and lived expenence, of women's 'organizational bodies'.

In this sense, women at work in the contemporary airline industry experience their bodies as both constraining and as facilitating. For instance, airlines market a contradiction, between responsibility for the safety and security of passengers on the one hand, and images of con-straint, confinement and fragility in the embodiment of their flight attendants on the other. The work of female flight attendants is thus underpinned by the need to maintain a 'glamorous' appearance while – and often in spite of – undertaking physically demanding labour in working conditions which are less than conducive to constant body maintenance. Drawing on research findings from the airline industry, the medical press and their own research, Boyd and Bain (1998: 26) have highlighted that

> cabin crew work is intrinsically demanding physically, and further affected by the universality of shiftworking, paucity of rest-breaks and an abysmal lack of facilities in which to take them, allied to the ever-present threat of contracting illness and disease due to polluted and unhygienic in-flight environmental conditions. Management pressure, sometimes reflected in a draconian disciplinary regime, also results in cabin crew members coming to work even when unfit to do so.

Clearly, an important theme running throughout much of the 'draconian' management of this contradiction between the requirements of gendered 'organizational bodies' and the working conditions of flight attendants is the idea and image of the 'perfect' organizational body, one which has a pervasive influence on women's consciousness of their bodies. In this respect, men and women in the airline industry were found to be subject to very different forms of regulation and control. Our research suggested that those techniques of somatic supervision through which the organizational bodies of flight attendants are managed are applied to male and female flight attendants in a gender-differentiated way. Male flight attendants have to look clean and 'socially attractive' – as the material signifiers of the antithesis of 'dirt' as metaphor (Douglas 1966) – whereas female flight attendants are specifically required to appear as sexually attractive – as desirable and as desiring (Weeks 1985) embodied commodities.

This suggests a direct relationship between the worker as a man or a woman and the form of regulative control, or somatic supervision, to which they are subject. This is indicated for instance, by the extent to which female flight attendants experience of their (sexually differentialized) organizational bodies is constantly saturated by images of the 'flawless professionalism' (as one particular advertisement for cabin crew recruitment put it) of other women at work in the airline industry (see Mills 1994). This difference between male and female flight attendants is significant because, in the case of the contemporary airline industry, while the former remain peripheral to the embodiment of the organization, the latter are required to epitomize an organizational ethos. For this to be managed effectively requires that female flight attendants seek and find pleasure in constructing and maintaining their organizational bodies and, in doing so, in conforming to an embodied, organizational aesthetic as indicated for instance, by the considerably more detailed uniform and grooming regulations issued to female flight attendants relative to male attendants at those airlines studied.

Various management strategies deployed in the construction and maintenance of organizational bodies involve not only peer but also self surveillance; female flight attendants in particular are managed through their own 'enjoyment' of their organizational bodies, and of the maintenance work which they are required to undertake as a condition of their employment in the airline industry. This inequality is perpetuated by the assumption that women enjoy this 'body work' and that it constitutes an aspect of their leisure rather than their working lives.

Those disciplinary practices that a female flight attendant must master in pursuit of an organizational body, suggest that art and discipline converge through a process of 'incorporation'. Through this process, a female flight attendant comes to embody the aesthetic standards of her employing organization; to present and perform her body according to a commercial logic which requires that she must develop a certain mode of being in her body which involves learning, practicing and internalizing a whole series of organizationally-defined 'body techniques' (Mauss 1973). As suggested above, this is largely because the female flight attendant's 'organizational body' is required, according to this logic, to act as the material expression of the airline by which she is employed, as the medium through which the employing organization is personified and through which it comes into contact with its highly segmented market. In the case of the flight attendant, her 'embodiment' is the primary instrument through which the airline encounters its passengers. This serves effectively to personify the organization (as employees are deemed to embody the organization's 'subjectivity'), and through the same process of embodiment, dehumanizes the employee who acts as an 'ontological subordinate', existing only to simultaneously personify and embody the employing organization.

What this suggests is an embodied process of organizational anthropomorphism, which simultaneously subjectifies the organization and objectifies the employee. In this respect, the management of embodiment within the flight attendant labour process can be seen as fundamental in engendering an 'organizational being'. The incorporation and expression of an organizational service ethos therefore appears to be a fundamental aspect of the role of the female flight attendant as a sexually differentialized labourer. Management must, therefore, incorporate the tacit skills of female flight attendants in performing 'body work' (Shilling 1993) in order to maximize the process – and profits – of 'incorporation' in a highly gendered way.

In conclusion: 'body work' and the gendered labour process

Thus, to secure employment as a flight attendant a woman must achieve and maintain a particular state of embodiment, prescribed primarily according to an instrumentally-imposed concept of a feminine body and practiced largely according to constraint, containment and concealment (Young 1990). This 'body work' must be undertaken in addition to, often in spite of, physically demanding manual labour, as well as the emotional and sexual labour (Hochschild 1983, James 1989, Adkins 1995) which flight attendants are required to perform. The maintenance of an appropriate state of embodiment demands both time and resources, yet, because this work is performed by women, the labour which is involved in performing and maintaining the appearance of a flight attendant is not remunerated as 'waged labour', but is perceived as an aspect of just 'being a woman' from which women are deemed to derive both pleasure and a sense of ontological security: 'investing in the body provides people with a means of self expression and a way of potentially feeling good and increasing the control they have over their bodies' (Shilling 1993: 7). As such, the 'body work' aspect of the flight attendant labour process is not remunerated as skilled labour. On the contrary, the 'body work' which flight attendants must undertake, perhaps as an example of what Marx called 'congealed labour' (Marx 1970: 11) – the labour required to transform one commodity into another – much like the 'emotional labour' aspect of their work (Hochschild 1983), constitutes 'concealed labour' to the extent that the better women are at its performance, the more invisible it becomes.

If we take the flight attendant as the epitomic sexually differentialized labourer (Tyler and Taylor 1998), we can observe the extent to which the bodies of flight attendants are moulded into material signifiers, not simply of the airline by which they are employed, but of the 'ethos' of contemporary capitalism more generally. Clearly, many workers – male and female – are trained to attire, intonate, and move their bodies and control their emotions in certain ways. However, sexually differentialized labour, of which we could argue the flight attendant's work is a notable example, specifically requires the management of the body – its presentation and performance – and this requirement is imposed in a fundamentally gendered way, at least in part, through organizational processes of incorporation. This process involves significant elements of 'body work' (Shilling 1993), through which the 'lived body' becomes the 'organizational body', engendering a bodily transformation (Ussher 1989) which is consequent upon the incorporation of the aesthetic standards of an employing organization.

In our consideration of these processes throughout this chapter, we have tried to argue first, that this work of incorporation suggests deficiency which is overcome through body work – yet, because this body work is performed by women, it is not recognized formally as 'work' – and second, that the moment that somatic surveillance is transformed into self surveillance may be seen as marking the moment when the 'lived body' becomes the 'organizational body'. Both aspects of incorporation – 'body work' (Shilling 1993) and somatic self surveillance –

we would argue are fundamentally embedded in both the relations of sexual difference and the structural properties of the flight attendant labour process. Intercorporation in the case of the airline industry can therefore be understood as a highly gendered process insofar as (i) the female organizational body acts as an organizational icon, as the embodiment of an organizational 'service' ethos, which is managed, at least in part, through (ii) gender-differentiated techniques of (formal and informal) somatic supervision which (iii) involve skilled labour which is naturalized *because* it is performed by women.

Bibliography

ACKER, J. (1990) 'Hierarchies, Jobs, Bodies: A Theory of Gendered Organizations'. *Gender and Society* 4:139–58.
ACKER, J. (1992) 'Gendering Organizational Theory', in A.J. Mills and P. Tancred (eds) *Gendering Organizational Analysis*. London: Sage.
ADKINS, L. (1995) *Gendered Work: Sexuality, Family and The Labour Market*. Milton Keynes: Open University Press.
BARRY, D. and M.A. HAZEN (1996) 'Do You Take Your Body To Work?', in D. Boje, R. Gephart, Jr. and T. Thatchenkey (eds) *Postmodern Management and Organization Theory*. London: Sage.
BOYD, C. and P. BAIN (1998) 'Once I get you up there, where the air is rarified: Health, Safety and the Working Conditions of Airline Cabin Crews'. *New Technology, Work and Employment*. 13, 1:16–28.
CASEY, C. (1995) *Work, Self and Society After Industrialism*. London: Routledge.
COCKBURN, C. (1991) *In The Way of Women: Men's Resistance To Sex Equality in Organizations*. London: Macmillan Press – now Palgrave.
DAVIES, M. (1979) 'Woman's Place is at the Typewriter: the Feminization of the Clerical Labour Force', in Z.R. Eisenstein (ed.) *Capitalist Patriarchy and The Case For Socialist Feminism*. New York: Monthly Review Press.
DE BEAUVOIR, S. (1988; first published 1949) *The Second Sex*. London: Jonathan Cape.
DE LAURETIS, T. (1989) 'The Essence of the Triangle or, Taking the Risk of Essentialism Seriously'. *Differences* 2:5–6.
DOUGLAS, M. (1966) *Purity and Danger*. London: Routledge and Kegan Paul.
ELIAS, N. (1991) 'On Human Beings and Their Emotions', in M. Featherstone, M. Hepworth and B. Turner (eds) *The Body: Social Process and Cultural Theory*. London: Sage.
FILBY, M.P. (1992) 'The Figures, The Personality and The Bums: Service Work and Sexuality'. *Work, Employment and Society* 6:23–42.
FOUCAULT, M. (1979) *Discipline and Punish: The Birth of The Prison*. Hamondsworth: Penguin.
GILBRETH, F.B. (1911) *Motion Study: A Method For Increasing The Efficiency of The Workman*. New York: D. Van Nostrand.
GOFFMAN, E. (1959) *The Presentation of Self in Everyday Life*. New York: Doubleday Anchor.

GOFFMAN, E. (1963) *Stigma: Notes on the Management of Spoiled Identity.* Englewood Cliffs, NJ: Prentice-Hall.
HALL, E.J. (1993) 'Waitering/Waitressing: Engendering The Work of Table Servers'. *Gender and Society* 17:329–46.
HEARN, J. and W. PARKIN (1995) 2nd edn *'Sex' at 'Work': The Power and Paradox of Organization Sexuality.* Brighton: Harvester Wheatsheaf.
HOCHSCHILD, A.R. (1983) *The Managed Heart: Commercialization of Human Feeling.* Berkeley: University of California Press.
JAMES, N. (1989) 'Emotional Labour: Skill and Work in The Social Regulation of Feelings'. *Sociological Review* 37:15–42.
MANWARING, T. and S. WOOD (1985) 'The Ghost in The Labour Process', in D. Knights, H. Willmott and D.L. Collinson (eds) *Job Redesign: Critical Perspectives on The Labour Process.* Aldershot: Gower.
MARX, K. (1970; first published 1864) *Capital: Volume One.* London: Lawrence and Wishart.
MAUSS, M. (1973; first published 1934) 'Techniques of The Body', *Economy and Society.* 2:70–88.
MAYO, E. (1933) *The Human Problems of an Industrial Civilization.* New York: Macmillan Press – now Palgrave.
MESSING, K. and J. STEVENSON (1996) 'Women in Procrustean Beds: Strength Testing and the Workplace'. *Gender, Work and Organization* 3, 3:156–67.
MILLS, A.J. (1994) *Duelling Discourses: Desexualization Versus Eroticism In The Corporate Framing of Sexuality: Images of British Airways.* Paper presented to the annual conference of the BSA, Preston, March.
PRATT, M.G. and A. RAFAELI (1997) 'Organizational Dress as a Symbol of Multilayered Social Identities'. *Academy of Management Journal* 40, 4:862–98.
PRINGLE, R. (1989) *Secretaries Talk: Sexuality, Power and Work.* London: Verso.
PRINGLE, R. (1993) 'Male Secretaries', in C. Williams (ed.) *Doing 'Women's Work': Men In Nontraditional Occupations.* London: Sage.
ROETHLISBERGER, F.J. and W.J. DICKSON (1939) *Management and The Worker.* Cambridge, MA: Harvard University Press.
SHILLING, C. (1993) *The Body and Social Theory.* London: Sage.
SHILLING, C. (1997) 'The Undersocialized Conception of The Embodied Agent in Modern Sociology'. *Sociology* 31, 4:737–54.
TAYLOR, F.W. (1911) *Principles of Scientific Management.* New York: Harper & Row.
TOWNLEY, B. (1993) 'Foucault, Power/Knowledge, and its Relevance for Human Resource Management'. *Academy of Management Review* 18, 3:518–45.
TSEELON, E. (1995) *The Masque of Femininity: The Presentation of Woman in Everyday Life.* London: Sage.
TURNER, B. (1991) 'Recent Developments on The Theory of The Body', in M. Featherstone, M. Hepworth and B. Turner (eds) *The Body: Social Process and Cultural Theory.* London: Sage.
TURNER, B. (1992) *Regulating Bodies.* London: Routledge.
TYLER, M. (1997) 'Women's Work as The Labour of Sexual Difference: Female Employment in the Airline Industry', unpublished doctoral dissertation, University of Derby.

TYLER, M. and P. ABBOTT (1998) 'Chocs Away: Weight Watching in The Con-
temporary Airline Industry'. *Sociology* 32(3):433–50.
TYLER, M. and S. TAYLOR (1998) 'The Exchange of Aesthetics: Women's Work
and The Gift'. *Gender, Work and Organization* 5(3):165–71.
USSHER, J. (1989) *The Psychology of The Female Body.* London: Routledge.
WEEKS, J. (1985) *Sexuality and Its Discontents: Meanings, Myths and Modern
Sexualities.* London: Routledge and Kegan Paul.
WILLIAMS, C. (1988) *Blue, White and Pink Collar Workers.* London: Allen and
Unwin.
WITKIN, R.W. (1990) 'The Collusive Manoeuvre: A Study of Organizational Style
in Work Relations', in B.A. Turner (ed.) *Organizational Symbolism.* New York:
Walter de Gruyter.
WITZ, A., S. HALFORD and M. SAVAGE (1994) 'Organized Bodies: Gender,
Sexuality, Bodies and Organizational Culture'. Paper presented to the annual
conference of the British Sociological Association, Preston, March.
WITZ, A., S. HALFORD and M. SAVAGE (1997) *Gender, Careers and Organisations.*
London: Macmillan Press – now Palgrave.
YOUNG, I.M. (1990) *Throwing Like A Girl and Other Essays in Feminist Philosophy
and Social Theory.* Indianapolis: Indiana University Press.

4
Sex, Talk and Making Bodies in the Science Lab.

Tom Delph-Janiurek

Introduction

The role of language, especially in the form of everyday talk, has been relatively neglected in work on the (re)production of embodied social identities. For instance in work on gender and everyday organizational life, linguistic interactions are often treated simply as the expressions of embodied social relations. Particular features of the way people talk to each other as gendered beings tend to be regarded as merely indexical of visibly, physically embodied gender and its associated power relations. The gendered identities and roles of interactants in conversations, therefore, tend to be regarded as fixed and static, as derived entirely elsewhere, as *possessions* brought to everyday interactions. However, recent work on language as social practice suggests that it is a prime means of through which separate and collective notions of gendered and sexualized identities are routinely and continually constructed, ascribed and may be resisted/contested. This approach treats gendered and sexualized identities and power relations as fluid *processes* that are continually (re)constituted through conversational behaviours rather than being more rigidly held possessions. This distinction matters because it seems to offer a fresh and productive way of addressing forms of routine, everyday oppression based on gender and sexuality. Furthermore, in the work of Judith Butler (1990, 1993) linguistic acts are implicated at the heart of the (re)constitution of gendered bodies.

What I explore here is how Butler's work and a focus on conversational behaviours can contribute to understanding routine, everyday ways through which people are (re)constituted as gendered and sexualized beings. Drawing on empirical work conducted in 'hard' science departments at universities in the north of England, I seek to move beyond simply considering bodies as sites at which gender is verbally and physically performed. What I want to draw attention to is how talk and bodies are both authored *and* audienced in particular ways relevant to gender, and how these processes are shaped by the specific discursive repertoires and meanings shared among particular groups. This is linked to the operation of power interactionally in that these groups also share 'rules' governing what kinds of gendered verbal and bodily perfor-mances will be collectively deemed intelligible and acceptable.

Talk and the (re)constitution of gender

Combining and expanding upon a diverse range of ideas such as those developed by Erving Goffman and Louis Althusser, Butler suggests that each time a person is addressed or referred to as a gendered being is cita-tional of 'authoritative' ascriptions of gender that begin with the 'found-ing medical interpellation' at birth (see Butler 1993: 7–8). In accordance with normative heterosexuality, infants are assigned one of two possi-ble genders according to sexually differentiated physical/biological fea-tures, what Tamsin Wilton (1996) has referred to as a 'genital identity'. The discourses that lie behind the selection of these criteria co-construct sex, so the distinction between sex as 'natural' given and gender as social construct disappears. This initial assignment of gender becomes an offi-cial statutory identity when recorded on a birth certificate, and prompts other authoritative performative acts through which gender is pre-scribed. For instance it is used to confirm that prospective marriage part-ners accord with the requirements of a legal marriage recognized by the state in Britain, by officially holding the status of woman and man. It is also used to determine whether individuals are sent to women's or men's prisons should they be given custodial sentences for some reason, notoriously in the case of those who have undergone surgical gender reassignment.

So rather than simply being used to name or refer to gendered bodies, gendered forenames, pronounal referents and terms of address can be regarded as citational hailings that actually work to (re)produce gendered bodies in everyday interactions. These performative speech activities must be matched by corresponding speech activities and performances by gendered subjects themselves, that work to constantly reaffirm and reproduce gendered subjectivity. Of course, all of this linguistic activity happens in conjunction with materially visible performances that include modes of bodily re-presentation such as dress, but it is important to recognize that the seemingly straightforward boundary

between language and the material is problematized and blurred.
Performances of gender include 'appropriate' ways of responding to the
hailings of others and ways of behaving as recognizably or intelligibly
gendered beings within the heterosexual matrix. The penalty for failing
to do this, of being unintelligible, is a form of excommunication, in
which bodies and subjects are removed to the 'unliveable' and 'unviable'.
This is also achieved through language, through the use of what Butler
refers to as 'prohibitive performatives'. They include homophobic hailings of subjects as 'masculine, phallic lesbians' or as 'feminine, effeminate gay men'. Butler also argues that 'racialized' bodies and subjects are
produced in a similar way, within a binary of white/non-white.

The process by which intelligibly gendered, heterosexualized, bodies
are (re)produced can thus be regarded as a kind of chain comprising
four linked components:

1. physiological bodies
2. the operation of hegemonic discourses of gender through official
   statutory powers, via authoritative performative acts that interpellate
   individuals as gendered subjects
3. much more everyday performative acts that are citational of these
   official interpellations
4. everyday performances through which individual bodies are
   authored as gendered in ways that match these gender ascriptions.

At each of these four points some form of disruption can occur to this
continual, repetitive process, creating slippage in the chain. There is of
course great debate among feminists, queer theorists and others concerning which interventionist techniques might best be applied, and
where in the chain (for example physically/visibly altering bodies
through medical/cosmetic intervention, amending the law, changing or
policing language, mis-performing gender) in order to dismantle the
oppressions and oppressive meanings of the hegemonic gender dualism
and normative, compulsory heterosexuality.

But one of the main criticisms often levelled at this account of the
(re)production of gendered/sexed bodies is that a sense of bodies as
physical 'things' seems to be erased. It is argued to be simply too much
of an abstraction away from the everyday world as we live in and understand it. This is particularly since Butler has further developed her work
mostly in relation to the authoritative interpellations of statutory legislation (see Butler 1997), rather than more routine everyday kinds of
conversation. A consequence is that bodies are presented as shaped by
the knowledges and workings of statutory, institutional forms of power

that are at a remove from everyday life and beyond the capacity of many people to challenge. Furthermore, they are also presented as subject to rather monolithic, 'macro' systems of meaning. Butler too seems to regard everyday talk as more of an outcome – it is merely 'citational' – rather than itself having the power to (re)produce bodies and subjectivities as gendered and sexualized within the time/space limits of each interaction. By focusing on features of everyday talk in a particular setting, or set of spaces, I will draw attention to how the verbal (re)constitution of gendered bodies is closely interwoven into everyday, repetitive conversational and bodily practices. Furthermore, I will highlight how this takes place in particular ways that are directly connected to local interactional 'rules' and much more 'micro level' systems of meaning as these operate within and between different groups. In turn this illuminates how power operates through verbal and embodied interactional behaviours and how this is linked to the (re)constitution of shared meanings concerning gender, along with other notions of sameness and difference.

Science laboratories at universities

This chapter examines some features of everyday talk reported in interviews with nine white postgraduate students and postdoctoral researchers working in four 'hard' science departments at three different universities in the north of England[1]. All names have been changed and the information provided about interviewees kept to a minimum in order to protect confidentiality. These interviews were conducted as part of empirical research into the role of language in the (re)production of gendered and sexualized spaces. There are several reasons for investigating conversational behaviours at science laboratories. They are ostensibly objective, highly rational domains in which the personal and the bodily, as these relate to workers themselves, may often be presumed to be unacknowledged or excluded. Along with a hierarchy of workplace roles (for example research team leaders, postdoctoral researchers, postgraduates, technical staff), workers in these spaces comprise 'communities' that might spend considerable lengths of time together, with a requirement for co-operation regarding the use of space and equipment within the laboratory. And as was especially the case at two of the research sites, they can also be very multilingual spaces, with high proportions of research workers for whom English may be only a second, third or fourth language.

In operationalizing Butler's theory, interviews have some advantages over the collection of actual conversational data. As many linguists have long argued, meanings in conversational interactions do not inhere within the actual linguistic structures of utterances but in the performative work that any utterance achieves. The significance of a piece of talk is not so much in what is actually said, but in what interactional activity or activities are intended and, crucially, how the talk is interpreted. Of course, sometimes great significance lies in the lack of accordance between authoring and interpretation. Interviews are therefore a way of collecting accounts of conversational behaviours that include highly relevant information concerning the encoding and interpretation of embodied interactional activities, features that sound and video recordings of conversational interactions simply do not capture.

Bodily and verbal organization

The physical layout of buildings and rooms in university departments, and the boundaries and internal divisions through which bodies are organized at their particular work locations, places restrictions on interactional patterns. Interviewees described the division of researchers into different laboratories, broadly according to their research topic. Researchers usually share laboratory work spaces on a routine basis, only retreating to individual desk or office spaces periodically to use computer terminals or engage in reading or writing tasks. Within this spatial organization of bodies, individuals may have very little control over whom they come into contact and share workspaces with on a routine daily basis. This may be particularly the case for postgraduates; all postgraduate interviewees lacked a notionally 'private' individual office space. This organization of work locations creates micro 'communities of proximity' within departments, that may have common research interests, share the same types of work and often occupy the same positions within the organizational hierarchy. But members of these 'communities' do not necessarily co-operate together as colleagues or mesh socially. As one postgraduate interviewee put it when talking about her work colleagues:

> *Cath*: [. . .] you can't pick and choose . . . you're stuck with them, it's like a family[2]

In addition to physical location, social attributes such as age can also be a factor in shaping conversational patterns. An interviewee in another department made this clear when he spoke about his relations with other male postgraduates:

Rob: Damien's older, he's got . . . he's done things in his life already, so he's from a slightly different sort of background to me . . . Dave's . . . more like me in terms of he's just left university and gone straight into a Ph.D., but he works at the other site so although I get on with him I don't really . . . I wouldn't say we were friends because I don't see him enough . . .

Along with this physical organization of bodies undertaking their workplace duties, the organizational positions of research staff, ancillary staff, postgraduates and technicians are continuously (re)produced in everyday ways through talk. Interactants collaborate in the production of a variety of language games, shaped by organizational regulations and codes governing the daily routines, rituals and practices of workplace duties. These formal rules and regulations determine matters such as the particular tasks members of the university population should engage in, how they should do them and to what standard, who may direct whom to perform particular tasks, and who may ask whom for particular types of information. These verbal interactional performances involve the continuous (re)production of patterns of domination and authority, equality, deference and subordination, in accordance with the positions that interactants occupy within the organizational hierarchy. These were the kinds of conversational behaviours that interviewees initially described when asked about their daily routines. They began by characterizing their everyday workspaces as peopled by stable, rational, diligent researchers and support staff, as spaces where notions of workers as embodied social beings were ostensibly erased with the donning of white lab. coats.

However they went on to describe how co-operative ways of working and repetitive, intelligible performances of organizational roles as embodied social beings often demanded degrees of sociability and the sharing of personal information. For instance verbal performances of the role of postgraduate in interactions with other postgraduates were described as usually being centered around talk unrelated to work and, therefore, often demanding the disclosure of items of more personal information. Sonia's is a typical characterization of this workplace 'chat':

Sonia: What do we talk about? It's just kind of . . . just stuff . . . we talk about going out or what we're going to do at the weekend . . . anything but work really [we both laugh] it's kind of a release I suppose from . . . from being at work.

Postgraduates often described themselves as highly sociable and willing to discuss personal details with each other (in one instance this included a frank discussion at lunch of personal methods of birth control). When postgraduates did talk with each other about their work this involved discussion of having problems with research projects and supervisors, and avoiding seeming confident and well-organized. For instance one interviewee described how work-related talk in her lab. was

> *Cath*: [. . .] about how you're work's going and how crap it is and you know [we both laugh] and nothing's working and there must be a curse or something on the lab at the moment . . . things like that.

In contrast to this easy, informal talk, postgraduate interviewees described how talk with supervisors and others higher up the hierarchy was usually closely related to work and often demanded degrees of preplanning and close self monitoring. In this way these conversational habits are characteristic of broad gendered language genres; namely 'feminine' and supposedly inconsequential 'chat' based around assumptions of equality, and 'masculine', pre-planned, 'important' talk. Within these kinds of 'communities of practice', groups or networks of colleagues or 'friends' interacting together on a regular basis, interviewees described how a great deal of talk unrelated to work comprised heavily stereotypical verbal performances of gender. Both women and men interviewees described men as frequently talking about 'public', 'masculine' topics such as politics, sports, cars and computers; women as frequently talking about 'feminine' topics that included television soap operas and more 'private' concerns such as relationships and feelings, shopping and children. These seemed to be the prime ways that interviewees recognized themselves and their colleagues engaging in vocal performances of gender and gendered power relations.

So to an extent, the sharing of personal information in conversations occurred in accordance with the findings of Halford, Savage and Witz (1997), whose work suggests that this is one way that hierarchical relations within organizations may be (re)produced. The broad idea is that senior workers maintain authority and social distance by avoiding personal disclosure to juniors. Junior workers share more personal information with each other, but tend to avoid disclosing any information that might compromise their position and prospects to seniors. However, the prescriptions of hegemonic versions of gender place constraints on the extent to which heterosexual men may talk about 'personal' matters such as emotions and relationships without compromising their masculinity.

It is noticeable how the stereotypical verbal performances of gender that interviewees described were shaped around men speaking about 'serious', public, impersonal and therefore 'masculine' topics and women speaking about 'the inconsequential', 'the personal' and the private, and therefore the 'feminine'. This obviously adds another dimension to the sharing of personal information, the performance of organizational roles and the (re)production of power relations. Furthermore, the patterns of social closeness and distance suggested by interviewees conversational habits were evidently defined in complex ways. Gender, position within the workplace hierarchy and age were just some of the dimensions along which degrees of sameness and difference were constructed. Interviewees described how these notions of sameness and difference operated in ways directly linked to conversational behaviours and the interpretation of meanings in talk.

'Discursive communities'

At a more complex level than 'communities of practice' are what Linda Hutcheon (1994) refers to as 'discursive communities'. These are groups of people that share highly complex sets of linguistic, rhetorical, ideological and social knowledges, perspectives and beliefs. Hutcheon develops this notion of discursive communities in relation to irony, suggesting that ironical meanings work among those who already share the same set of presuppositions and the same semantic and semiotic frame. She suggests that membership of discursive communities is often shaped around notions of gender, sexuality, 'class', 'race', ethnicity, and may also relate to profession, ethics and morals, that configure what she calls 'micropolitical complexities that do not have ready labels'. An illustration of the difference between being a member of a community of practice and a member of a discursive community, as this relates to gender and sexuality, was supplied by Cath. She described a common occurrence reported by several interviewees, talk featuring a kind of 'ironic' banter between women and men engaging in 'playful' gendered rivalry and enacting gender solidarity:

> *Cath*: I mean there's the general banter [. . .] you know, lads and girls and they're always picking on each other, you know . . . it could be construed as sexist but nothing serious, do you know what I mean?

I mean there's things up on like the wall like lab rules, you know and there's one girl called Francine who, she's a great laugh and she'll, er you know . . . I think the blokes kind of tend to target as er taking the piss out of her . . . but not in a nasty way at all, it's all done in a, it's a very jolly way . . . it's like 'Oh Cine, you've done this wrong' and so there's a lot of lab rules up saying Francine must do all the menial tasks and things like this, you know, and then there's the one next to it saying that Paul must do all of them you know, it's all that kind of . . . you're sort of forever . . . man, woman kind of, you know . . . 'men are crap, women are great' sort of thing, you know . . . that goes on.

Engaging in this kind of 'banter' is of course another way that gendered identities are (re)produced through talk. However, the production of something as being ironic or playful rather than hurtful or oppressive is subject to authors and readers belonging to the same discursive community. 'Getting' the irony and 'sharing the joke' therefore involves sharing a kind of social competence. In the case of Cath, an 'out' lesbian in her lab, what I interpreted as a resigned tone in her voice as she described this suggested to me that there was perhaps a deeper level of irony in operation when she participated in this kind of banter.

Language codes and modes

Membership of both 'communities of practice' and 'discursive communities' demands competence with the dominant codes and modes of talk. These abilities are also fundamental elements of what is a kind of localized social competence. Two interviewees whom I interviewed together drew attention to issues surrounding linguistic competence. Sally, an English woman postgraduate and Marten, a Dutch man postdoctoral researcher who had been living in England for several years, were working in a laboratory along with ten other research workers, the majority of whom were drawn from other European countries, and half of whom were men. All members of the lab took their coffee and tea breaks together in a part of the lab. where work desks were located, there being no 'proper' coffee area. Within this informal break-time space, seats were organized in a rough circle. Marten reported that a prime feature of the usual arrangement of bodies was the segregation of women and men, although Sally made it clear that this was not something she was aware of until it was mentioned by Marten. This bodily performance of gender to some extent followed the pattern of occupation of work desks, in that two women's desks were located close to the drinks machine, whereas a cluster of men's desks were located towards the other side of the room. During these breaks Sally and Marten agreed that there was a considerable requirement for some form of conversation to take place:

> *Tom*: Do people try and avoid silence in coffee?
> *Marten*: Yeah
> *Sally*: Yeah [. . .]
> *Sally*: Mmm . . . especially if there's like twelve of you in (. . .) sat there all silent . . . yeah, it's shit, yeah . . .

The dominant language during these breaks was English, this was the one language that most speakers had at least some ability with. But this meant that some members of the laboratory were effectively excluded from conversation because of their low levels of ability with English, although Sally suggested that for two French women this exclusion was self-imposed:

> *Sally*: [. . .] Gabrielle and Beatrice won't join in because they think that their English isn't good enough [. . .]

For women, being excluded from conversation places them in the traditional 'feminine' position in 'public' speech domains, namely that of non-participants lacking a voice. However for men to be silenced runs contra to the 'scripts' of hegemonic versions of masculinity, and silencing can therefore operate to remove men towards the realms of the unintelligible. This seemed to be evident in the case of one man in particular:

> *Marten*: Theo never speaks . . .
> *Sally*: Theo never does, yeah, I don't know what's wrong with Theo but . . .
> *Tom*: Is he just quiet all the time?
> *Marten*: He's . . . he's a bit weird in the sense that . . . he's definitely not quiet all the time . . . he's got certain people that he talks quite a lot with . . . well he's got a bit of a problem I think in that sort of group situation so . . . he shuts up and . . . sits at the end . . . in front of his computer and stares at the screen . . . and drinks his tea or coffee or whatever . . .

Theo's non-participation in group conversations, in conjunction with bodily distancing himself from the rest of the group, contrasts with his behaviour towards a more selective audience. His silence during work-breaks marks him out as lacking social abilities and as evidently being something of a 'puzzle'. His eye-gaze is described as averted from the group, and there is a sense of a stereotypically gendered 'nerdiness' or 'geekiness' in the attention he is reported to give to his computer screen.

Participation in multi-party conversation also demands competence with the dominant mode of speech. Marten and Sally drew attention to speech rate when they described talk with a member of the lab. for whom English was a first language but who had impaired hearing:

Marten: [. . .] with Claire, she's deaf . . . if you want to draw her in first of all you have to repeat.

Sally: Yeah, you can't do it naturally, the conversation becomes really stilted, cause first of all she hasn't got a clue what . . . what's been said before, yeah, and then you have to sort of break the conversation . . . in order to get a point across to er . . . and even when she answers you can't follow it up very easily because you have to ask the same question twice . . . and she won't wear her hearing aid for some reason, [. . .] so . . . it's quite difficult to . . . on a one-on-one it's a bit . . . a bit easier, but I still . . . it's still very . . . stilted because it just doesn't . . . the conversation . . . doesn't go fast somehow, yeah, it feels unusual because it's so slow . . .

Individuals can also be excluded from key conversations at which the collective identity and membership of dominant workplace social groupings are defined. A marked feature of interviewees accounts of their workplace friendships was how often these were accomplished away from the workplace itself, and the extent to which this accomplishment involved the exchange of personal or 'private' information. In general, the closeness of particular friendships were largely defined around the degree to which information exchanged was felt to be private and personal. Conversations in which groups engage in the exchange of close personal information are instances in which ideas and assumptions concerning gender and sexuality, particularly as these relate to those present and other individuals at work, may be circulated and negotiated. They are social events at which individual, embodied gendered identities can be more fully 'fleshed out', as individuals share (auto)biographical narratives. But Rob described how one woman was excluded from participating in this kind of key conversation when he spoke about socializing in the pub after work with colleagues:

[. . .] we play games like 'Truth', right when we've been absolutely pissed out of our heads and gone round in a circle telling each other inappropriate bits of information [laughing] that we probable shouldn't mention anyway [...] there's some personalities in the department which are not part of that erm ... Lisa Ahmed because of her religious up-bringing erm although she's very erm ... without being patronizing, she's very Westernized and ... and is very amenable to sort of going to the pub and not drinking herself but being there [...] we're having this conversation around her ... in some respects that's a bit inappropriate.

What Rob describes is conversational behaviour that is 'feminine' to the extent that it is centered on the disclosure of personal information. This takes place as part of a social event – heavy drinking in public – that used to be more associated with 'masculinity' but which might now be associated with newly emerging forms of femininity. However, this is 'masculine' behaviour, in that the purposes of this kind of conversation are geared towards humorous effect and embarrassment rather than being to do with more 'feminine' matters such as mutuality or empathy. And the suggestion is that those who do not participate fully are constituted as 'other' in some way. I suggest that these kinds of conversations may often be crucial in the establishment and continuation of dominant workplace cultures.

Conversational subtleties

However, it is not only lack of abilities with the dominant codes and modes of talk that may limit participation in conversation. An ability to decode and encode shared, locally dominant meanings that may often be expressed in quite indirect and subtle ways is also required in order to avoid being constituted as 'other'. Negotiating social relations in conversation includes understanding the implicit, indirect, moment-by-moment subtleties of verbal and gestural performances. These include the subtleties and potential ambiguities of encoded citational hailings and positionings as social beings 'samed' or 'othered' along the lines of gender, sexuality, 'race', 'class' or age. The extent to which participation in effortless, 'relaxing' social conversation or 'chat' demands a knowledge of the complexities of the constitution and negotiation of interpersonal meanings was highlighted when Marten and Sally spoke about conversation with members of the lab. who were fluent in English, but who did not have 'first language' abilities:

Marten: [...] you have to make an effort to get into a conversation with them ...

Sally: I mean okay they can talk it and they can understand what you're saying but they don't understand sometimes like [. . .] your conversation as like sarcastic you know, cause a lot of the way that you communicate sometimes is through sarcasm you know when you go out to say to people you just say it for a laugh, you know what I mean? and er you know, you can't do that so you sort of have to conduct the conversation without any sort of nuances in it, it's just a very straight forward conversation.

These people were obviously grammatically competent users of English as a code with a set of ostensibly 'fixed' meanings. But they lacked the kind of social competence that permits the possibility of levels of irony, ambiguity and the destabilization of 'fixed' meanings, dimensions along which a discursive community may often operate. In contrast, talk with members of the same discursive community was much more satisfying because it was easier to negotiate social relationships with someone sharing the same codes, modes and subtleties of talk:

Sally: [. . .] if I was talking with Marcus for instance, yeah, half of our conversation would be . . . well maybe not half of it, but a lot of it we'd be taking the piss out of each other, yeah, then that leads on to more serious conversation, yeah, but you can't do that in conversation [. . .] with Claire for instance . . . and that . . . in that, it tends to be partly . . . boring [laughs] because there's no . . . there's like a complete lack of all the other sort of erm . . . social signs of talking . . . not necessarily the facial expression but . . . the way . . . I don't know really how to describe it . . .

What Sally describes is how she and Marcus negotiate their interactional relations through 'inconsequential' talk in the form of traded insults, what could be regarded by an outsider as offensive, aggressive interactional behaviour. What I take her to be describing here is how she and Marcus engage in subtle bodily and other displays of close listenership and full comprehension in these conversations, and that these contribute to verbal and other processes through which they are continually mutually constituted as 'same'.

The verbal constitution of sexualized difference

So far, as the everyday stories and comments of my interviewees illustrate, talk and bodily behaviours are very closely implicated in the everyday interactional (re)production of gendered and 'othered' bodies. A key point is that 'getting on' with work colleagues and participating in workplace communities of practice and discursive communities demands a complex mixture of abilities. These communities are partly based around shared assumptions concerning gendered and sexualized intelligibility. Non-participatory behaviours (particularly for those that embody masculinity), or performances as social actors that do not use the same codes and modes of talk, are read as evidence of 'otherness' and can remove individuals towards the domains of the unviable. Sally provided a clear example of this when she talked about contrasting attitudes towards two gay men, Tim and Mike, who had previously worked in her department:

> *Sally*: [. . .] there's one guy er Tim, I think he's left now, but he was like . . . you know, he was always gay priding and that . . . I think in Tim's case everyone was fine about it because they . . . they knew he was gay and . . . he's not effeminate or at all, but you know he was just . . . he was ringing up his boyfriend and whatever [. . .]

Sally describes Tim's behaviour at work as according with shared notions of 'appropriacy' and some of the prescriptions of hegemonic forms of masculinity, in that his modes of bodily (re)presentation are described as not including any 'feminine' signifiers. For these reasons he was afforded at least some degree of acceptance among his work colleagues. In contrast she described how Mike's workplace self presentation included the misperformance of gender in the form of 'feminine' verbal characteristics, some of which she reproduces in the interview. These contributed to highly marked verbal performances of a 'camp' gayness, and in turn to him not being accepted by colleagues. This was along with what is perhaps regarded as his 'failure' to participate in social networks at work:

> *Sally*: . . . he likes his own particular circle of friends, yeah, and it's all like really sort of *lovey* yeah? . . . 'Oh Lovey' you know 'Can I?' and very . . . yeah, I don't know [. . .] he's very over the top . . . in his show of affection for certain people and stuff . . . and that pisses a few people off, I don't know why, it just does . . . yeah . . . because he's not just . . . it's not just affection . . . he just goes too far . . . it just really grates on your nerves after a bit . . .

Mike, unlike Tim, had been the subject of homophobic comments and 'jokes'. Sally went on to describe how negative attitudes towards Mike also stemmed from a particular incident at work. Mike was regarded as having infringed social 'rules' by attempting to place restrictions on who was to attend an out-of-work social gathering:

> [. . .] this person was leaving and (Mike) was his friend and this person said 'Oh, you know, I'm going to have a party and everyone's going to be invited' but Mike went around saying 'Oh specifically such-and-such and such-and-such is *not* invited to this', you know . . . very sort of exclusive, and people disliked him because of that, and that's why . . . I don't think it's right that they take the piss out of him . . . but they latch onto the fact that he's gay as something to sort of hold against him.

What this suggests is that failure to cohere with the prevailing dominant social 'rules' at work (which in the case of the research sites discussed here tended to be shaped around Anglophonic, masculine heterosexual norms) also constitutes individuals as 'others'. Non-conformative performances of gender and, as in the case of Mike, sexuality, may then be taken as additional 'proof' of this otherness, though perhaps the social conduct of those classed as gendered or sexualized 'others' tends to be placed under closer scrutiny. In contrast to Mike, who undoubtedly is relegated to the domains of the unviable and the unliveable through the verbal behaviours of his colleagues, both Tim and Cath, as an 'out' lesbian, enjoyed much more acceptance from their heterosexual colleagues. Cath herself felt that her ability and willingness to participate in dominant kinds of conversation (such as the gendered 'banter' discussed earlier) contributed to this acceptance.

Conclusion

Several points emerge from these interview narratives that support Butler's theory and suggest ways it might be developed further. Quite clearly routine forms of talk, in conjunction with bodily behaviours and modes of (re)presentation, are central to the everyday (re)production of gender and sexuality. These interviewees describe how being intelligible as a social being at work demands participation in conversations in which personal information, including details relevant to gender and sexuality, are shared. They describe verbal performances and hailings, along with patterns of conversational participation and behaviour, through which beings are continually (re)constituted as gendered, within the time/space limits of workplace conversations.

In addition, the comments of these interviewees suggest that these verbal processes can undoubtedly be subject to highly 'localized' sets of expectations, assumptions, informal 'rules' and shared knowledges, as these operate among communities of practice and discursive communities. These verbal processes may evidently be closely bound up with the interactional operation of power, and the (re)constitution and circulation of dominant workplace cultures and associated processes through which individuals are repetitively (re)constituted as 'others'. And quite clearly notions of sameness and difference might be highly complex among people spending relatively long periods of time together. These are situations in which the significance of the visible of bodies may recede and the linguistic become more central. Gender and sexuality undoubtedly intersect with a variety of other axes along which sameness and difference may be constructed. Interviewees' comments illustrate how notions of difference can be constituted linguistically, for instance through (lack of) abilities with the dominant codes and modes of talk. But in addition to abilities with English, notions of sameness can also be constructed through far less explicit linguistic means, through subtleties of expression and meaning operating among members of the same discursive communities, and through the extent to which individuals cohere with informal social 'rules'. The suggestion here is that full linguistic competence includes the ability to perform and hail others as gendered beings in very subtle, implicit ways that go beyond the formal features of talk such as word-choice or grammatical structure.

Regarding the notion of intelligibility, clearly there can be many 'local' factors involved when collectively-held notions of intelligibility are agreed, and those identified as gendered/sexualized 'others' either accepted or ostracized. The ostensibly 'neutral', though implicitly heterosexual, workspaces of my research sites were subverted to the extent that 'out' lesbians and gay men were present among the workforce. However, it was those whose performances of gender tended to accord with hegemonic, heterosexual prescriptions, and who seemed willing to participate in the dominant 'conversational culture' who were deemed acceptable at work. It was verbal misperformances of gender and breaches of informal workplace social 'rules' that constituted individuals as unviable. What this in turn suggests is that subversive, embodied authorings of gender and sexuality, aimed at creating slippage in the production chain of gendered and sexualized bodies, must be tailored to suit particular discursive communities. This is so that a given audience will derive the subversive meaning intended by the author(s). On the part of the author(s), this demands a kind of social competence, an understanding of how power, gendered and sexualized meanings operate within any given group of people.

Acknowledgements

I wish to express very grateful thanks to the research participants and to the following, who generously and patiently supplied comments and encouragement at various stages in the drafting of this chapter: Gill Valentine, Peter Jackson, Tina Skinner, Ulf Strohmayer, Allen White and of course, the editors of this volume.

Notes

1. This research is funded by the Economic and Social Research Council (grant number R00429534083). These three institutions were each large (by UK standards) universities.
2. I have used the following symbols in interview extracts:
   ? = questions marked by tone/pitch movements.
   [. . .] = speech omitted.
   . . . = short pause (less than 0.5 seconds).
   italics marks intonational stress.
   [laughs] = items in square brackets describe attitudinal expression within the interviews.

Bibliography

BUTLER, J. (1990) *Gender Trouble*. New York: Routledge.
BUTLER, J. (1993) *Bodies that matter*. New York: Routledge.
BUTLER, J. (1997) *Excitable Speech*. New York: Routledge.
HALFORD, S., M. SAVAGE and A. WITZ (1997) *Gender, Careers and Organisations*. Basingstoke: Macmillan Press – now Palgrave.
HUTCHEON, L. (1994) *Irony's Edge*. London: Routledge.
WILTON, T. (1996) 'Genital Identities' in Lisa Adkins and Vicki Merchant (eds) *Sexualising the Social: Power and the Organization of Sexuality*. Basingstoke: Macmillan Press – now Palgrave.

5
Paradoxical Stories of Prostitution[1]
Joanna Phoenix

Analysis of the main sociological and criminological writings on women's involvement in prostitution suggests that a continuing and unresolved question has been whether, and to what extent, prostitute women are like or unlike other non-prostitute women. In this chapter I examine the issue of prostitute-women's difference from, and similarity to, other non-prostitute women in academic discourse and in prostitute-women's own accounts of their lives. I argue that while academic discourse has constituted prostitutes as either different from *or* similar to other women, prostitute-women themselves accommodate the contradiction of being both like *and* unlike other women.

Academic explanations

There has been over a century of published research findings and theoretical analyses of prostitution from both criminological and sociological perspectives. Many of these explanations are interlinked ideas and suppositions about prostitutes and prostitution. While any particular contribution to the field is distinct and unique, it is also linked to earlier and later contributions. Each contribution picks up and develops constructions and understandings of earlier work at the same time as indicating new questions that, in turn, provoke new and different explanations. Hence, academic discourse on prostitution forms a chain of explanations in that such literatures are often interlinked via the types of questions that are pursued.

It is my argument here that underpinning the academic discourse on prostitutes and prostitution is one central, fundamental question: in what ways are prostitute-women like or unlike other women? To date there have been three ways that questions of difference (or similarity) have been addressed and with that there have been three different constructions of prostitutes. Prostitutes have been constituted as though they are:

1. unlike all other women because prostitutes are pathological or inhabit a unique social milieu;
2. the same as all other women because prostitutes are merely working women;
3. in some respects unlike other non-prostitute women because of the effects of involvement in prostitution while in other respects like other non-prostitute women because their lives are structured by the same constraints.

In the following section I examine each of these constructions via a deconstruction of the dominant explanatory models in which they appear (see Phoenix 1999a for a fuller deconstruction of these models).

Prostitutes as other women

The construction of prostitutes as different to other women occurs in two ways: prostitutes are (i) abnormal women engaged in pathological activities or (ii) socially deviant and, at times pathological, women existing within deviant and/or criminal subcultures. The construction of prostitutes as essentially different to other women by virtue of their abnormality was formalized in the early nineteenth century. As Bell (1994) and Spongberg (1997) report, early writers analyzed and categorized prostitute-women in opposition to the then dominant notions of femininity and in particular in relation to archetypal images of 'the good wife' and 'the virginal daughter'. Indeed, in an analysis of nineteenth-century medical discourse, Spongberg argues that it was prostitutes' very bodies that were constructed as absolutely distinct to other non-prostitute women. She writes:

> Medical anthropologists attempted to define prostitutes in ways that distinguished them from all other women. Prostitutes came to be seen not only as sexual pariahs, but also as women exhibiting a variety of other forms of deviancy and excess, such as lesbianism, alcoholism and other forms of addiction. No longer could prostitutes be sympathetically viewed as frail women who 'fell' in a moment of moral weakness – rather, they became abnormal women who could be regarded as less than human. This of course created a gulf between the upright woman and the fallen woman. (Spongberg 1997: 6)

It was against such a backdrop that the first criminological explana-tions for women's involvement in prostitution were developed. In the century that has elapsed there have been explanations put forward that took as their object of knowledge the assumed pathology of prostitutes. Underpinning these explanations was a basic conflation between the activity of selling sex (that is prostituting) which in itself is constituted as an abnormal activity and the individuals who do so (that is prosti-tutes). Thus, a category of women became known by the activity they engaged in. So, for example, Lombroso and Ferrero (1895) explained women's engagement in prostitution by claiming that they were individual women possessed of a physically pathological nature that resulted from their evolutionary degeneracy.[2] In a later text, S. and E.T. Glueck (1934) argued that prostitutes were poor women who were also psychologically pathological. They were women who were raised by parents of 'low mentality', in broken homes where the 'moral standards' were 'low', where conflict abounded and where disciplinary practices were 'unintelligent'. Such backgrounds created 'feeble-minded' and 'psychopathic' women who 'find it difficult to survive by legitimate means' (299). In their final analysis, they asserted that these factors alone compelled women into prostitution because possessing a psycho-logical abnormality reduced women's 'inhibitions' and 'constraints' so that when such women experienced poverty, it was likely that they would engage in prostitution. Indeed, even as little as thirty years ago, Benjamin and Masters (1964) argued that prostitutes could be divided into two categories: 'voluntary prostitutes' and 'compulsive prostitutes'. 'Voluntary prostitutes' were, according to Benjamin and Masters, 'normal women' who voluntarily became prostitutes because they had a need to economically provide for themselves, whereas 'compulsive prostitutes' were women suffering from pathological psychological problems. 'Compulsive prostitutes' were driven into prostitution by their own 'psycho-neurotic', 'masochistic' and self-degrading' needs which had resulted from a deep trauma in early life.

At the same time as these pathological explanations were developed, there was another set of writings which also constituted prostitutes as different to other women. Rather than focusing on prostitutes' assumed psychological or biological abnormalities, these later writings focused on their social deviancy and criminality. It was assumed that the dif-ference between prostitutes and other women inhered in prostitutes' relationship to, and position in, the wider society. Prostitutes were understood as women who were cut off from, or had slipped through, 'normal' constraining relationships and institutions (such as the family

and motherhood). These more sociological analyses of prostitution conflated prostitute-women with a social location (that is deviant subculture) and thus, prostitutes became known by the social subculture they
inhabited. Moreover, in common with other subcultural theories of
delinquency, such subcultures were assumed to exist *beyond* mainstream
society. Hence, being a prostitute meant belonging to and being
integrated within illicit and illegitimate relationships, social networks
and normative systems. So, for instance, in a work commission by the
British Social Biology Council, Wilkinson (1955) asserted that women
became prostitutes after experiencing a 'drifting, disorganized state'
of 'social irrelation' caused by possessing a 'disorganized personality'
which was 'unable to benefit from the social organization of life'
(108).[3] After drifting for a while, such women were introduced to prostitution, often through a friend, and found that they could obtain the
'belongingness' within a new social group that they were lacking before-
hand. It is important to note however, that even while stipulating that
prostitutes were different to other women because they belonged to a
deviant, criminal, prostitution subculture, Wilkinson also recognized
that they were like other women in the sense that prostitutes, too,
searched for ways of belonging to social groups. Thus she wrote:

> Once a girl has become a professional prostitute, one perceives the
> phenomenon of stabilisation. . . . She becomes a member of that
> society of which she has been on the fringe in her state of instabil-
> ity. . . . Local geographically cohesive groups may form in this society,
> but transcending this is the fact that the woman's status is now
> defined, she belongs to the group of prostitutes and is able to talk
> about 'us'. (1955: 108–9)

Constituting prostitutes as different to other women, either by virtue
of an assumed psychological or biological pathology, or by virtue of
being members of deviant, criminal subcultures, has the effect that the
similarities between prostitutes and non-prostitute women remain
forever outside the reach of the analysis. Invoking explanations that
take as their object of knowledge the manner and means by which prostitutes are unlike other women ultimately results in the theoretical
occlusion of the ways in which prostitutes are like other women.

Prostitutes as the same as other women

The construction of prostitutes as the same as other women is a more
contemporary construction. It has occurred in relation to researchers

picking up and developing the notion that prostitutes are poor women and in relation to an examination of the economics of prostitution and women's relative poverty. It is assumed in such explanations that poverty channels women into prostitution, particularly societies in which there are few, if any, realistic options for women to earn an income independently of their male relatives. Rather than demarcating prostitutes from non-prostitute women, proponents of most economic explanations (such as Finnegan 1979, McLeod 1982, Roberts 1992, McKeganey and Barnard 1996) collapse any such distinction. Combined with this, there has also been a notable collapsing of any line of demarcation between work (as a set of economic activities that individuals engage in in order to earn income) and prostitution. Thus, prostitution becomes, simply, an economic activity and prostitutes become workers. Such assumptions have opened the theoretical space to pursue questions about how women's involvement in prostitution is structured by similar social, material and ideological processes that structure and condition all women's economic participation.

McLeod (1982) presents the reader with the clearest example. She argued that women's involvement in prostitution had nothing to do with personal or social deviancy, but rather could only be understood in the context of a society which structures women's economic dependency on men. In other words, she asserted that women's involvement in prostitution is best understood by examining women's wider socioeconomic position in society. She wrote:

> Recruitment to the ranks of prostitutes is not appropriately characterised as only concerning a small group of highly deviant women. It is secured by women's relative power still being such that for large numbers, sex is their most saleable commodity. (1)

McLeod further claimed that 'women's generally disadvantaged social position in the context of a capitalist society is central to their experience as prostitutes. Women's entry into prostitution is characterized by an act of resistance to the experience of relative poverty' (25). Hence, in a society where the labour market is structured by notions of male breadwinning and female dependency, women are excluded from effective economic participation. When this is combined with the segregation of childcare and domestic responsibilities from the labour market, women's relative poverty is created. This means that some women will, of necessity, need to find alternative and less than conventional means of earning a living. For some women, this means engagement in prostitution.

In addition to this, McLeod (1982) argued that prostitution holds certain attractions for women: it presents women with the opportunity of combining childcare responsibilities with full time work and permits them to earn larger amounts of money than are otherwise obtainable in the legitimate labour market. Hence, for McLeod (and others) involvement in prostitution becomes a rational economic act resisting women's poverty and prostitutes become 'economic entrepreneurs'. More than this however, there is also the notion that prostitutes are the same as other women because prostitution itself is the same as, or at least very similar to, other forms of women's work. McLeod (1982) argued that many of the aspects of engagement in prostitution that seemingly distinguish prostitutes from other women are experiences *all* women share. Indeed, even selling sex is not the unique preserve of prostitutes. Comparisons are drawn between prostitutes who sell sex directly for money and wives who barter sex for economic stability and dependency within marriage (see also Bell 1987, Phetersen 1989, Jenness 1990, Phoenix 1999a). Similarly, violence from punters and ponces to prostitutes is understood as the same as other forms of male violence (see also ECP 1997).

Explaining women's involvement in prostitution as epiphenomenal to women's socio-economic position relative to men within society begs the question of difference. For if prostitutes are the same as other women, and prostitution is the same as other women's work, then all women are prostitutes. However, clearly there are differences. Interestingly, the manner in which the question of difference is dealt with has had the result of, ultimately, totalizing the sameness between prostitutes and other women. Again, McLeod (1982) provides a very clear example. For her, what differences that may exist between prostitutes and other women are the result of the legal discrimination that prostitutes suffer. She argued that the law, and its enforcement, enshrines 'sexist attitudes' and was 'shaped by sexist assumptions regarding women's sexuality' the result of which creates a 'scapegoating stigma [that] defines prostitutes as responsible for prostitution' (91–119). More importantly however, the stigma, itself, is derived from the sexist ideology that affects all women. Thus in the process of analyzing the formal legal responses to prostitutes, McLeod ultimately erased the possibility of difference via a theoretical move which stipulated that prostitutes were only unlike other women in as much as they were *more* vulnerable to the state-sanctioned oppressive practices affecting *all* women. Such arguments are echoed by many contemporary writers (for instance, Bell 1987, Delacosta and Alexander 1988 and Phetersen 1989):

> Financial dependency or despair is the condition of a majority of women, depending on class, culture, race, education and other differences and inequalities. . . . The financial initiative of prostitutes is stigmatized and/or criminalized as a warning to women in general against such sexually explicit strategies for financial independence. Prostitution is a traditional female occupation. Some prostitutes report job satisfaction, some consciously chose prostitution as the best alternative open to them (International Committee on Prostitutes' Rights, cited in Phetersen 1989: 192)

In the end, within most economic explanations, prostitute women are inscribed and constituted as the same as other women. The space to examine how and in what ways prostitutes may be unlike other women is ultimately foreclosed by the very conceptual demarcations that enabled such writers to understand prostitution not as an abnormal or deviant activity, but rather as a form of paid work.

Almost different: almost the same

The third and final set of explanations for women's involvement in prostitution that I will examine here are those which bring into the analytical foreground the related issues of male violence and gender. Within these explanations, prostitutes are constituted as in some respects unlike other women, while in other respects like non-prostitute women. Specifically, within this set of explanations there is the assumption that while on the whole there is nothing to distinguish prostitutes and non-prostitutes, differences do emerge when the effects of involvement in prostitution are examined. Prostitution is understood to be both a manifestation and effect of men's control over women's sexuality – the dynamics of which apply equally to all women within a given social system. So, for example, it is argued that male domination, which in part produces women's poverty, rests upon the sexual commodification and objectification of women within society generally. This then generates a structure whereby some women are forced or compelled into prostitution through financial and physical coercion.

These sets of ideas link together such that prostitution becomes the central metaphor for male power, female sexuality and women's subordination within a patriarchal social structure. Real prostitutes (as opposed to imaginary, metaphoric 'prostitutes') are, thus, represented as 'casualties' of male domination in that they are women with few, if any, resources to resist the social forces which commodify all women. There are many writers who examine women's involvement in prostitution using such a theoretical framework, such as Barry 1979, Dworkin 1979, Schrage 1989. In what follows I focus on one particular example: *Backstreets: Prostitution, Money and Love* by Hoigard and Finstad who began their study with the aim of understanding both the similarities *and* differences between prostitution and heterosexual relations more generally.[4]

Hoigard and Finstad (1992) constructed prostitutes as the same as other women in that prostitutes are neither pathological individuals, nor women engaged in deviant or abnormal activities. Within a social structure that ensures that women's sexuality is commodified, all women engage in trading their sexuality for something else because women 'have to create access to the benefits of society via men's use of women's sexuality' (187). Indeed, such a construction is notable in the writings of other radical feminists. For instance, Edwards (1997) claimed that prostitution was 'part of wider systematic abuse, commodification and objectification of women as a "sex class"' (69). Wynter, in a position statement on behalf of WHISPER ('Women Hurt in System of Prostitution Engaged in Revolt') asserted that 'Prostitution isn't like anything else. Rather everything else is like prostitution because it is the model for women's conditions' (268).

Hoigard and Finstad constructed prostitutes as unlike other women in two ways. First, in an explication of the processes that lead to women's entrance into, return to or continuation with their involvement in prostitution they asserted that women who become prostitutes have statistically atypical backgrounds. Prostitutes come from the working class, have irregular home lives and difficulties in adjusting to school or work, and have been placed in institutions such as 'orphanages, women's homes, reform schools, child and adolescent psychiatric institutions, drug and alcohol rehabilitation clinics and prisons' (16). Their experiences of institutions are important because, as argued, it is here that women learn to be prostitutes via exchanging information about ways to survive. Hoigard and Finstad further specified the process of becoming involved in prostitution as:

[. . .] a process in which the women's experiences cause a breakdown in their respect for themselves, for other women and also for men. Such individual experiences are seldom sufficient reason for prostitution. It is only when the experiences are translated and incorporated into the collective experience which girls share with other youths that prostitution becomes a viable option. (17)

Fundamental to this process, Hoigard and Finstad claimed, is incorporation into the self-image of the dominant ideology that a 'woman's body is her most important asset'. In this respect, the biographies of individual prostitute-women are not like the biographies of other non-prostitute women. More than this, however, Hoigard and Finstad explicitly argued that prostitutes are unlike other non-prostitute women because the effects of engaging in prostitution are, to some extent, unique. Within the male violence and gender explanatory model and the theoretical framework that Hoigard and Finstad draw upon, prostitution is understood as neither a form of deviancy (or abnormality) nor a form of work. It is, first and foremost, a form of violence against women. Hence, organizations like WHISPER not only refuse to demarcate forced and voluntary involvement in prostitution, but focus almost exclusively on the effects of prostitution-related exploitation and oppression. It is asserted that prostitutes are victimized, in the traditional sense, in that they are more likely to suffer assaults, attacks, harassment, exploitation and rape than non-prostitute women are. The regularity of such violence and brutality are understood to produce specific effects. These range from the complete shattering of an individual's personal life, the destruction of their self-image and self-respect and a tremendous burden of guilt, shame and self-disgust (see, for example, Bell 1994, Hoigard and Finstad 1992, McKeganey and Barnard 1996, O'Neill 1996). Hoigard and Finstad asserted that these effects are so overwhelming, lasting and devastating that 'it makes it reasonable . . . to say that customers practice gross violence against prostitutes' (1992: 115). Indeed, they concluded their argument by claiming that:

> The similarities are there [between prostitutes and non-prostitute women]. But they can easily be exaggerated. Prostitutes' experiences and destitution are so overwhelming that important qualitative differences become apparent. . . . [In short] the manner in which the prostitute relates to her sexuality as a commodity for trade does not differ from how other women relate to their sexuality because it is atypical: it differs because it is overwhelming and dominating. (117, 186)

In common with the previous models examined, this theoretical model is haunted by the problem of erasing difference in the service of a totalizing construction of sameness and vice versa. So, although

Hoigard and Finstad expressly intended to theorize prostitutes as both the same and different to other non-prostitute women, ultimately, they were unable to do so. The failure was generated, in part, by the very theoretical innovation they explored, that is that prostitution can be used to illuminate normality for women. Hoigard and Finstad (1992) failed to fully distinguish prostitution from dominant ideologies and images of women's sexuality more generally. According to their explanation, prostitution is only possible because a society views women's sexuality as subordinate to men's. It is part of a wider structural and systematic sexual commodification of women. The very logic of this explanation collapses the distinction between prostitution and how women's sexuality is experienced and expressed. Ironically, the consequence of collapsing the line of demarcation between sexuality and prostitution is that the sameness of prostitutes and non-prostitute women is totalized. For if the existence of prostitution is premised on the structurally conditioned economic subordination and sexual commodification of women, then there can be no women who are not prostitutes. The logical conclusion is as MacKinnon wrote: 'prostitution [is the] fundamental condition of women' (1989: 243).

The empirical study

This chapter draws on empirical data that was collected for a wider project on the conditions in which women are sustained within prostitution (Phoenix 1999a). That project examined how prostitute-women were able to make sense of their engagement in prostitution; thus, it offered an analysis of how a group of prostitute-women came to understand their involvement in prostitution and make the types of choices they made in the context that they inhabited. To that end, 21 partial life-historical interviews were collected with prostitute-women who did not identify as drug dependent. The women all lived in MidCity and worked in a variety of settings such as from the street, from their own homes, from saunas and massage parlours and in brothels. They ranged in age from 18–44 years old. They had been involved in prostitution for between nine months and 25 years. Each of the respondents was contacted through one of two gatekeepers (one a probation officer running a day drop-in centre for prostitute women and other offending women, and the other a sexual health outreach worker working within a local project). In addition to these 21 life-historical interviews, supplementary data was collected through three months observation.

The women's voices

In the preceding sections, it has been shown that academic discourse has constituted prostitutes as (i) different to other women; (ii) the same as other women; and, (iii) in some respects similar and in other respects different to other women. Interestingly, the prostitute-women who were interviewed were also intrigued by the question of difference and similarity. However, unlike academic discourse, the prostitute-women saw themselves as both different from *and* similar to other non-prostitute women. In what follows, I trace some of the ways that the women identified themselves. I do this in order to illuminate how the women were able to speak of themselves as both like and unlike other women; and, how they were able to contain the contradiction within such a conceptualization.

Before proceeding however, it is important to mention how the data was analyzed and how the term 'identity' is used in this chapter. Analytical protocols were adopted from what has been loosely called a 'discourse analysis' perspective. Application of these protocols permitted the realism of autobiographical narratives (or life historical interview materials) to be suspended. Questions were asked not about what the specific events and processes were that the interviewees recounted as important in conditioning their engagement in prostitution, but rather about the symbolic landscape and nexus of meanings that permitted the interviewees to tell the types of stories that they did.[5] These protocols for analysis also impact upon how 'identity' is conceptualized. Within this chapter, the term 'identity' is not used to denote the 'essence' of a person or a set of personal characteristics; nor is it used to signify the central author (or self) who elaborates and gives meaning to their story as in the identity that is created when individuals turn themselves into 'socially organized biographical objects' (Plummer 1995: 34). The reason that these conceptions of identity were rejected is that they are premised upon two assumptions that run contrary to the perspective taken herein. Specifically, they rely on a notion of an essential self who is situated at the centre of awareness of an individual and who has mastery over the symbolic communication (see especially Plummer 1995).

To put it simply, by suspending autobiographical realism, the notion that the narrative that is produced is a 'simple' mirror image or is referential of the 'self' is also suspended (see Sampson 1989). The concepts 'identity' and 'identification' are used within this chapter to signify the *portrayed* self in the women's stories, or the constellation of the different, diverse and multiple ways in which the women represented themselves in their stories. It is the person constructed *within* the autobiographical narrative by, and within, the ways in which the respondents positioned themselves in their texts relative to others within a specific symbolic landscape (see Langenhove and Harre 1993) and in so doing demarcated and differentiated the boundaries between self and others (Habermas 1987). Without wanting to over-state the point, this 'prostitute-identity' is not the immediately expressed, self-conscious articulation of subjectivity. Instead, it is the personhood imagined in the narratives of the women and made possible by the constellation of different meanings for and connections between 'men', 'money' and 'violence'. I now trace the three different ways that the women I interviewed spoke about themselves as both like *and* unlike other women.

Sex, income, working and rented vaginas

All of the women interviewed led lives that were torn apart by the aggregate effects of poverty, homelessness, violence, living on inadequate social security benefits, lack of access to adequately paying legitimate jobs and so on. They also faced regular arrest for prostitution related offences (and thus were sentenced to financial penalties). In short, they had very few options open to them to sustain their material security in legitimate ways. Within this context, underpinning and making possible the prostitute-women's identification of themselves as both like *and* unlike other women was a symbolic landscape in which the meanings for men and money were conflated so that 'men' became 'money'. It was a construction of particular men (that is punters) that was universalized, mythologized[6] and applied to all men so that men were constituted as both income (that is sources of money) and as income which could only be generated through exchanging sex for money. This particular nexus of meaning was encapsulated in the often-repeated claims of the women that: 'all men are punters'.

The claim that 'all men are punters' was made possible by the women's acceptance of dominant discourses of masculine sexuality. Here, men are constructed as a constellation of their sexual needs which if left unmet threatened the stability of individual relationships and, indeed, society itself. The women portrayed men as driven by their sexuality which, in turn, was defined as instrumental, aggressive, functional and devoid of any meaning. In short, men were talked about as though they were little more than their sexual needs: men were 'always on the prowl', 'always looking for the latest shag'. This was noticeable in the women's euphemistic descriptions of the sex punters buy from prostitutes as 'relief' or 'satisfaction'. It was also noticeable in the way that the women declaimed that punters were not unfaithful to their wives or partners by going to prostitutes.

> Men who come to me are generally faithful to their wives. They don't see coming to me as being unfaithful. To be honest, I don't either. It's non-committal and he's just getting a little extra relief that he probably needs. (Sophie, aged 28)

Combined with this understanding was the women's belief that men, as a group, have easier access to more money than women. Intertwined within all the women's narratives were discussions of men's relative economic privilege, which these women suggested, was as a result of men having fewer impediments to work. It was noted that men could go out to work more easily because they did not have to arrange childcare. It was also noted that this applied to men's capacity to get money illegitimately. Indeed, Olivia (aged 28) spoke very eloquently about how men could 'do burglary and drug selling and get away with it' whereas women could not.

The construction of all (normal) men as being driven by their biological need to have sex and the women's recognition of men's greater financial and economic resources permitted the women to decontextualize the prostitute–punter relationship. Specifically, the relationship was transformed into nothing more and nothing less than a series of episodic, routine economic exchanges in which normal (that is statistically typical and ordinary) men purchased necessary 'outlets' for their physical needs (see Faugier and Sargeant 1997) from women who needed to earn money. This is important because it provided the symbolic landscape in which the women could talk about themselves as both like other women, in that as prostitutes they were merely working women *and* unlike other women because their work had turned them into little more than rented vaginas.

Prostitutes' discussions of themselves as 'working women' have been noted in many other texts and places. It forms the central and fundamental tenet of prostitutes' rights campaigning groups (such as the English Collective of Prostitutes in the UK and Call Off Your Tired Old Ethics (COYOTE) in the USA). Indeed, it was the title to one of the foremost pieces of social science research into prostitution in the early 1980s.[7] In terms of the women interviewed for this project, such identification was encapsulated and made visible in the women's talk about the differences between the sex that they sell to punters and 'real' sex.

> At the end of the day, you're getting money from a punter. It's not sex, it's money – it's *work*! (Ruthie, aged 25)

> You don't think about it, you think of it as work . . . because you think of it as a job, it's just like doing paperwork. (Andrea, aged 27)

Because men and income were symbolically fused together and because the sex punters buy is merely a routine economic exchange, the women were able to portray themselves as workers. In this respect, the prostitute-women were able to locate themselves as no different than other ordinary working women. They, like other women, were just doing their jobs and getting paid for it.

However, the same symbolic landscape also permitted the women to tell a very different story in which they were utterly unlike other non-prostitute women. This can be seen by tracing the ways in which the men as income nexus of meaning permitted the women to talk about themselves as reduced to being commodities. A more contextualized recognition of the punter/prostitute exchange as taking place between (anonymous) men who were interested only in relieving their own physical needs created the conditions in which 16 women talked about themselves as such.

> It's not easy to go out and do a client and then do another one and keep that up. You have to keep up the smiling and the chat. You turn yourself into something to sell. (Janet, aged 37)

More than this however, the same women also discussed whether they owned and controlled the commodity that they had turned into. A concomitant symbolic division between the women's 'selves' and their 'bodies' permitted 15 of the 16 women to talk about both owning and controlling their commodified bodies. Witness Lois:

> When I work, I wear makeup. When I'm done I take me makeup off and I am just me – Lois. But when I put my makeup on and do my

hair, I become someone totally different – I'm Daphne. I'm sort of split into two. The one is like an ordinary everyday twenty-one year old and the other is just something to get money with. (Lois, aged 21).

An alternative symbolic subsumption of self to body permitted 11 of the 16 women to talk about themselves as owning, but *not* controlling their commodified bodies. Instead, the anonymous, instrumental punters had control.

You end up becoming the hustler. You think of yourself as just a body all the time. . . . But you end up losing yourself to your body and having no control over it anymore. The punters just do what they want to with you. (Georgia, aged 37).

There was a third and final variation in the women's location of themselves as commodities. This variation occurred, not in relation to recognition of the contextual specificity of the punter/prostitute relationship, but rather in relation to the recognition of some of the practices resulting from poncing relationships in which the women had been involved. The women neither owned nor controlled their commodified bodies as these were both controlled and owned by their ponces. Although most of the 21 women interviewed talked about the practice of buying and selling prostitutes between different ponces, four women discussed their own experiences of being traded like chattel property. In their talk, such practices were not treated as particularly out of the ordinary or even as troublesome. Barbara simply remarked: 'Oh yea, I was sold. That was rife down there.' The point at which these four women located themselves as neither owning nor controlling their commodified bodies occurred when the women discussed how much they had been sold for. The amount signified to them a measure of their commodity value. Lois remarked: 'Can you believe it? Kevin sold me to Steve for just fifty pounds! I was worth more than that!'

The identification of themselves as commodities created the conditions in which the women located and constructed themselves as very different to other non-prostitute women. It was prostitutes' experiences engendered by their involvement in prostitution, their recognition of the specificity of those experiences and their understanding that the effects of those experiences that meant that they were not like other women. By their own accounts, their experiences within prostitution had turned them into rentable vaginas.

Relationships, expense, business and love

Earlier it was seen how men were defined in relation to money that is as income. In what follows, I shall outline how men were also defined as 'expense'. On one level, it was a mythologized construction of men in that involvement with men in general (rather than in the context of engagement in prostitution) was understood as generating expense. As Jasmine explained: 'If you get involved with any of them [i.e. men], in any way, it costs you in the end.' More specifically however and in the context of engagement in prostitution, involvement with men was understood as incurring 'opportunity costs' (that is payments made for the purpose of achieving something) or 'hidden costs' (that is payments which are unknown at the time of calculation but which become apparent later).

What type of cost was incurred depended on which type of men the women were positioning themselves in relation to. Thus, involvement with men as ponces, boyfriends and police was constructed as a form of 'opportunity costs'. These groups of men were understood as providing women with 'sanctuary' from prostitution or protection from various prostitution-related risks (such as violence, exploitation, intimidation and threats from other ponces and so on), but it came with a cost. Most of the women talked about the 'sanctuary' that boyfriends provided by financially supporting them (and thus helping them to leave prostitution), but the price was the women's independence. Others talked about the protection that ponces offered from other ponces trying to exploit them; the violence of punters; and being victimized by other street criminals. Eleven women talked about costing the type and quality of protection that individual ponces could offer against the financial exploitation and possible violence that the women might be subjected to.

> After Dagger [that is a previous ponce] got arrested for poncing me, I paid Germaine. Germaine was somebody that was friends with Dagger, but I paid him to watch us girls while we was out, for a little extra protection like. (Gail, aged 28).

Similarly, involvement with the police was understood as being occasionally necessary for the women, in order that they could provide themselves with protection against particularly exploitative, violent ponces or particular punters who were known to be violent. The cost in this instance was not, counter-intuitively, that the police would ask the women to make statements or press charges against their ponces, or indeed, that the police would ask the women to supply information about the local drug scene. Rather, it was being 'indebted' to particular policemen. Christine explained the implications of this. After she had obtained the help of one policeman with a violent ponce, he had 'kept coming around and asking questions'. She said, 'He was on my back all the time' and when she stopped giving him information, he 'made it harder for me on purpose', 'he nicked me *all* the time man – sometimes three times a night'.

On the other hand, involvement with men as partners was also defined as incurring 'hidden costs'. Two of the 21 respondents talked about how being involved with particular men resulted in their initial entrance into prostitution. Both women talked about 'having the knickers charmed off' them. Thus the cost of their relationships was engagement in prostitution. Seventeen other respondents discussed how their continued engagement in prostitution was the hidden cost of maintaining their involvement with particular men.

> You meet a man. . . . You're working, and first of all you give them a tenner or whatever coz they're skint. And then you think, 'Oh I love you' and you give them fifty or a hundred pounds. And eventually . . . you're having to raise a certain amount and you're keeping, maybe, five or ten pounds for yourself. (Andrea, aged 27)

Twelve of the respondents also discussed how leaving their intimate relationships incurred the hidden cost of returning to or continuing with prostitution. In short, most of them commented that their relationship breakdowns caused their engagement in prostitution. Hence, Georgia (aged 35) remarked: 'What could I do? I had two children, nowhere to go and no money of my own. Sometimes I think that I bought myself out of that marriage by selling myself on the streets.'

The conflation between involvement with men and 'expense' is important because it provided the conditions in which the women could position themselves as both like *and* unlike other women. They were like other women because they fell in love with men and that cost them money. The men as expense articulation of meanings conditioned the universalization of the message that all heterosexual relationships are founded upon costs surrendered by the women. Indeed, nine of the 21 women talked about how they, like all other women, made their choices and took what actions they deemed necessary based on the love they felt for the men they were involved with. Drawing on discourses in which heterosexual love is experienced as a sublimation of the women's desires and a concomitant centralizing of the men's desires, these women talked about their willingness to sacrifice everything for their partner regardless of how they were treated. Indeed, there was a notable blurring of the boundary between love and money so that giving men money was transformed into a primary signifier of loving them. With that, exploitative and/or violent prostitution-related relationships (that is poncing relationships) were re-inscribed as non-prostitution related relationships (that is ordinary heterosexual relationships). Ingrid's and Georgia's quotes below demonstrate how they identified as the same as all other women by erasing the exploitation of their prostitution-related relationships and transposing them into 'normal' relationships.

> He used to kill me. I mean I stayed for nine years and he was always beating on me, took all my money, but I stuck it out. **[Why?]** You do, don't you? You wanna be loved – a girl just wants to be loved. (Ingrid, aged 44)

> You meet someone and they're the type of people that you like. . . . You know, they talk very, very nice to you and make you feel special. Then before you know it, you fall for them, you work for them and you give them all your money because you've fallen for them. (Georgia, aged 35)

In a different fashion, the same symbolic landscape (that is men as expense) permitted the women to locate themselves as unlike and different to other non-prostitute women. Their experiences in prostitution had 'taught' them of the necessity to approach *all* heterosexual relationships (prostitution related or not) with a degree of scepticism. So, unlike other women, they calculated the costs and benefits of particular courses of action, of involvement with different types of men, of ways of maximizing their incomes while minimizing their risks. They were 'smart' women, in business for themselves, working 'the right way'. How such sentiments found specific expression varied according to whether or not the women were being ponced at the time of the interview. The non-ponced women prioritized the risk of financial exploitation that was associated with involvement with any and all men (prostitution-related or not). For them, being smart meant not getting involved with any man.

When I was younger, I lived with men that took advantage – I didn't see it coming. But once it happened again and again, I'd seen I'd been taken for a right cunt. You put it down to experience and say 'No more'. You can't be innocent about men and you have to run your life like a business. (Janet, aged 37)

Margie showed how the suppositions put forward by Janet permitted these women to locate themselves as different to other women.

I have this friend. She goes out on a Friday night for the sole purpose of finding a man to fuck him – anyone! I think 'Well I wouldn't do that!' Coz half these straight women, they give it away. Fucking no – I'm sorry, it will cost you more than that for me. (Margie, aged 33)

In contrast, the women who were being ponced at the time of the interview talked about how they, unlike non-prostitute women, were smart because they did get involved with ponces. They highlighted the dangers of involvement in prostitution, prioritized reducing their risks of violence and thus, were able to use their involvement with ponces as a signifier of their business success.

It's the done thing where I work. Every girl has an old man – she needs one if she's going to do it properly. Ya need someone to watch out for you coz there are too many creeps out there. (Sammy, aged 18)

I have worked with ponces for most of the time I've worked. But there is girls that work without ponces. But the majority of them that don't – it's because they're that heavy on drugs that a ponce wouldn't touch them coz they wouldn't be getting anything if they did! (Andrea, aged 27)

Whether ponced or not, via identifying themselves as 'business-women', these prostitute-women were able to talk about and locate themselves as unlike other non-prostitute women. Unlike other women, their experiences in prostitution (of violence from punters and ponces and financial exploitation) had given them valuable insights into the relationships between men and women, and they realized the necessity of calculating the costs and benefits of any relationship with men and of prioritizing risks. They were not like other women, because as prostitutes, they were smarter.

Risk, violence, victims and survivors

All of the women interviewed for this project had experienced some type of violence as a result of their involvement in prostitution. Typically, this was from punters and ponces, although they also recounted stories of violence they suffered at the hands of the police, of local neighbours and even local school children.[8] In this respect, violence was 'normal' to the women. Moreover, most of the women had experienced some type of financial exploitation, usually from landlords and ponces, but also from friends, boyfriends and even family members. It is hardly surprising given this context that underpinning the narratives of all the women interviewed was a symbolic conflation between 'men' and 'danger' in which the boundaries between 'normal men' and 'abnormal men' were dissolved. Hence, 'men' were 'dangerous', in that they threatened women's overall material and physical safety and 'suspect', in that they were not trustworthy.

The conflation of men with riskiness and danger was most evidently seen in the women's discussion of ponces. Although the term 'ponce' has been used to describe an individual who financially exploits (through threat or charm) a prostitute woman, it is also a crucial and important symbolic character within the 21 women's narratives. The 'ponce' was used to denote all the dangers, tragedies and pitfalls for women that came with prostitution. 'Ponces' were sadistic men who rape, kidnap, brutalize, impoverish and entrap women. It was claimed that there was no escape from ponces, no effective resistance and no protection. In constituting this symbolic category, the women drew on discourses which constructed ponces as male criminals and male criminals as 'tough', 'outsiders' – all of which conjoined under the expression 'bad' and positioned ponces as 'aliens' to ordinary morality (Katz 1988: 80–113). The women also deployed discourses that essentialized masculine violence. Hence, 'ponces' were masculine Others who were always and already violent.

> Ponces are not like other men. They ain't got no heart. They only ever want money. Like once, there was this young girl, she had a ponce, and he used to beat her up all the time. There was one time she hurt her leg really badly and we told him to take her to the hospital. He wouldn't. He shoved her back on the street and she fell running for a punter. Her leg was broken! All he

could say was, 'Leave her alone, she's gotta earn money'. (Helena, aged 35)

What you gotta understand is that he was a *ponce*. I mean, if I didn't make enough he'd send me back out. He was the proper order ponce. He wanted – I got. And if I didn't get, he'd kill me. (Ingrid, aged 44)

Here we see the women maintaining a strict demarcation between 'ponces' and other men. 'Ponces' are somehow different to other men. However, in tracing the women's comments about and discussions of boyfriends and partners we can see the collapse of this line, and with that the collapse of the distinction between 'normal' and 'abnormal' men. The women continually suggested that involvement with any and all men was 'risky' because it carried with it the threat of violence and financial exploitation. To be precise, underpinning the women's stories were notions and assumptions that boyfriends were especially suspect because the women could never trust them not to become ponces. The women attributed this to the way in which prostitutes were willing to share their money.

I didn't mind giving him money. I mean we were together, but when he started expecting it off me. That's when I realised, that's when I knew it, that's when I knew he was a ponce. (Christine, aged 23)

Everyone's really down on ponces. . . . Women made men into ponces – it's not the opposite way round! You start giving your boyfriend money and eventually, there's never actually any say so, eventually you're having to raise a certain amount and you're keeping less and less. (Andrea, aged 23)

Hence, the symbolic boundary between normal and abnormal men is dissolved via a construction of all men as suspect and risky. For, by the women's own accounts, there is no difference between boyfriends and ponces in terms of the specifics of the relationship (that is violence and financial exploitation do not mark some relationships as poncing ones) because all intimate relationships with men are marked by the exchange of money. Ponces were merely and only boyfriends who 'got greedy'. In other words, they were men who took more than was their due. (Phoenix 1999b).

There was a further dissolution of the boundary between normal and abnormal men that occurred in relation to punters. The women stridently asserted that they could never be certain whether their punters were 'funny punters' (men who were pathologically violent and sadistic). Underpinning the women's stories were notions that *all* punters were, at least potentially, *also* funny punters.

> I've had one guy – he was a headmaster. You know, really nice guy, respectable family man. He wanted caning and afterwards he tried to rape me. He said, 'I want sex and I swear to God I'll kick the shit out of you unless I get it.' Just goes to show you, you can't tell, they can all be funny. (Sophie, aged 28)

Yet, at the same time as recognizing this, and as we have seen earlier in this chapter, punters were also understood as ordinary men 'doing what comes naturally'. Thus, all men were both normal and abnormal, both natural men and funny punters.

The conflation of men with risk, danger and suspicion created the conditions in which all relationships between men and women were encoded as being dangerous and sites of abuse or exploitation. The message from such constructions was clear. As Ingrid said:

> Men, bastards, the bloody lot of them. You can't trust them. They just use and abuse women. You can't tell me there's a man out there who hasn't (or won't one day). (Ingrid, aged 44)

Within this symbolic landscape, by locating themselves in relation to a notion of 'men' as risk, the women were able to identify themselves as 'victims' of men's exploitation and violence. Twenty of the 21 women did so and talked about themselves as women who were unable to control the events of their lives because they were controlled by others who hurt, mistreated or injured the woman to exact such control. In many cases, these women connected the victimization that they had experienced in their families growing up or in their adult relationships to their initial, and at times sustained, engagement in prostitution.

The identification of themselves as 'victims' permitted these women to recount stories in which they understood themselves as being *like* other women because if all men were both normal and abnormal, both threatening and risky, then all relationships were characterized by violence, abuse and exploitation.

> Men are a waste of time. They're out taking our money, beating us and raping us – or judging us. And I don't mean just working women

– they'll do it to any woman. Men are all bastards when it comes to women. (Sammy, aged 18)

However, the same symbolic landscape permitted these women to iden-tify as, contradictorily, survivors and not victims. This can be seen in tracing not how the women discussed themselves in relation to men, but rather how they demarcated and distinguished between themselves and other non-prostitute women. In this respect, the prostitute-women interviewees were also able to imagine themselves as *unlike* other women.

Eighteen of the respondents identified themselves as 'survivors' in that they talked about themselves as women who managed successfully to negotiate the risks and uncertainties posed by men (and in particu-lar posed by specific men within the institution of prostitution). This identification occurred primarily in relation to the notion of other non-prostitute women as 'weaker', 'not surviving' and 'not strong'. The respondents asserted that non-prostitute women, (unlike prostitute-women) 'don't know what men are really like', 'don't know how to make it for themselves' and 'can't cope'. Witness the following statements:

I think we are better at surviving than ordinary women. We've been around and we see. And I think ordinary women, they wouldn't tackle a man where we would. . . . We can cope with violent boyfriends better than ordinary women. I ran after my last one with a hatchet knife! I can't see no ordinary woman doing that! We're sur-vivors and they're not. (Janet, aged 37)

I think all women have a way of going about things, but I think pros-titutes are better at surviving coz we're more honest. We don't say, 'Oh I love you'. The only difference is that the punter's not a stranger for straight women. (Gail, aged 28)

Working women are better survivors than straight women. We know a lot more about men than straight women. Well, we would wouldn't we? We have just loads more knowledge. We know how to get them, how to keep them and how to get rid of them if we're in trouble. And we know how to survive without them. (Sammy, aged 18)

In these quotes, Janet, Gail and Sammy are clearly spelling out the dif-ferences as they see them between themselves and other non-prostitute women. Prostitutes know more. All women are victims of men's violence and exploitation, and prostitutes know that whereas other women do not. Prostitutes are survivors.

Conclusion

In the introduction to this chapter I commented that sociological and criminological analyses of prostitution, and prostitute-women themselves have been intrigued by the question of the difference (or not) between prostitutes and other women. It was apparent, even during the preliminary analysis of the interview materials, that the prostitute-women I spoke to were able to live both within and outwith the contradiction of being both like *and* unlike other non-prostitute women. The contradiction was accommodated in as much as the symbolic landscape that underpinned the women's narratives created in the conditions in which such a paradoxical statement could be made and still make sense. Thus, the 21 interviewees who took part in my research described themselves as like other women in that they, in common with all other women, lived lives that were structured by money and violence. And, these 21 women were also able to talk about themselves as *unlike* other women because by their own accounts, their specific experiences as prostitutes enabled them to penetrate the veils of ideology. They, unlike other women, realized that both financial considerations and men's potential for violence shape many of the dimensions of the sexual relationships between all men and all women.

Notes

1. This is a revised version of a paper submitted to the British Sociological Association Annual Conference, 1998. It has been substantially altered as the original version was subsequently published in the *British Journal of Criminology*. In order to comply with copyright regulations, I have developed an argument that was referred to in the original BSA conference paper and introduced new data in the explication of that argument.
2. In all fairness, Lombroso did not apply the notion of individual pathology exclusively to women; nor did he argue that 'degeneracy' was the sole cause of criminality and prostitution. He also claimed that social and environmental factors were important. Moreover, Lombroso's study of prostitutes was part of his wider theoretical project that attempted to search for and understand the 'natural' and 'organic' causes of crime. Thus, he explained male criminality and prostitution (which he took to be the equivalent of criminality in men) in similar terms.
3. See also Bryan (1967) and Jackman (1967).

4. It is a false dichotomy to distinguish too fully between the economic and male violence explanatory models. Theoretical analyses of prostitution are not so simply reduced into two opposing positions. Most explications that examine prostitution and draw on a male violence framework also recognize the poverty of many. Similarly, many economic explanations also recognize the violence that prostitutes experience.
5. See Phoenix (1999a) for a much fuller description and discussion of these protocols for analysis, the theoretical justification for them and how they apply to the analysis of prostitute-women's autobiographical narratives.
6. Walkowitz, in an early article, wrote about the mythologizing that went along with the Jack the Ripper murders in London in the late nineteenth century. She used the term to denote how constructions of the specific are then translated into the universal in such a way as to contain a specific message (Walkowitz 1983).
7. McLeod, E. (1982).
8. In MidCity, during the fieldwork stage of this project, a 'vigilante' group, whose aim was to 'clean up the streets' had just been formed. Although most of their strategies were low-level and non-confrontational, there were some members of the group that took much more direct action by at first intimidating and then attacking the local street working prostitutes.

Bibliography

BARRY, K. (1979) *Female Sexual Slavery* New York: New York University Press.
BELL, L. (ed.) (1987) *Good Girls/Bad Girls: Sex Trade Workers and Feminists Face to Face* Ontario: The Women's Press.
BELL, S. (1994) *Reading, Writing and Rewriting the Prostitute Body* Indiana. Indiana University Press.
BENJAMIN, H. and R. MASTERS (1964) *Prostitution and Morality: A Definitive Report on the Prostitute in Contemporary Society and an Analysis of the Causes and Effects of the Suppression of Prostitution.* London: Souvenir Press.
BRYAN, J. (1967) 'Apprenticeships in Prostitution' in W. Simon and J. Gagnon (eds) *Sexual Deviance.* London: Harper and Row.
DELACOSTA, F. and P. ALEXANDER (eds) (1988) *Sex Work: Writings by Women in the Sex Industry.* London: Virago.
DWORKIN, A. (1979) *Pornography: Men Possessing Women.* New York: Perigee Books.
ECP (1997) 'Campaigning For Legal Change' in G. Scambler and A. Scambler (eds) *Rethinking Prostitution: Purchasing Sex in the 1990s* Routledge: London.
EDWARDS, S. (1997) 'The Legal Regulation of Prostitution: A Human Rights Issue' in G. Scambler and A. Scambler (eds) *Rethinking Prostitution: Purchasing Sex in the 1990s.* London: Routledge.
FAUGIER, J. and M. SARGEANT (1997) 'Boyfriends, "pimps" and clients', in G. Scrambler and A. Scrambler (eds) *Rethinking Prostitution: Purchasing Sex in the 1990s.* London: Routledge.
FINNEGAN, F. (1979) *Poverty and Prostitution: A Study of Victorian Prostitutes in York.* Cambridge: Cambridge University Press.
GLUECK, S. and E.T. GLUECK (1934) *Five Hundred Delinquent Women.* New York: Knopf.

HABERMAS, J. (1987) *Philosophical Discourses of Modernity*. Cambridge: Polity Press.

HOIGARD, C. and L. FINSTAD (1992) *Backstreets: Prostitution, Money and Love*. Cambridge: Polity.

JACKMAN, N. (1967) 'The Self-Image of the Prostitute' in W. Simon and J. Gagnon (eds) *Sexual Deviance*. London: Harper and Row.

JENNESS, V. (1990) 'From Sex and Sin to Sex as Work: COYOTE and the Re-organisation of Prostitution as a Social Problem' *Social Problems*, vol. 37, no. 3, pp. 403–20.

KATZ, J. (1988) *The Seductions of Crime*. New York: Basil Books.

LANGENHOVE, L. and R. HARRE (1993) 'Positioning and Autobiography: Telling Your Life' in J. Nussnaum and N. Couplan (eds) *Discourse and Life Span Identity*. London: Sage.

LOMBROSO, C. and G. FERRERO (1895) *The Female Offender: The Normal Woman and the Prostitute*. London: Fisher Unwin.

MACKINNON, C. (1989) *Towards a Feminist Theory of the State* Cambridge MA: Harvard University Press.

MCKEGANEY, N. and M. BARNARD (1996) *Sex Work on the Streets: Prostitutes and Their Clients*. Buckingham: Open University Press.

MCLEOD, E. (1982) *Working Women: Prostitution Now*. London: Croom Helm.

O'NEILL, M. (1996) 'Researching Prostitution and Violence: Towards a Feminist Praxis' in M. Hester, L. Kelly and J. Radford (eds) *Women, Violence and Male Power*. Buckingham: Open University Press.

PHETERSEN, G. (ed.) (1989) *A Vindication of the Rights of Whores*. London: Seal Press.

PHOENIX, J. (1999a) *Making Sense of Prostitution*. London: Macmillan Press – now Palgrave.

PHOENIX, J. (1999b) 'Prostitutes, Ponces and Poncing: Making Sense of Violence' in J. Seymour and P. Bagguley (eds) *Relating Intimacies: Power and Resistance*. London: Macmillan Press – now Palgrave.

PHOENIX, J. (2000) 'Prostitute Identities: Men, Money and Violence' *British Journal of Criminology* vol. 40, no. 1.

PLUMMER, K. (1995) *Telling Sexual Stories: Power, Change and Social Worlds* Routledge: London.

ROBERTS, N. (1992) *Whores in History* Harper Collins: London.

SAMPSON, E.E. (1989) 'The Deconstruction of the Self' in J. Shotter and K. Gergen (eds) *Texts of Identity*. London: Sage.

SCHRAGE, L. (1989) 'Should Feminists Oppose Prostitution?' *Ethics* 99, pp. 347–61.

SPONGBERG, M. (1997) *Feminizing Venereal Disease: The Body of the Prostitute in Nineteenth-Century Medical Discourse*. London: Macmillan Press – now Palgrave.

WALKOWITZ, J. (1983) 'Jack the Ripper and the Myth of Male Violence', *Feminist Studies* 8, no. 3.

WILKINSON, R. (1955) *Women of the Streets*. London: British Social Biology Council.

WYNTER, S. (1989) 'WHISPER: Women Hurt in Systems of Prostitution Engaged in Revolt' in A. Delacosta and P. Alexander (eds) *Sex Work: Writings by Women in the Sex Industry*. London: Virago.

Part II
The Social Construction of Gendered Bodies: Signs and Symbols

6
The Working Body as Sign: Historical Snapshots
Carol Wolkowitz

This chapter brings together two case studies in which the representation of labouring bodies in class-, race- and gender-specific terms is particularly pronounced.[1] The first case study concerns images of female manual workers which circulated in Victorian Britain and the second examines the photographs of men and women at work produced by the American social reformer Lewis Hine. While I hesitate to generalize from these few examples from still photography – especially since counterinstances come to mind – they do remind us that the construction of masculine and female bodies takes place in relation to work as much as other areas of social life. I want to demonstrate not only that bodies are inscribed by ideas about the work which people do, but also that particular constructions of labouring bodies then come to signify anxieties about the changing nature of work and employment. Images of men's and women's bodies have come to play important rhetorical functions in debates about the meaning of work and the adequacy of its rewards at particular historical conjunctures.

My underlying concern is that the sociology of the body has too readily simply reproduced late twentieth-century ideologies which highlight the malleability of bodies, mainly through constant *self*-control, *self*-surveillance and judicious consumption (for example Giddens 1991), failing to pay attention to the relation between paid labour and the social construction of bodies. As Scarry (1994) suggests, we tend to associate bodies – sensuousness – with play, desire and spontaneity, rather than work, which is instead associated with the opposite, numbing routine. Based partly on her analysis of Marx, Scarry's *The Body in Pain* insists upon the relation between human sentience and the making of artefacts – human creations – which are 'the memorialization of . . . embodied work; while tools, land and the material object are all extensions or "prolongations" of the worker's body' (1985: 247). She also reminds us that man remakes his body (which is therefore itself a kind of artefact) in his activity of providing himself with sustenance and use-values to renew his body. Recognition of the absolute necessity of real, feeling human bodies' involvement in production is obscured by commodification and the capitalist structure. However, Scarry's account is almost completely gender-blind, and consequently neglects the role of gendered representational practices in constructing – and not just capturing – the body's labours.

In contrast, feminist analyses have focused on the codes through which images of bodies are gendered (see Kuhn 1985) and documented the extent to which gender and sexuality are appropriated by employers as part of the employment contract (for example Hochschild 1983; Pateman 1988; Brewis and Kerfoot 1994; Adkins 1995; McDowell 1997). However, the meanings conveyed by gendered bodies need to be contextualized historically, and the role of images of work and employment in the construction of long-standing connotations of male and female bodies, deserves more exploration than it has been given so far. 'Race' and class as aspects of the representation of bodies are essential parts of the analysis.

Photography and power

Sociologists have been paying increasing attention to the relation between sociology and photography, but it is hard for sociological research to accommodate the contradiction between the photograph's appearance of 'surface validity' and the indeterminacy of its meaning (Plummer 1983; Walker and Wiedel 1985; Harrison 1998). 'Making sense of the body' using photographic material has been concentrated in cultural theory, in which work inspired by 'photographic theory' (Burgin 1982) has been happy to reject the apparent literalness of documentary photographic representations for an exploration of the social relations of their construction. Even here, however, photographs of working people can be seen as part of the documentary tradition, separate from representations of 'the body' (compare, for example, Clarke 1997 and Pultz 1995). Yet the two are brought together, at least indirectly, by some theorists intent on clarifying the power relations embedded in the visual image. Many key writers follow Foucault in seeing photography as an example of the 'material elements and techniques that serve . . . and support . . . the power and knowledge relations that invest human bodies and subjugate them by turning them into objects of knowledge' (Foucault 1979, as cited by Schatzki and Natter 1996). For instance, Tagg's (1988) well-known study of the power relations of representation concentrates on the development of photography in relation to the surveillance of the bodies of subordinate peoples, especially the sick or insane, the orphaned, the criminal, the colonized or enslaved.

Long established conventions structure many of the images we have which are related to work, although we sometimes have to look to the history of painting for explication of, for instance, the going-to-work-at-dawn and coming-home-in-the-evening-light pictures which are a staple of both genres, or the 'Othering' of the worker already noted (Treuherz 1987; Pollock 1993; Scarry 1994)[2]. Nostalgia deeply permeates photographs of work, many of which seem to have been occasioned by awareness of the rapid disappearance of labouring communities. These include most notably Salgado's (1993) 'Archaeology of the Industrial Age' but also the Depression-era photographs of American tenant farmers, or those of male craft workers in the same period. Sekula insists that the photograph's rhetorical function depends partly on context; for instance, the same photograph can function both as a report, bearing witness or, when presented as an aesthetic object, celebrate a 'bogus Subjecthood' in terms acceptable to the dominant classes (1982: 109). His writing on industrial photography explores the relationship between photographic culture and economic life, in particular the contradictory implications of the photographic archive, in which can be seen the rationalizing impulse of the time-and-motion study, the emotional investment of workers and their families and the construction of an imaginary landscape; the harmonious community projected by industrial capital (Sekula 1983).

However, more recent writing has begun exploring bodies at work. Pollock (1993) highlights the centrality of fantasy in the construction of photographic images, even those of working people, which is crucial to her understanding of sexual difference. As she (and also Trachtenberg 1989) comment, *which* bodies are pictured is as important as *how* they are represented. Powerful personages are more often figured in photographs based on head-and-shoulders shots. These images of work at work, where portraits of past presidents and so on line the boardroom, are not accidental; following Scarry one could say that they naturalize and legitimate the absence of the capitalist's bodily labour from the production process. When the entire body is shown these images never document the actuality of the subject but represent rather the 'fantastic bodies' produced by unconscious desire. This makes them especially rich as a way of tapping historical constructions of working bodies.

The 'fantastic body' of Hannah Cullwick

If we want to understand the *bodily* aspect of labour in class-, gender- and race-specific terms, the fascination of bourgeois Victorian men with the bodies of working-class women, especially women who worked out-of-doors in 'masculine' manual jobs, is a good place to start. As David-off (1983), Pollock and others highlight, 'images of laboring women's bodies circulated from Parliamentary report to popular journalism to the walls of official galleries and the pages of private albums . . .' (Pollock 1993: 5). Just as the body of the prostitute was a contested site, a terrain for the playing out of Victorian class and gender anxieties (Walkowitz 1980; Nead 1988) so too the bodies of female manual workers were a subject for 'the bourgeois deployment of the technologies of sexual regulation of the body of the proletariat' (Pollock 1993: 5).

An important resource for examining the era's obsessive interest in working-class women's bodies has been the collected papers of A.J. Munby (1828–1910), a Victorian civil servant who moved at the fringes of London artistic circles of the time (Hudson 1972; Stanley 1984). He left his papers to Trinity College, Cambridge, with the reservation that they not be revealed for forty years. His secret relationship with and marriage to a domestic servant, Hannah Cullwick, with whom he lived but briefly, is documented through their correspondence; the diaries she kept for him, in which she described – indeed celebrated – her gruelling day-to-day tasks in obsessive detail; his own diaries; and his sketch books. Munby's papers also contain his collection of 600 photographs of working women – for example, colliers, fisherwomen, mill workers, acrobats and servants. Although the eroticized master–servant relationship between Munby and Cullwick raises a huge number of questions, especially insofar as it was played out in terms of gender, class and racial symbolism, my main concern here is with the ways in which writers using the archives have illuminated the complex and highly contradictory connections between social structure and the construction of labouring bodies.

Leonore Davidoff's 'Class and Gender in Victorian England' (1983, first published in 1979), concentrates on Munby's obsessions with the construction of the classed female body through certain kinds of manual work. Davidoff's use of these documents to explore the ways both class and gender were inscribed on the bodies of female domestic servants gives a lie to the idea that scholars have become interested in 'the body' only recently. The continuing popularity of the Munby–Cullwick relationship as a subject of study is also due to the readiness with which we can assimilate the construction of Cullwick's clearly eroticized classed body to the concepts through which bodies and their representation have been theorized more recently: the labouring body is brought within the domain of psychoanalysis, performance and sexuality where current thinking simply assumes the body belongs. Davidoff explores the ways Victorian working-class women literally embodied class difference, through, for instance, diet, labour and the learned postures of deference. Munby himself was fascinated by working women's physical features – their 'rude strength', broad backs, 'ruddy countenance' and suntanned skin and, especially, their hands and feet, which contrasted greatly with the dainty white hands and smaller, more delicate feet of the middle-class girl. (He wrote approvingly, for instance, of a colliery girl in boots, 'shod like a horses hoofs' [Davidoff 1988: 42].)

Equally compelling is the way in which the demeaning nature of their domestic labour and confinement to the 'back passages' of the house polluted domestic servants. Like prostitutes, they stood at the nexus between classes: whereas the prostitute was in close body contact with the bourgeois male, the labour of the domestic servant preserved the privacy of the middle-class household. In bringing the water indoors for the family to wash, dealing with stained linen, removing rubbish and body wastes from the house, she enabled the middle class to keep their own bodies out of the public eye; she was a kind of conduit between the private and the public, a kind of sewer. Servants'

> most important job was to remove dirt and waste: to dust; empty slop pails and chamber pots; peel fruit and vegetables; pluck fowl; sweep and scrub floors, walls, and windows; remove ash and cinders; black lead grates, wash clothes and linen. (Davidoff 1988: 44)

It was not surprizing therefore that working-class women had a particular place in the Victorian map of the social body. As Davidoff says, the head was the middle-class male; the hands, the unthinking, unfeeling 'doers'; the heart the middle-class woman responsible for the emotional, tender side of life. The working-class girl represented the 'nether regions' of bodily functions, sexual and cloacal. Her degradation was constituted by both the work she did – it was only her labour which allowed the middle class woman to develop an image of disembodied purity, to signify femininity for the age – and the servile social relation in which it was embedded.

Ann McClintock (1995), like Davidoff, stresses the extent to which, through the equation of dirt, sexuality and blackness, the working-class woman's body was racialized and the middle-class woman whitened. Racialization was explicit in the relationship between Hannah Cullwick and Munby; she called him 'Massa' in imitation of her idea of a 'Negro' slave word for master. She had her photograph taken for him posing as a slave (as well as in other roles). In Munby's own sketches his working-class women appear to be racialized as well as masculinized. (The figure of Boompin' Nelly, for instance, 'is entirely blackened: she squats hunched and brooding, her colossal arms resting on enormous, wide-spread, foreshortened legs' [McClintock 1995: 107], and in his sketches of middle-class and working-class women, class is figured as racial as well as gender difference.

Analyses of the particular relationship between Hannah and Munby and the photographs of her have undergone significant shifts. Although some commentators agree that his fantasies of masculinized working-class women allowed Munby to enjoy his unacknowledged homosexual desires, the further question arises: who was empowered by these images? (Mavor 1996: 980). Tagg (1988: 92) takes it for granted that Munby's collection of photographs embodies 'the procedures of objecti-fication and subjection' and Davidoff assumes not only that Munby himself took the photographs, but that Cullwick was a passive victim of Munby's obsessions. More recent analyses challenge a too-ready equa-tion of woman with victim. It appears that the photographs of Hannah Cullwick were not taken by Munby himself, but by professional photog-raphers, either in their shops, to which Hannah often took herself and her props, or outdoors. For instance, the photograph shown in Plate 1 was taken when Hannah thought to 'please Massa' by asking a passing photographer to take a picture of her 'in her dirt' scrubbing and whiten-ing the front doorsteps of the house where she was employed (Hiley 1979: 67; see also Mavor 1996). Similarly the relationship is seen as one best understood through Foucault's concept of power (Dawkins 1987) or as reflecting Cullwick's own sexual desires as much as Munby's: let us 'grant Hannah some "perversions" of her own' Mavor says (1996: 86).

McClintock argues that the power relation between Munby and Cull-wick can be best analyzed using the model of sadomasochism, in which the scenarios directed by the S/M couple are orchestrated and controlled as much by the 'bottom' as the apparent master. Although the symbols they used in their games are drawn from the wider social structure,

Plate 1 Hannah Cullwick cleaning the front steps on her knees, 1864 (Reproduced by kind permission of the Master and Fellows of Trinity College Cambridge)

Munby did not always play the master; for instance he liked to be held by Cullwick in scenarios now associated with the practice of 'babyism'. McClintock (1995: 154) insists, therefore, that the ways in which the photographs and diaries make Cullwick's work visible, the ways they eroticize that work which ought to be invisible, is Hannah Cullwick's own achievement:

> Smeared on trousers, faces, hands and aprons, dirt was the memory
> trace of working class and female labour, unseemly evidence that the
> fundamental production of individual and imperial wealth lay in the
> hands and bodies of the working class, women and the colonized.
> Dirt, like all fetishes (e.g. money) thus expresses a crises in value, for
> it contradicts the liberal dictum that social wealth is created by the
> abstract, rational principles of the market and not by labour
> (McClintock 1995: 154).

The servant's work was supposed to be invisible, undertaken before
dawn or late at night, dodging the employer when 'in her dirt', appearing to open the door only in clean clothes. Moreover in a context in
which the Victorian middle-class obsession with dirt symbolized a
refusal to acknowledge the source of their wealth, Cullwick's ritualized
counting of the number of boots she had blacked, parading her blackness, guiding Munby round the household sites of her labours, is her
way of claiming a presence and making her labour visible.

The photographs and diaries also seem to present Cullwick's labour
as a kind of performance, albeit not quite in Butler's (1991) terms, the
success of which is validated by her relationship with Munby. This is
partly because the photographs of Hannah Cullwick performing her
domestic duties, like photographs of other Victorians, look so staged,
due to long exposure times and the use of props in studio photography,
but there is more to it than this. The photographs of Cullwick in different dress, that is playing different roles of lady, milkmaid, slave and
so on, clearly prefigure the work of the American photographer Cindy
Sherman, who photographed herself in stereotypical situations constructed through props, dress and expression. In this context the
photographs Hannah had taken of herself as a domestic servant picture
this as one of several possible roles, one adopted willingly from a position of strength.

In another interpretation of the archives Pollock (1993) sets the
Munby–Cullwick relationship in the context of the images of women
manual workers which Munby collected, most taken by local photog-
raphers and sold to visiting businessmen, as well as the tradition of
painting working people. From Pollock's point of view this obsessive
interest demonstrates the role fantasies about working-class women
played in the construction of the subjectivity of the middle-class male.
The context of Munby and Cullwick's relationship was widespread
concern about the female labouring body and especially her relation to
sexual difference. This was part of wider semiotics in which 'hardship

and poverty signified in and on the bodies of miners' and other working people. Their bodies stood for 'the radical alienness of industrial labour', locating it, through an anthropological gaze which racializes the social other not as an effect of capitalism but as the natural traits of their bodies (Pollock 1993: 24). While at first sight Pollock's discussion seems to imply that the body is only a text onto which signs of social relations and their effects have been 'displaced' she does not deny either the material effects of these social relations or indeed the social effects of particular representations. The most obsessive concern was for females, and among them the Wigan colliery pit-brow women who, because they wore divided skirts, were seen as half girl, half man. For instance, Plate 2 shows several pictures of female mining workers in the trousers which so exercized Victorian gentleman. In these pictures and others of their type the young women are always pictured with the tools of their trade, but one cannot help, I would argue, reading the shovel and round sifter as male and female symbols connoting the women's ambiguous gender identity. As Pollock and Davidoff both argue, the otherness of the worker is signified by their unnatural sexuality.

The overt concern was about moral danger, with respect to either the de-sexing of these girls or the way their work and costume led to the revealing of it, but the concern was saturated with disgust. One famous passage in the 1842 Parliamentary enquiry into labour conditions in mining noted that

> The chain, passing high up between the legs of two of these girls, had worn large holes in their trousers and any sight more disgusting, indecent or revolting can scarcely be imagined than these girls at work. No brothel can beat it. (Davidoff 1983: 51)

Pollock argues that the obsessive disgust these working women generated also has to be understood psychoanalytically. For Pollock the fascination of the photographs of mining women to Munby and other collectors was related to the way it played on their unconscious anxieties. The artifices adopted by the middle-class lady, the wide skirts and corsets, meant safety; although they confirmed gender difference they also hide the female's sexed body. In contrast, the trousered legs of women manual workers challenged the inevitability of man's difference from and superiority over the female; the trousers both reveal the artificiality of gender difference and makes evident 'what happens between their legs', sexual difference. Since it is recognition of the girl's lack

Plate 2   Carte portraits of pitbrow workers, Wigan and Shevington, 1867–78 (Reproduced by kind permission of the Master and Fellows of Trinity College Cambridge)

Plate 2 Continued

which precipitates the boy's fear of castration and the Oedipal stage, the female genitals are seen in psychoanalysis to excite male anxiety, deflected through fetishization. Pollock argues that along with the more usually cited reasons for getting women out of the workplace we have to consider the unconscious anxieties this resolved for men of the time. She argues that what was threatening about working women was not simply the challenge to male social and economic privilege but the way fears about their bodies challenged the stability of masculine psychic structure. The nineteenth-century disjunction between women and work, which feminists tried to challenge, is of course, mostly a matter of economic and social independence, but it is also a matter of body politics, men's hostility being partly a function of the role 'our bodies are obliged to perform or transgress . . . [in] masculinity's projected fantasies' (Pollock 1993: 47). What is at stake is the reduction of women's bodies to the position of signs in the masculine formation.

These are not so much competing accounts of the Munby–Cullwick relationship nor of the obsession with the bodies of working-class women as attempts to uncover further layers of meaning. What they share is the perception that gender and (fantasies about) sexual difference were essential to the representation of the labouring body and its altereity. These writers demonstrate that the analysis of gendered bodies is not simply postmodernist play, but concerned to explain the conflicts with which sociology and labour studies conventionally deal.

The manly worker as sign

If Hannah Cullwick's work, and that of domestic servants generally, was domestic, demeaning, servile, repetitious, ideally invisible, what work represents the opposite of all these – the heroic triumph of man (!) over nature? Although images of the heroic worker go back to at least Victorian times, for instance the famous painting 'Work' by Holman Hunt (Treuherz 1987), some of the most interesting examples come from twentieth century United States. Barbara Melosh (1993: 156) outlines the inflection of work with nobility through images of masculine bodies in the classical heroic mould in some detail, focusing on the public art sponsored by the American New Deal's Treasury Section of Fine Arts in the US, which from 1935 to 1943 awarded commissions for 'embellishments' for new buildings. As she documents, the broad, bare-chested, heavily muscled figure of the 'manly worker', became a key icon precisely at a time when male unemployment was at its height, skilled craftsmen were being replaced by semi-skilled operatives and manual workers by clerical and professional employees in the growing service sector. Unlike the iconography of Soviet socialist realism, which along with Mexican muralists was a key influence, the representation of work as mastery, 'the ability to reshape the material world and to make one's own destiny', was always represented as male, and almost always as white male. African-American male workers were not infrequently portrayed, but never cast in such a monumental role (see also Natanson 1992). Women were never represented as emblematic of a community – they were very occasionally included as factory workers, for instance in one part of a large mural, but more typically as members of families in early American frontier settings.

In the American documentary photography of the Depression era, however, this manly worker does not figure very strongly. The best-known photographs of the period, by Dorothea Lange, Walker Evans, Margaret Bourne-White, Russell Lee and Arthur Rothstein, who were employed by the Farm Security Administration under the tutelage of Roy Stryker, more often dealt with migrant, tenant, dispossessed *families*, serving, Tagg argues, to legitimate their status as dignified but passive recipients of state financial support. In some ways more vivid and interesting comparison with the Victorian images of working women comes earlier, in the photographs of Lewis Hine (1874–1940). Active from about 1907 to 1932, Hine became better known once the documentary style had established institutional categories for his work (Trachtenberg 1989). As a social reformer documenting the lives of the poor he is also sometimes characterized as a sociologist, and his writing on the 'types' of people he photographed was indebted to John Dewey and George Herbert Mead.

My interest is in two distinct series of pictures. The first is his series of pictures of the paid homeworking done mainly by women and children, which Hine undertook as the staff photographer for the National Child Labor Committee. As Boris (1994) highlights, American campaigners wanted to stop homeworking entirely; they campaigned not just against child labour, but against suppliers who tried to cut costs by giving out work to adult women either in their homes or in the factory sweatshop. Their most famous poster, 'Sacred Motherhood', for instance, made the point that the exploitation of women by suppliers destroyed family life and rendered the husband-father idle (Boris 1994). Hine's photographs convey this definition of the situation well. Photographs intended to document the existence of homeworkers and the condition of their families had to be taken on site, in this case tenements where there was little light. The photographs show heavily shadowed, gloomy interiors, slovenly housekeeping, degrading work. As Trachtenberg (1989) says, they show in a 'frozen moment' how un-absorbed the women and children are in the work, lacking in joy or satisfaction. Men are either absent, idle or out of place. As Trachtenberg goes on to say, although these photographs show work being done, those doing it are not pictured as workers.

After the First World War, however, Hine published another series of photographs which could not be more different. His series of pho-tographs of the making of the Empire State Building in New York City in 1930 were commissioned by the building's owners and first published in 1932 as the main part of Hine's book for children, *Men at Work: Photographic Studies of Men and Machines* (1977). These bodies in motion are everything Hine's homeworkers (or Victorian working women) were not: work makes man transcendent. Feeling of space and light and movement show them embodying positive values of work. As Trachtenberg says, the explicit message in the accompanying text as well as in the photographs identifies industrial workers as modern heroes. This notion

> finds its realization in the display of the working body in motion, in acts of concentration, muscular co-ordination, balance, strength, a repertoire of spontaneous gestures that show the body's experience, skill, training. (1989: 210)

Whereas Hine's homeworkers are bound down by their bodies, literally sagging in their chairs, the men atop the Empire State Building are exis-tential giants, transcendent figures flying through space. In some shots (for example, Plate 3) the worker looks almost like a flying angel; in others, in which workmen are pictured at the edge of mile-high plat-forms they resemble the statues which sometimes ring the roofs of urban buildings.

These different images, the male worker and the working mother, were deployed at different political moments and in relation to differ-ent critiques. According to Trachtenberg, the earlier photographs come out of a more radical, although reformist, politics than the later ones. Hine's earlier work was located within the institutional framework of the American Progressive reform movement, which critiqued and sought to control the destructive forces let loose in America by urban industrial capitalism. Although a bourgeois movement set against socialist politics it sought to shift public opinion in favour of legislative change. However, by the late 1920s, partly as a result of the First World

Plate 3 Lewis W. Hine The Sky Boy, Empire State Building 1931
(Courtesy George Eastman House)

War, which produced and intensified corporatist links between state and the owners of industry, former radicals now sought only recognition of the contribution of labour to the capitalist system. The 'moral realism' of the period sought to overcome the fissiparous tendencies of the increasing industrial division of labour by spiritualizing labour. The recognition of – indeed the glorification – of the manly worker was part of this attempt at symbolic integration.

One is tempted to generalize and argue that when photographs present work as problematic, this takes the form of focusing on women (and children), whereas the bodies of (white, skilled) male workers signify social solidarity. However, as in the case of the Victorian photographs examined above, it is not only male and female bodies but gender-stereotyped feminine and masculine poses and dress which connote the character of a workforce or which comment upon their relation to the wider society. For instance, in a posthumous collection of Hine's photographs, *Women at Work* (Doherty 1981), packaged as a companion volume to *Men at Work*, many of the photographs do show respect for women as workers and for their right to work. But the women workers are most frequently photographed sitting down, heads bowed to their handiwork or machine, which effectively replicates the postures of demure femininity typical of portraits of women in domestic settings. When pictures show male workers in such poses, such as in some photographs of clothing factories, they tend to be read as pictures of a docile workforce. It is surely signficant that the photographs produced during the Second World War (and also paintings in Soviet socialist realism) which project women's integration into the industrial workforce in positive terms do so partly through masculinizing women's dress and body shape. For example, Dorothea Lange's pictures of wartime California shipyards (for two examples, see Tagg 1988) show women workers wearing overalls and hard-hats, as mainly masculine in stance and staring straight at the camera.

Conclusion

In this chapter I have looked at pictures of men's and women's work and male and female workers, at differences in how their bodies are represented and at the use of their bodies as representations. In these examples women's work and women workers are curiosities, scrutinized, often immediately recognizable as signs of actual or potential social ills and altereity. We inspect the bodies of the women in Munby's collection of postcards and intrude into the homes of Hine's homeworkers, who appear too discouraged and passive to tell us to go away. Women's bodies seem to operate as a kind of magnetic pole, attracting anxieties about a range of problems and standing as a sign for them. Men's bodies in contrast deflect anxiety, for they represent the positive virtues of work and the incorporation of the worker into social mainstream. Men are pictured using skill and courage to enable them to use their work to shape the world, and as a route towards their own transcendence. The immanence/transcendence of female and male bodies is paralleled by other binaries – between flesh and spirit, shame and pride. At least until very recently, when the gender associations of these concepts are being shifted, many images still retain maleness as the sign of labour.

What are we to make of analyzing such material, as feminists? We obviously want to free ourselves from constructions of the past by making them visible. But there are dangers. Concentrating on the bodies of workers risks saturating ourselves in sexual difference, thereby reproducing rather than challenging the notion that one has to be 'defined by one's body' (Dyer 1997: 5). To this it can be countered that we need to show the extent to which the bodies by which we are defined are in any case partly imaginary. Looking at visualizations of working bodies can help to illuminate how far our understanding of embodied workers is a product of representational practices as well as actual differences in the sexual division of labour.

Notes

1. I am grateful to those University of Warwick MA students who have discussed this material with me in seminars, to colleagues who raised useful questions at the Edinburgh Conference, and to Eileen Boris for bringing Hine's photographs of homeworkers to my attention.
2. Note for instance Van Gogh's comments on his painting *The Potato Eaters* (1885): 'I have tried to emphasise that those people eating their potatoes in the lamplight, have dug the earth with those very hands they put in the dish, and so it speaks of *manual labour*, and how they have honestly earned their food. I have wanted to give the impression of a way of life quite different from that of us civilised people.' (cited by Treuherz 1987: 123–4)

Bibliography

ADKINS, L. (1995) *Gendered Work: Sexuality, Family and the Labour Market*. Buckingham: Open University Press.
BORIS, E. (1994) *Home to Work: Motherhood and the Politics of Industrial Homework in the United States*. Cambridge, New York and Melbourne: Cambridge University Press.

BREWIS, J. and D. KERFOOT (1994) 'Selling Our Selves: Sexual Harassment and the Intimate Violations of the Workplace'. Paper presented at the Conference of the British Sociological Assocation, Preston.

BURGIN, V. (ed.) (1982) *Thinking Photography*. London and Basingstoke: Macmillan Press – now Palgrave.

BUTLER, J. (1991) 'Imitation and Gender Insubordination' in Diana Fuss (ed.) *Inside/Out: Lesbian Theories, Gay Theories*. London: Routledge.

CLARKE, G. (1997) *The Photograph*. Oxford and New York: Oxford University Press.

DAVIDOFF, L. (1983) 'Class and Gender in Victorian England' in Judlh Newton, Mary Ryan and Judith Walkowitz (eds) *Sex and Class in Women's History: Essays from Feminist Studies*. London: Routledge & Kegan Paul.

DAWKINS, H. (1987) 'The Diaries and Photographs of Hannah Cullwick' *Art History* 10:154–87.

DOHERTY, J.L. (1981) *Women at Work: 155 Photographs by Lewis W. Hine*. New York: Dover Publications.

DYER, R. (1997) *White*. London: Routledge.

GIDDENS, A. (1991) *Modernity and Self-Identity*. Cambridge: Polity Press.

HARRISON, B. (1998) 'Re-visioning the Body: Photographic Representation and Resistance' British Sociological Association Annual Conference, University of Edinburgh.

HILEY, M. (1979) *Victorian Working Women:Portraits from Life*. London: Gordon Fraser.

HINE, L.W. (1977) *Men at Work: Photographic Studies of Modern Men and Machines*. New York: Dover Publications.

HOCHSCHILD, A. (1983) *The Managed Heart*. Berkeley: University of California.

HUDSON, D. (1972) *Munby: A Man of Two Worlds*. London: Gambit.

KUHN, A. (1985) *The Power of the Image*. London: Routledge & Kegan Paul.

MAVOR, C. (1996) *Pleasures Taken: Performances of Sexuality and Loss in Victorian Photographs*. London: I.B. Tauris.

MCCLINTOCK, A. (1995) *Imperial Leather: Race, Gender and Sexuality in the Colonial Context*. New York and London: Routlege.

MCDOWELL, L. (1997) *Capital Culture: Gender at Work in the City*. Oxford: Blackwell.

MELOSH, B. (1993) 'Manly Work: Public Art and Masculinity in Depression America' in B. Melosh (ed.) *Gender and American History since 1890*. London and New York: Routledge.

NATANSON, Nicholas (1992) *The Black Image in the New Deal: The Politics of FSA Photography*. Knoxville: Universiy of Tennessee Press.

NEAD, L. (1988) *Myths of Sexuality*. Oxford: Blackwell.

PATEMAN, C. (1988) *The Sexual Contract*. Cambridge: Polity.

PLUMMER, K. (1983) *Documents of Life*. London: Unwin Hyman.

POLLOCK, G. (1993) 'The Dangers of Proximity: The Spaces of Sexuality and Surveillance In Word and Image' *Discourse* 16, 2 Winter: 3–50.

PULTZ, J. (1995) *Photography and the Body*. London: George Weidenfeld and Nicolson.

SALGADO, S. (1993) *Workers: An Archaeology of the Industrial Age*. London: Phaidon.

SCARRY, E. (1985) *The Body in Pain.* New York and Oxford: Oxford University Press.

SCARRY, E. (1994) *Resisting Representation.* New York and Oxford: Oxford University Press.

SCHATZKI, T. and W. NATTER (1996) 'Sociocultural Bodies, Bodies Sociopolitical' in T. Schatski and W. Natter (eds) *The Social and Political Body.* New York and London: The Guildford Press.

SEKULA, A. (1982) 'On the Invention of Photographic Meaning' in Victor Burgin (ed.) *Thinking Photography* London and Basingstoke: Macmillan Press – now Palgrave.

SEKULA, A. (1983) 'Photography Beween Labour and Capital' in Benjamin Buchloh and Robert Wilkie (eds) *Mining Photographs and Other Pictures 1948–1968.* Canada: The Press of Nova Scotia College of Art and Design and The University College of Cape Breton Press.

STANLEY, L. (ed.) (1984) *The Diaries of Hannah Cullwick: Victorian Maidservant.* London: Virago.

TAGG, J. (1988) *The Burden of Representation: Essays on Photographies and Histories.* Basingstoke: Macmillan Education.

TRACHTENBERG, A. (1989) *Reading American Photographs: Images as History.* New York: Hill and Wang.

TREUHERZ, J. (1987) *Hard Times: Social Realism in Victorian Art.* London: Lund Humphries Publishers Ltd, in association with Manchester City Art Galleries.

WALKER, R. and J. WIEDEL (1985) 'Using Photographs in a Discipline of Words' in Robert Burgess (ed.) *Field Methods in the Study of Education.* London and Philadelphia: The Falmer Press.

WALKOWITZ, J. (1980) *Prostitution in Victorian Society.* Cambridge: Cambridge University Press.

7
Walking on the Beaches Looking at the . . . Bodies

Paula Black

Introduction

Why tourism? Why the body? Both of these areas have become 'fashionable' in sociology to the extent that it is now not strictly accurate to describe them as under-researched (Scott and Morgan 1993). My concern with tourism and the body stems from a research question designed to investigate the sexual experiences of British travellers and tourists abroad, their sexual risk taking and the potential for HIV transmission (Black 2000; 1997). As an aspect of this research I have theorized the body as one which belongs to a specific class and gender and is also constructed in relation to sexuality. Despite the fact that travel involves the removal of the physical body into a situation where heightened sensuality is a prime motivating factor, tourism theory has included relatively little mention of the body. In contrast to an emphasis upon the tourist gaze (Urry 1990), Veijola and Jokinen argue for the embodiment of tourism theory:

> [The] tourist *gaze*? Isn't it rather the tourist *body* that breaks with the established routines and practices? We do gaze at dance performances and museums at home, don't we? But instead, hardly ever engage ourselves in singing and dancing together; very rarely at home do we share the feeling of being together in this big, wild, incomprehensible world, full of strangers whose words and gestures don't say anything. Here, we know it in our conscious bodies that are temporarily united in an utterly physical ritual. (1994: 133).

It is this focus upon corporeality which will be my theme.

Methodology

I will draw upon research conducted in two Genito-Urinary Medicine (GUM) clinics in the south east of England outside London.[1] Fieldwork was conducted in 1994 and 1995. All clinic attendants who had travelled abroad in the previous two years were invited to take part in the research by either myself or the clinic staff.

A questionnaire was used as the basis for 141 structured interviews. Areas covered include biographical details; sexual partners in the UK; contraception in the UK; travel history; sexual behaviour abroad; contraception use abroad; sources of knowledge about health advice for travellers; previous treatment for an STD and attendance at a GUM clinic; and alcohol and drug use both at home and abroad. The total interview sample consisted of 66 men (47 per cent) and 75 women (53 per cent). Their ages ranged from 17 to 79, with an average of 31. A total of 88 per cent described themselves as British, and 91 per cent were permanent residents of the UK. Sexuality was ascribed to the interviewees on the basis of reported sexual partners in the previous two years. Using this form of assessment, 32 per cent of the total sample were heterosexual men, 52 per cent heterosexual women, 13.5 per cent gay men and the remainder reported partners of both sexes.

In-depth interviews were conducted with 10 women and 8 men, or 13 per cent of the questionnaire sample. These interviews were begun by using an 'opening out' question which asked the interviewee to discuss one travel experience. Even though identical questions were not asked in each interview, a mental checklist evolved which was then covered. This was derived from what Strauss and Corbin call 'theoretical sensitivity', or a combination of relevant literature, professional experience and personal experience (1990). The areas include:

- how does travel fit into the biography of the individual?
- the details of sexual encounters
- perception of 'difference'; would the interviewee behave in the same way at home? Were they a different person on holiday or while travelling?
- the experience of cultural differences. Do these influence who the traveller interacts with, has sexual contact with, and do they influence the negotiation of the sexual encounter itself?
- do they see themselves as a 'traveller' or a 'tourist' and do they recognize a difference between the two?

- perception of risks; does this influence choice of destination, travelling companions and (sexual) behaviour while travelling?

Analysis of the interview material followed the grounded theory method advocated by Strauss and Corbin (1990).

The body in traveller and tourist narratives

A key distinction to arise from the research is that made between 'traveller' and 'tourist'. These labels were accepted by all interviewees, but the qualitative differences between them were most vehemently defended by self identified travellers. Though I accept that the label traveller was a crucial aspect of identity, and a structuring tool for travellers' narratives, I shall argue later that such differences in fact reflect class positions. These labels have implications for the type of journeys conducted, the experiences described, the sexuality of the individual and the role of the body within the travel type. For travellers, the purpose of the journey, while undoubtedly partly motivated by pleasure seeking, is also intrinsically bound up with the self concept and self actualization. Learning about other cultures and languages is seen to be part of the process where travel develops the inner life of the individual. Those who took on the identity of traveller also claimed an ideological position for themselves in opposition to the Western Judaeo-Christian tradition. This is an important factor in self definition as traveller which does not refer to specific activities, but to an ideological position. It is difficult to disentangle the actual opinions and experiences here from the dominant discourse surrounding travel. In traveller circles these are the oft repeated mantras of the values of travelling and the superiority of the travel experience over tourism.

What travellers are generally trying to distance themselves from is a specific form of tourism, and one that is generally thought of as constituting tourism *per se*, that is of tourism to resorts. Resorts are locations, often purpose built, with the role of providing accommodation and entertainment for visitors. The characteristics of the resort may be seen as an ideological construct which are designed to service and construct a particular type of travel, that is, that of mass tourism as opposed to individual travel. The resort represents an homogenized form of tourist experience where the excesses of local culture are screened out in favour of living conditions and means of socializing familiar to the tourist from their home environment. Resorts are isolated from the local culture and have more in common with each other than they do to other non-resort locations within the same country.

These two Ideal Types of travel are differentiated in the narratives, and are returned to frequently in order to distinguish between bodily experiences. For example, Jonathan clearly contrasts the two:

> A traveller's been through pain, a tourist hasn't. A traveller's arrived at a perception of himself somewhere and been through misery and has got somewhere and has chilled out. They've growed (sic) their hair long, they've lost their Western clothes, that's not true, well they've lost, they've fitted in with the culture. They've kept their eyes open. They would no more upset that culture than upset their own parents, you know. A tourist demands service, you know, I despise the idea of service, I think everybody in a foreign country should (laughs), should serve the locals, you know, I'm just resolute about this. Travellers are people, they're just, they're tolerant, they pick up litter. I mean I'm glamorizing it but I'm trying to get the point across that you become tolerant of everybody around you and culture, you become aware of the fact that you're being treated as a guest and that you should behave with a code of conduct and you should give people on the road the respect to talk about what they wanna talk about, you know, its just brilliant.

For Jonathan and for all other self-identified travellers, travel could be seen as both an activity and a defining aspect of identity. A key aspect of travel is the modification of the body in keeping with traveller style. For Jonathan this includes growing his hair and losing his Western clothes. A view of the traveller lifestyle which echoes Jonathan's comments comes from Mark:

> I think the travellers are, they're sort of a bit more 'right on' shall we say. The tourists go there and they just take the piss really. Well look, tourists are working people, travellers are people who enjoy life and sort of, you know, without abusing what's around them so much. I mean you can't say everybody, I'd say I'm definitely generalizing. Yes, tourists are a complete fucking nightmare they really are, they stand out more so than anybody and they make so many problems for travellers.

Mark's claim here that tourists 'stand out', I would argue actually refers to their class identity and to the way that this is displayed through rituals of the body. He is inferring that their mode of dress, their manner of speech and their cultural values locates tourists firmly within the cultures they have left behind for the brief duration of their stay. This not only marks out their bodies as different from local people, but also contrasts them to the lifestyle of travellers. The difference between 'working people' and 'people who enjoy life' is an echo of the workers and 'leisured classes' distinction. 'We pick up the languages' implies that travellers are more highly educated and have a greater aptitude for learning from their travel experiences. In contrast, 'they're on a package holiday' implies a mass mentality where the crowd is followed at the expense of individual betterment. In contrast, it is home responsibilities and the restrictions imposed by economic factors or work commitments which the holiday maker is wishing to remove themselves from. Resort holidays, therefore, are motivated by the desire to escape from the routines of everyday life in contrast to the traveller's motivation to engage in new situations because of some intrinsic value they may hold. Nick explains his attraction to resort holidays:

> It gives you the chance to relax, do things that you want to do on your own, erm, a bit of privacy away from you know all relations and all the other outside influences and just get away from it all. I always look at holidays as totally being escapist, to get away from everything.

He goes on to explain how a large part of this relaxation for him comes through bodily activities ranging from sport (rugby tours with 'the lads') to drinking and visiting nightclubs and bars.

Authenticity and the body

Both travel and tourism, therefore, imply specific relationships to the body and to lifestyle forms. One of the key claims made by travellers is that travel leads to more 'authentic' experience and that resort holidays are 'shallow'. The authenticity of travel may relate more to the traveller discourse than to any qualitative difference between traveller and tourist activities. Travellers claim authenticity as an intrinsic characteristic of their identity. Authentic experience is seen to be fostered by anything which enables the traveller to engage more closely with local culture. This claim to authenticity is justified with reference to body experiences rather than simply relying upon the tourist gaze. Direct involvement in local culture is prized and tourists who place an emphasis upon the visual at the expense of the experiential are scoffed at.

Heather had given some thought to her lifestyle and how this contrasted to the experiences of tourists:

> I don't think tourists tend to interact so much with the local environment and the local culture, erm, its very much the interface between the tourist and the place they're in, you know, it's very much looking at it through a camera lens or looking at it through a bus window or going through a guide, a tour guide. It's also, erm, a much shorter space of time as well so they don't really have the time to get to know the people so much and I think they tend to stay in, er, hotels that tend to cater to them in the way they're accustomed to in terms of Western civilisation, rather than actually getting to know about the culture and staying with local families and learning the language. The real place is the people and the way of life rather than just the history or the architecture or the art, you know, or whatever. I think the real crux of the place is getting to know the people and the way of life.

Heather here is reinforcing Urry's insistence on the primacy of the tourist gaze in characterizing tourism, and she contrasts this with traveller experience (1990). The viewing of sights through the windows of the tourist bus or through the lens of the camera removes the physical sensing body from the 'authentic' experiences of travelling. She also mentions that accommodation should be as close as possible to the local standards of living, if not actually living with local people. This is qualified by the proviso that authenticity means living as close as possible to nature, and so by local forms of accommodation travellers generally refer to standards of living of either the poorest people in the locations they visit, or forms of life in less developed regions. This again reinforces the view that to have an authentic travel experience the body must be as close as possible to the 'natural' surroundings of the location. To be placed in standard tourist accommodation removes the body from the physical sensations which define authenticity. Encapsulation in hotels reproduces the standard of living experienced at 'home' and so throws doubt upon the traveller's claim to authenticity, or upon the claimed difference between home culture and travel culture (Eastern culture and Western culture). The preference for less developed modes of life implies an avoidance of over developed areas, and in particular those locations with high levels of tourist saturation. Through these techniques travellers believe that they can avoid the staged spectacles of the tourist world.

Shallowness relates most directly to resort and mass tourism forms of holiday and even those who sometimes chose, or by circumstance found themselves, engaging in such holidays criticized them for their 'tackiness' or lack of substance. Ingrid here explains her travel preferences:

> I wanna go travelling sort of backpacking, do that sort of holiday where you see stuff. I wouldn't go on that sort of thing where, you know, you're down the bar every night and down the disco. I mean I've got nothing against going out clubbing and whatever and I do it in [town], but I don't know, I felt it [resort holiday] was all really rather cheap and sort of shallow whereas if you like go proper travelling and that you meet people that are just like wanna see the world.

This accusation of shallowness then does not simply relate to activities, such as clubbing, as these are engaged in at home without reservation. Rather, what appears to give rise to the 'shallow' label is the context within which these activities occur.

The beach

The beach is an often mentioned location for either socializing or sexual contact. It has been argued that the seaside and the beach in particular have been created as liminal zones which encourage the display of the 'carnivalesque'. These liminal zones differentiate themselves from other spaces in their link to pleasure and the distancing from spheres of production and regulation (Shields 1990). The beach may also be seen as a zone which separates nature in the raw (the sea) from civilization (the city) through the differentiation of the zones in between. The beach is an intermediate stage between nature and culture (Fiske 1989). Certainly, the beach was mentioned by the interviewees as a highly important social location where normal codes of dress, levels of activity, and privacy of sexual contact were over-turned. The beach has also been linked to sexual possibility and the disclosure of the body, particularly the female body. 'Dirty' postcards represent a long tradition of sexual excess and female nudity which contribute to the sensuality of the beach and to the male 'gaze' focusing upon the bodies of women (Rojek 1993). Beaches are places for looking, and particularly in terms of looking at bodies, it is the female body which is on display (Fiske 1989).

The beach and sunbathing are linked to having fun, particularly through the conduit of the body. They may play a role in the first social contact leading to meeting a sexual partner. When potential partners are encountered in bars and restaurants, a 'walk on the beach' acts as a sexual euphemism in enticing the partner away from the watching eyes of others. The following quote illustrates the location changes involved in Anna's increasing intimacy with a local man during her trip to Colombia and the part played by the beach:

> About four in the morning he [partner] said let's go for a walk on the beach, which basically means lets get off together, it was sort of, erm, a pretty obvious pick up line and, erm, I was really into him by then. The beach there is never empty, there's always people on it all night so you, even if you wanted to go further you couldn't because, you know, its too public. So yeah, we had a bit of a snog and came back to the night-club and met my cousins and then he arranged to meet me the next night, and we met up on the beach at those lovely little bars on the beach, and he booked a hotel for us that night which was very nice of him.

For gay men, particularly those who were unlikely to engage in penetrative sex, the beach formed a significant site to engage in sexual activities and an important meeting place to encounter other gay men seeking sexual contact. It seems that in certain areas of the beach here, as with other gay cruising areas, the move to a private place out of the view of others is less relevant than moving to an area that is recognized as a sexual arena. As Adam uneasily describes:

> It [Sitges] was very cruisy, I mean I don't like the sort of like casual sex on beaches and things, I mean if you went down the promenade at night it was quite amazing, there was just rows of men sort of like having sex on the beach.

Fiske outlines how the beach may be divided into different areas according to their proximity to culture (the city). Those that, for example, permit nude bathing are furthest away from roads and towns. For all of the interviewees who experienced sexual contact on the beach, there was a clear sense of certain times and certain locations where sex was permitted. These areas were also differentiated in terms of whether it was heterosexual or gay sex taking place there. An interesting distinction between types of beaches is also raised by Rojek (1993) in his contrast between 'suburban' and 'non-suburban' beaches. The attraction of the suburban beach lies in cultural stimuli including the proximity of other bodies, and the activities and facilities provided close to the beach. This form of socializing on the beach may be linked to a tourist form of travel where the beach forms an important location for meeting others, for engaging in sexual contact and for signifying membership of the tourist group through the acquisition of a suntan. The non-suburban beach derives its value from more 'natural' stimuli which relate to the lack of crowds and the 'unspoilt' location. This type of beach may be related to a traveller form of experience. While the beach still acts as a venue for sociability and sexual contact, the forms of these contacts are based upon the exclusivity of the location and experience. Both types of relationship to the beach also reflect claims to authenticity by travellers. Rojek argues that in the late twentieth century the beach has become an 'axis of consumption and transformation' (Rojek 1993: 190). The accusations of shallowness and uncritical consumption levelled at tourists by travellers are reflected in the type of beach designed as an integral part of the tourist holiday. I would, however, doubt the claims to such a distinction as facilities provided for travellers and designed specifically for their needs are often located along or upon beaches even if their form differs to those demanded by mass tourism.

Fun and the body

One of the perceived characteristics of the resort holiday which contributes to viewing it as shallow is the fact that interaction takes place in highly mediated social environments, with sexual contact presumed to be the desired outcome. For travellers the claimed interest in socializing lay in learning about a different culture or in the intrinsic characteristics of potential partners. To be seen to focus purely upon the body, and specifically upon the sexual body is seen as 'tacky'. Despite this, the body becomes an important means of assessing the attractiveness of potential partners for both travellers and tourists, even though for both groups a striking lack of physical descriptions were evident when discussing partner attractiveness. Only occasionally were physical characteristics mentioned. Descriptions of partners generally centred around what happened, where they met, and what kind of person they were. Rarely within these descriptions were references made to how a partner looked, or to their body. However, the selection of a partner was heavily influenced by cultural symbols displayed on and through the body.[2]

Characteristics which were considered attractive often denoted a specific form of travel and the social activities linked to it. For example, the body image associated with tourism social activities was important. Partners were described as tanned which locates them within a holiday environment where sunbathing is a common activity, and contributes to attractiveness in that in the late twentieth-century at least, a tan is associated with leisure activities and good health (Carter 1995). In a travel context the symbols of 'traveller' such as clothes worn and locations visited allow attractions to develop within a culturally defined group. As attractiveness is judged according to context, a lack of familiarity with the surrounding culture may lead to ambiguities in choosing a partner. After the experience gained from her relationship with an older Tunisian man Rachel comments:

> It's incredibly easy to have a one night stand abroad, probably easier than it is here because you don't, I mean if, you know, if you're down the town on a Saturday night you know you can tell whether or not they're a twat do you know what I mean? But like when you're abroad you haven't got the same sort of, you know, its a different culture, he might be a twat but you don't realize it yet.

Here, Rachel describes how part of the reason for the failure of her relationship was that she had been unable to judge her partner's characteristics in the same way as she would have done at home. Part of the reason for this was that she was unable to read signs relating to gender, class and sexuality in an unfamiliar body culture.

Sexuality and its expression within a travel and tourism context are closely related to the types of socializing which take place. Interaction with others in a social environment is often the precursor to meeting sexual partners (this is not necessarily the case in commercial sexual encounters or in gay cruising). The display of the body in highly regulated forms is a vital part of this socializing. The signs of class, gender and sexuality are constantly read and interpreted by others in a social situation, and this is an intrinsic part of having fun. This fun in a tourism and resort context centres around 'going out' which often means to bars, clubs and restaurants or to other places where the main purpose of the activities is to interact with others, 'to meet people'. Fun involves a high level of body awareness which contributes to feelings of pleasure. Having fun includes preparation for that fun which is centred upon the body. In preparing to go out much work is often done to the body, particularly for women, in order to achieve a body image to be presented to others in the social arena. This may include the styling of hair, application of make-up, paying attention to the clothes to be worn, as well as shaving, deodorizing and other methods of rendering the body socially acceptable (Holland *et al.* 1994).

Sunbathing is an activity centred around the body and body image. As sunbathing takes place during daylight hours, at a location frequented by many others on the same type of trip and with similar preferences for activities, sunbathing itself counts as a form of sociability. It may also act as a precursor to the socializing to occur in the bars and clubs later in the day as overt and covert contacts may have been made during this time. The suntan is an important symbol of having engaged in leisure, and of the health of the individual who sports it (Fiske 1989; Carter 1997).

While undoubtedly also a constituent of travel, in contrast to tourism, fun in the travel context is seen by travellers to be more of a by product of the process of travel rather than central to its evaluation and motivation. Having fun may also involve visiting bars, lying on beaches and preparing the body, but is defined in different terms by those who would see themselves as travellers. Sunbathing is not a central activity and when lying on the beach, the inactivity itself is the *raison d'etre* for the activity rather than the suntan. Visiting bars may occur only at certain times and in certain locations during a trip. The bars visited will be frequented by other travellers and the standards of facilities which are provided are much more basic than those experienced by tourists. Certain liminal areas, such as the islands of Koh Phangan and Koh Samui off the coast of Thailand are recognized as 'party zones' in themselves and attract either travellers whose favoured activity while travelling is the attendance of 'raves' and parties, or other travellers at times when a specific form of fun and interaction is required. To some extent such areas function as the nightclubs of the world for travellers. Correspondingly, certain times may be described as liminal, and are celebrated by travellers in all locations. For example, full moon parties are frequently celebrated, and commonly act as a source of intense fun and potential sexual contact. In attending to the body image, travellers refer to different types of cultural and bodily symbols which rely less upon make-up and comparatively expensive clothes. In common with tourists, these bodily symbols serve to identify group membership. An area of Bangkok, the Khao San Road, serves as an illustration of how location, fun, body image and tourist/traveller identity are interrelated. This area is isolated from the world we know as 'Bangkok' and certainly from that of local people. Travellers who have journeyed extensively meet here. They carry upon their bodies symbols which have meaning for other travellers and identify them as belonging to a similar identifiable culture. Such symbols include 'scruffy' or 'hippie' clothes, earrings made locally or in other traveller destinations and the wearing of friendship bands. Mark describes his observation of these symbols while staying in another area of Bangkok. The ability to read these symbols and to carry those of traveller were important for Mark to place himself within the traveller culture, which acted as a significant source of his self identity:

> You'd just be there all day hanging out in the pub and you'd see new fresh people come off the plane, you can spot them a mile away, they just look so, even back-pack travellers you can still spot them when they come off the plane, they come into town, they just always stand out a mile, they smell of Western countries and they come there and they're just sort of, they don't know what's going on, they don't know anything and they're too vulnerable.

To local people the travellers are simply seen as dirty; the bodily symbols are read according to a different discourse. Locals define themselves in contrast as clean and smart. Of course linked to these distinctions is the claim by travellers, and the image held by many others, that for tourists in resorts the main outcome of having fun, and a specific form of fun in itself, is sexual contact (Ford and Eiser 1996). This is reinforced by the heightened bodily awareness experienced away from home; an awareness which is experienced by travellers on a more continuous basis. The key point here is that the desire for fun brings together people often searching for similar experiences, in the types of situations that heighten social contact and interaction with others. As Hollands argues in his study of young peoples' nights out in the north east of England:

> It is important to reiterate the yawning gap between public perceptions of the relationship between promiscuity and nights out and the actual reality of sexual contact. This is not to argue that sex does not happen or that sexuality is unimportant. On the contrary, symbolically it is probably one of the most central components of going out. However, much of the investment made here is displaced into clothing, posture, interaction, innuendo and conversation. (1995: 58)

The social situation is not unproblematically a signifier for sexual contact. Rather, the rituals of sociability may signify other underlying factors, of which the byproduct, but not necessarily the primary intention, is to meet a sexual partner.

The body in tourism: conclusions

To summarize, I have looked at the nature of tourism theory and the role of the body within it, particularly in reference to authenticity. I have drawn upon in-depth interviews with British travellers and tourists in order to outline the distinction that they make between travel types. I have also looked at sexual encounters abroad. The role of the body has been considered in these different areas and I have questioned the primacy of 'the gaze' in tourist experience (Urry 1990; Crawshaw and Urry 1997).

A clear distinction emerged from the in-depth interviews between travellers and tourists. It was the self-defined travellers who were most concerned to emphasize this distinction. Travel was seen as embodying a form of freedom and self expression absent from tourism. In this way travel was not seen by my interviewees simply as an activity to be engaged in uncritically, but as a means of creating the self in a dialectical relationship between place and the individual acted out within the discourse of travel. The term traveller describes identity rather than simply an activity engaged in. By investing so much of themselves in the process of travel, the visitor seeks a return and in the case of travellers the rewards were seen to be authenticity of experience. By expending more time and energy than tourists, travellers believed they could escape the packaged nature of not only the tourist experience, but of *all* experience. Travellers and tourists expressed a different relationship to the tourist gaze. In their claims to authenticity and in the culturally mediated definitions of traveller and tourist categories, the interviewees in this study continuously referred to the role of the body. Though this reference was not always explicit, in their narratives the display of cultural symbols on and through the body is evident. A reliance upon the gaze is seen to imply shallowness and is attributed to mass tourism. In contrast, immersion of the body in local culture through sexual contact with local people, living with host communities and sharing their food, a level of authenticity is claimed. The use of the body as a form of display in social settings as a precursor to sexual contact is seen to be a characteristic of tourism and the use of the body in this way is denigrated by travellers.

Urry (1990) and Munt (1994) argue that individualistic travellers are products of the rise in the service class in Western societies. By advocating individuality, the middle classes formulate their own travel experiences in opposition to the mass tourism of the working class. Munt, however, points out the irony in this position:

> The practices of travellers are best conceived within a 'cult of individualism' through which it is deeply ironic that they are largely indistinguishable from each other by virtue of their discourse, dress codes and the informal 'packages' that they follow through travel guides. (1994: 114)

Class remains an implicit form of categorization between traveller and tourist. Though it would not necessarily be expressed in class terms by the travellers themselves, the indicators they use in categorizing individuals may be related to a specific form of 'habitus' (Bourdieu 1984). Self actualization, new experiences, learning about other cultures and languages all create 'cultural capital' in the eyes of this service class. Among my interviewees the distinction between traveller and tourist was at least partly based upon class and the display of the body while travelling corresponded to differing approaches to body projects, and to the self imposed identity in relation to travel. Gender also plays a role here. As Jokinen and Veijola (1997) point out, the tourist body is not a universal category, but is rather a gendered body.

The common image of the permissive young person on a package holiday drinking, taking drugs and having sex to excess is often accepted with little critique by the media, the general public, and even health professionals and academics. If there is a pure form of liminal zone which encourages such behaviour it could be seen to be the resort aimed at young people, or what Wickens has described as 'ravers' (1997). The display of the body in a social environment is often read unproblematically as a sign for 'shallow' experience including casual sexual encounters. From a closer study of interactions within these contexts however, it is clear that much of the sexual abandon presumed to be liberated within the liminal zone is either displaced into sexual innuendo, dress and socializing, is exaggerated in the accounts of those involved, or is a figment of the age and class bias of writers on the subject. Resorts are based upon mass tourism, and as such are generally associated with 'the gross values of the welfare state' (Rojek 1993: 175). The working class has long been associated with 'ribaldry' and an aggressive sexuality. The view of the tourist resort as fostering extensive sexual encounters and risk taking behaviour, while the middle-class walking holiday embodies 'pure' forms of mind and bodily enjoyment, is to simply reproduce class stereotypes within social theory.

Notes

1. GUM clinics were selected as the site for the research because they provide a 'captive sample' of people who either have engaged in sexual risk taking, or believe themselves to be at risk. Other clinic studies with a predominantly quantitative focus have also been conducted in London and several other sites in the UK (Hawkes *et al.*, 1995; Mendelsohn *et al.*, 1996; Carter *et al.*, 1997). This provides material for comparison.
2. A large area of consideration for women is the potential risk involved in being alone with a male partner. Assessment of the level of risk posed by the partner is decided by categorizing men in to 'good bloke/bad bloke' or assessing the potential strength of the person in terms of physical risk. In order to achieve this a woman may take into account the age and size of the man, or she may get to know his friends in order to place him within a familiar moral framework. For the move to a more secluded area which precedes sexual contact, a woman must be as certain as she can be that she is in no danger from her partner. This is a process which is occurring at the same time as she is attempting to decipher the sexual messages being received and interacting in a busy social situation. She may draw upon as many cultural cues as necessary, but at the same time 'intuition' plays a part in her assessment of the safety of her situation. It is not possible here to go into detail, but the vulnerability of the female body to violence and sexual attack from men was an all pervasive sense of risk for women when travelling.

Bibliography

BLACK, P. (2000) 'Sex and Travel: Making the Links', in S. Clift and S. Carter, *Tourism and Sex: Culture, Commerce and Coercion*. London: Pinter.

BLACK, P. (1997) 'Sexual Behaviour and Travel: Quantitative and Qualitative Perspectives on the Behaviour of Genito-Urinary Medicine Clinic Attenders', in S. Clift and P. Grabowski (eds) *Tourism and Health: Risks, Research and Responses*. London: Pinter.

BOURDIEU, P. (1984) *Distinction: A Social Critique of Taste*. London: Routledge and Kegan Paul.

CARTER, S., K. HORN, G. HART, M. DUNBAR, A. SCOULAR and S. MACINTYRE (1997) 'The Sexual Behaviour of International Travellers at Two Glasgow Clinics'. *International Journal of STD and AIDS* 8:336–8.

CARTER, S. (1997) 'Who Wants to be "Peelie Wallie"? Glaswegian Tourists' Attitudes to Sun Tans and Sun Exposure', in S. Clift and P. Grabowski (eds) *Tourism and Health: Risks, Research and Responses*. London: Pinter.

CARTER, S. (1995) 'Becoming Brown: A Short History of the Sun-Tan'. *Annals of Tourism Research* 18:345–78.

CRAWSHAW, C. and J. URRY (1997) 'Tourism and the Photographic Eye', in C. Rojek and J. Urry. *Touring Cultures: Transformations of Travel and Theory*. London: Routledge.

FISKE, J. (1989) *Reading the Popular.* Boston: Unwin Hyman.

FORD, N. and J. EISER (1996) 'Risk and Liminality: The HIV-Related Socio-Sexual Interaction of Young Tourists', in S. Clift and S. Page (eds) *Health and the International Tourist.* London: Routledge.

HAWKES, S., G. HART, E. BLESTOE, C. SHERGOLD and A. JOHNSON (1995) 'Risk Behaviour and STD Acquisition in Genitourinary Clinic Attenders Who Have Travelled'. *Genitourinary Medicine* 7:351–4.

HOLLAND, J., C. RAMAZANOGLU, S. SHARPE and R. THOMSON (1994) Power and Desire: The Embodiment of Female Sexuality, *Feminist Review*, 46, 21–38.

HOLLANDS, R. (1995) *Friday Night, Saturday Night: Youth Cultural Identification in the Post-Industrial City.* Newcastle: University of Newcastle.

JOKINEN, E. and S. VEIJOLA (1997) 'The Disoriented Tourist: The Figuration of the Tourist in Contemporary Cultural Critique', in C. Rojek and J. Urry (eds) *Health and the International Tourist.* London: Routledge.

MENDELSOHN, R., L. ASTLE, M. MANN and M. SHAMANESH (1996) 'Sexual Behaviour of Travellers Abroad Attending an Inner-City Genitourinary Medicine Clinic'. *Genitourinary Medicine* 1:43–6.

MUNT, I. (1994) 'The "Other" Postmodern Tourism: Culture, Travel and the New Middle Classes'. *Theory, Culture and Society* 11(3):101–23.

ROJEK, C. (1993) *Ways of Escape: Modern Transformations in Leisure and Travel.* Basingstoke: Macmillan Press – now Palgrave.

SCOTT, S. and D. MORGAN (1993) *Body Matters: Essays on the Sociology of the Body.* London: Falmer.

SHIELDS, R. (1990) 'The System of Pleasure: Liminality and the Carnivalesque at Brighton'. *Theory, Culture and Society* 7:39–72.

STRAUSS, A. and J. CORBIN (1990) *Basics of Qualitative Research: Grounded Theory Procedures and Techniques.* London: Sage.

URRY, J. (1990) *The Tourist Gaze: Leisure and Travel in Contemporary Societies.* London: Sage.

VEIJOLA, S. and E. JOKINEN (1994) 'The Body in Tourism'. *Theory, Culture and Society* 11(3):125–51.

WICKENS, E. (1997) 'Licensed for Thrills: Risk-Taking and Tourism', in S. Clift and P. Grabowski (eds) *Health and the International Tourist.* London: Routledge.

8

The Fabric of Love: a Semiotic Analysis of the Suspender Belt

Dana Wilson-Kovacs

Introduction

This chapter focuses on the evolution of the suspender belt, an artefact which has circumscribed the female body for the last hundred years. Born out of practicality, this article of clothing has come to signify, albeit controversially, the assertiveness of female sexuality. The development of this artefact triggered not only a different perception of the female body but has also moulded ideas of femininity and eroticism. Embracing the view that the female body has become 'the site on which feminine cultural ideas can be literally manufactured' (Betterton 1987: 8), and the place where stereotypes, presentation and codes of behaviour can be recycled and reinforced, this study aims to reveal the complex process by which some of these cultural practices have developed.

Inspired and modified by the cultural practices which define them, Western ideas of femininity are reflected in representations of the female body, while femininity itself is determined through display and ornamentation (Berger 1973). A substantial amount of sociological research has been conducted into the specific ways in which changing images, codes and ideologies relate to the display and ornamentation of the female body (for example Brownmiller 1984; Betterton 1987) but few studies have analyzed how the artefacts accompanying this process have been materially and symbolically produced. This is so in the case of female underwear and its erotic connotations.[1] Though historians of female underwear have provided insights into Western cultural discourses about the handling, packaging and presentation of the female body, sociologists have shown little interest in this field.[2] The artefact that has attracted most interest in sociological literature has been the laced corset (Kunzle 1982; Steele 1985), but no studies have attempted to analyze the development and semiotics of the suspender belt – another female garment which remains in common use. Such an

120

approach can reveal the ways in which the suspender belt both reflects and determines social organization and cultural values pertaining to gender and sexuality. It can also provide important insights into the relationship between artefacts and their use by explaining the ideological construction of a specific need; it can disclose how the changing value of a commodity has articulated distinct modes of consumption; and it can provide new ways of interpreting the evolving value and symbolism of a commodity and its relevance to current cultural iconography.

This chapter will deal with some of these aspects of cultural production and consumption, and it will explore how material objects are valued in cultural contexts. It will analyze the processes involved in the emergence and development of erotic female underwear, paying particular attention to the suspender belt. Its premise is that in order to understand the contemporary iconography of underwear and its role in the cultural construction of femininity it is important to understand its development. The main contention will be that the production of the iconography of women's underclothes has been conditioned not only by the development of ideas of cleanliness, sexuality and the body, but also by a parallel surge in technical innovation, industrial processing and advertising techniques, which have all contributed to contemporary ideas of femininity.

This chapter is divided into four sections: the first will discuss the ideological premises for the development of underwear, the second section will give an insight into this development until the Edwardian era, the third part will follow the individual trajectory of the suspender belt since its conception, and the last section will deal with more theoretical issues derived from this development. The historical exposé presented below is by no means a complete one: controversial claims regarding the birth of the suspender belt and the gaps in the general development of underwear remain to be substantiated by further research. Lying beyond the presentation of a complete historical account of these aspects, the aim of my research is to provide a frame for understanding the consumerist ideologies behind the artefacts themselves and their changing significance.

Factors in the early development of underwear: the shame frontier, consumerism and the new ideologies of the body

The development of underclothes has been the result of a complex cultural process which has primarily involved the intensification of the shame frontier, the appearance of modern consumerist ideologies and the articulation of middle-class values and modern attitudes towards sexuality and the body. These factors have operated together, influencing each other, and producing a new ideology of the body. 'The shame frontier' (Elias 1978) was articulated in early modern times. Whereas before the sixteenth century 'women aroused desire with the idea that they were almost naked under their dresses' (Saint-Laurent 1968: 162), over the next three hundred years this attitude gradually disappeared, at first in the upper classes, and then in the middle and lower classes. Comments Elias:

> Up to then 'the whole mode of life, with its greater closeness of individuals, made the sight of the naked body, at least in the proper place, incomparably more commonplace than in the first stages of the modern age. . . . People had a less inhibited – one might say a more childish – attitude towards the body, and to many of its functions' (1978: 164).

The dynamics of the shame frontier have contributed to the perception of erotic lingerie. However, they have not been the single factor in its development.

The new attitude to nudity developed along with the emergence of the culture of mass consumption, whose rationale focused on material accumulation, innovation and choice. This growth of material culture echoed a similar development in philosophical materialism and rationalism. From the seventeenth century materialist thinking has been part of technological and economic innovation, and inherent in the recognition of the concept of consumer demand. As Mukerji showed, eighteenth century Europeans 'changed their style of dress with a rapidity that Veblen would call a form of conspicuous waste', thus establishing 'the modern form of fashion or fashionable change' (1983: 169). Fashion and novel fabrics inspired not only changes in dress, they also promoted novel modes of personal appearance and cleanliness which intensified the shame frontier. Class differences became less pronounced as the middle classes sought to emulate upper-class dress and manners, and 'new meanings were given to objects, capital goods and commercial opportunities, for these could give people power for making social claims and facilitate new varieties of economic action' (Mukerji 1983: 257). Not only was it the shame frontier that was modified as a result of these innovations: as the middle classes became more economically influential, their values became paramount in the construction of body ideologies.

The period between the sixteenth and the nineteenth centuries marked the end of a society in which physical intimacy prevailed. Whereas previously behaviour was generally regulated by recourse to religion and the body disciplined through a mixture of rational and religious agencies, during this period materialist philosophy, science, and the demands of trade and industry made their impact, encouraging an organic perspective on the body.[3] The sexual impulses had to be rationally contained and explained. By being increasingly seen as the site of both sexual contact and conduct, the 'new' body was ambiguous. It had to be protected as well as disciplined in order to control its sexual impulses (Craik 1994: 115). The moral problematic of containing the sexuality of the body shifted from the religious to the scientific. Novel methods were required to control the sexualised body. They were provided by the scientific advances of the nineteenth century which, instead of liberating the body from external control, intensified social regulation. According to Foucault (1990), the discipline of the body through higher agencies (such as religion) was replaced by a discipline operating at the discursive level (prevalent in the medical and scientific texts of the time), and at the material level as reflected in aspects of material culture related to both the body and to the discursive agencies.

Primarily as a result of the problems resulting from the emergence of modern gender roles, which influenced the ideologies surrounding the sexualised body, the female body and sexuality were of special concern. As well as introducing production constraints and novel urban and industrial experiences, early capitalism led to an expansion of the middle-classes and the separation of their public and private spheres (Mulvey 1989). These changes were accompanied by a polarization of gender roles: men were identified with activity, production and the public domain, and women with consumption and the intimacy of the domestic sphere. In the nineteenth century female sexuality itself, became the object of a growing field of material culture based on economic development and the new ideologies of the body. These processes were echoed in the fashions of the day. While menswear became generally more functional, women's attire was oriented towards conspicuous consumption and artifice, and loaded with sexual overtones. With the imposition of Victorian morality 'the image of restrained and respectable womanhood contrasted with the elaborate and highly decorative underclothes worn by women' (Craik 1994: 121). The shame frontier became an area of especial concern for women, and this was reflected in the role and variety of female underwear. While it was justified as being functional – emphasizing health, comfort and practicality – underwear also drew attention to the body by modelling it and creating new forms and codes of desire. Through their constructionism and artifice they presented the female body as a symbol of the crisis which marked the breakdown of the divisions between low and high culture.[4] The result was a new discipline of the body and a consumerist structure which persist still.

The first items of lingerie: drawers and corsets

The next section presents the general development of underwear and within this the emergence of the suspender belt, an artefact that has contributed to the production of these codes of femininity and reflected the ideologies which underline the female body and its sexuality. Though articles of underwear were commonly used by men, at a time when leggings were worn, and occasionally by women when dancing, to cover the genitalia, the first specific items of female underclothing – drawers and corsets – were introduced on a mass scale only in the nineteenth century. In the early 1800s drawers were somewhat reluctantly accepted as feminine undergarments in Britain after they had been worn in France. At first they were used only by young girls, but a combination of severe winters and medical advice encouraged their use by mature women – as the following extract of the 1841 *Handbook of the Toilet* shows: 'drawers are of incalculable advantage to women preventing many of the disorders and indispositions to which the British females are subject' (Carter 1992: 46).[5] The reluctance to accept drawers is documented by *Cassell's Magazine* as late as the 1880s, when it recommends that they be used instead of flannel petticoats.

Like many other commodities – and especially those that dress and shape the body – drawers were not universally popular. For some, such as the anonymous author of *My Secret Life*, they were regarded as an obstruction which hindered access to the genitalia: 'Formerly no woman wore them, but now whether lady, servant, or whore, they all wear them. I find they hinder those comfortable chance feels of bum and cunt, of which I have had so many' (in Marcus 1974: 98).[6] Whether or not this attitude was typical of Victorian sexuality, it was to be paralleled by a subtler construction of sexual desire in which the garment itself was a source of erotic appeal. This is suggested by the prudery of Victorian advertisements which portrayed drawers as 'rather shyly drawn folded with just parts of the embroidery or lace showing' (Carter 1992: 64) – just waiting to be unfolded and used.

Similar innuendoes are found in representations of the corset, a garment which shapes the body into an erotic object. Unlike drawers which symbolized containment and cleanliness, the corset had no functional value. This unalloyed eroticism is perhaps the reason for the popularity of the corset among historians and social analysts. The corset is the only item of underclothing which has been widely, and somewhat controversially, documented.[7] Tight-lacing had been popular intermittently since the sixteenth century,[8] and for Victorian women the tight-laced corset was an essential item of fashionable wear.[9] The popularity of the corset with women across the social and moral spectrum made its message ambivalent: while it helped construct fashionable concepts of beauty, it was at the same time associated with scandal.[10] The corset blurred the demarcation between the respectable and the disreputable women, and the boundaries between the private and the public domains. Through its ambiguity – being both seen (in the shape of its wearer) and unseen (hidden under other garments) – the corset took on erotic overtones, swiftly becoming an object of fetishist enthusiasm.[11]

In the advertisements of the time sexual curiosity and desire were aroused by portraying corsets floating in space as if inhabited by invisible bodies. By alluding to the shape of the body without actually representing it, the advertisements of the period not only encouraged the fetishist appeal of the garment, they also established an unstated link between underwear and sexuality and facilitated the construction of popular codes of desire.[12] The corset created a prototype for an everyday pleasurable body which, though it was not confined to academic art nor in itself necessarily artistic, reflected an aesthetic ideal. More importantly, it also contained and disciplined the female body. This prototype was later to be taken by the suspender belt, at first in combination with the corset and then with the brassiere.

The conception of the suspender belt

The obsession with health and hygiene which took hold in the latter half of the nineteenth century gave rise to a growing anxiety over constricting garments such as the garter and the fashion for tight corseting. Attempts were made to hang the stocking by various suspender devices. Already in 1862, Parisian garters with buckles 'had ribbons that attached to or clasped the bottom edge of the corset and, slotting through the buckles, helped to support the stockings' (Hawthorne 1993: 74). It was not, however, until the invention of vulcanized rubber that a viable replacement for the garter was devised. By weaving strands of this resilient substance into fabric an elasticised ribbon was devised that proved ideal for underwear waistbands, braces and suspender belts.

In 1876 female French dancers caused a stir by appearing at the Alhambra Theatre in stockings suspended from clumsy shoulder harnesses, rather than wearing tights (Pearsall 1981). Within a few years, suspenders, at first attached to a belt worn over the corset and later attached to the corset itself, were items of everyday wear. By the 1880s they were being championed by the National Health Society as a replacement for the constricting garter (Farrell 1992), and by the turn of the century women's stockings were being routinely manufactured to serve the suspender, reaching to the upper thigh with a welt four centimetres deep to accommodate the clip. By bridging the gap between the stocking and the mysterious recesses of the female anatomy, the suspender would seem to have obvious erotic potential. Claims, however, that it gained early recognition as an erotic garment can be dismissed. The furore that greeted the Alhambra performance of 1876 was a response to the naked thigh rather than to the device which achieved its display. The popular image of the suspender as an accessory of the French can-can dancer of the 1890s is a Hollywood fiction; for such erotic displays of the period the garter was not only preferred but considered indispensable.

While corsets and articles of lingerie which had already established themselves were promoted with suggestions of eroticism, in the case of the newly invented suspender belt the emphasis was upon its utilitarian virtues. The suspender was generally presented as an artless accessory to the corset package and any erotic response it may have elicited was subsumed within the generality of female underwear. Even after the turn of the century the suspender was still very much an innovative piece of apparatus for which '(e)very sort of cunning arrangement is advertised, from the sublime to the ridiculously complicated. Such marvels as the Portia Combined Stocking Suspender and Shoulder Harness, which in 1900 is described as "very useful for little boys".' (Hawthorne 1993: 79)

The development of the suspender belt

At the end of the nineteenth century in France the corset was for the first time split into two different undergarments to improve its functionality by allowing more movement in the back and waist, but it was only in the 1920s that the modern suspender belt[13] and brassiere[14] entered mainstream fashion. In 1904 the Kleinert Rubber Co. marketed their keyhole loop and rubber stud to which to attach the stocking, and in 1912, in the USA, the modern combined suspender and belt was patented (Hawthorne 1993). The corset, employing new manufacturing techniques that involved elasticised materials, was simplified. Many young women abandoned it altogether, wearing only a brassiere, a suspender belt and a pair of brief loose 'camiknickers' beneath minimal dresses.

The choice of suspender belt was possibly prompted by financial considerations – the belt retailed for half the cost of the corset. Its popularity along with that of lighter underwear can also be related to the mass marketing of sanitary pads in the 1920s and 1930s (Brownmiller 1984: 194)[15] which were developed from absorbent wartime field dressing and superseded the bulky 'rags'. But the most important factor in the evolution of the suspender belt was the booming stocking industry. By 1925, with new mass production techniques, 150 pairs of stockings per day could be manufactured per operator. Stockings made of artificial yarn, first manufactured in the USA in 1912, created look-alike silk stockings, and for the first time glamorous hosiery at reasonable prices was available to the working girl (Hawthorne 1993: 87). The proliferation of elastic materials and the introduction of nylon in the 1940s (a new artificial fibre superior to rayon in its weight, versatility and strength) further improved the composition and the look of stockings and suspender belts.[16]

After the constraints of the Second World War the undergarments industry boomed. The period between 1947 and 1964 is renowned for its foundation garments. In this period some of the most erotic and stylish underwear appeared. Nylon was used in the manufacture of glamorous lingerie and suspender belts, and whereas the pin-ups of the 1930s stimulated their patrons with a glimpse of their suspenders, the 'girlie mag' models of the 1950s featured the full suspender belt. The suspender belt was being promoted in the 1960s by such improbable artifices as the Kayser Bondor Teenage Advice Bureau, which aspired 'to help schoolgirls "sort out their underwear problems" [and] 'Teenform', an American range of undies [marketed in Britain] that concentrated on the between-ager – 10–11 and 12-year-old bras, roll-ons and suspender belts' (Hawthorne 1993: 108).

The period between the mid 1960s and the 1980s saw the emergence of minimalist underwear: 'built-in panties, halter-neck bras . . . and the arrival of moulded undergarments – seamless, one-piece bras and panties, almost invisible in wear and very comfortable' (Carter 1992: 116). Women began to wear tights, which had been introduced in the early 1960s as children's wear, and they swiftly superseded the nylon stockings that had previously been considered an essential part of the female wardrobe. The stocking, 'once regarded as essential to the well-dressed woman, dropped from holding 72 per cent of the stocking market in 1964 to holding a mere 5 per cent of tights and stockings in 1971'. By 1978 a fashion writer could state that 'Today [the stocking] only just survives, having to be sought out by the dwindling tiny minority of older women faithful to tradition' (Ewing 1978: 169). Yet by the end of the 1980s the stocking/suspender belt combination was back in fashion. 'In 1988 it was reckoned that women under the age of twenty-five bought one pair of stockings to every three pairs of tights. . . .' (Farrell 1992: 80)

While the 1980s concern with health and hygiene may have contributed to the revival of the suspender belt, it was mainly marketed with reference to its supposed eroticism. Suspender belts now have limited practical value, and have come to reflect instead a nostalgia for glamorous fashions and to symbolize the archetypal essence of sexuality: 'They are so darned uncomfortable . . . but I sometimes put them on . . . just to please him.' (Hawthorne 1993: 126)

The iconographic development of underwear: media and technology

During the first three quarters of the nineteenth century the introduction of technical innovations and the evolution of advertising greatly stimulated the general development of underwear. Shifts in fashion were facilitated and sometimes even initiated by technological advances, such as the introduction of vulcanized rubber in the 1840s and chemical dyes of the 1880s.[17] Early methods of mass production and the growth of a cottage industry based on the sewing machine led to a substantial increase in the manufacture of items of clothing and a fall in retail prices. Expense was consequently of less consideration when indulging in fashion novelties, and as the nineteenth century progressed underclothes were gradually differentiated into a range of separate garments.

By the end of the nineteenth century the underwear industry had became extremely sophisticated and was promoting itself by extensive advertising. Consumer psychology was further encouraged and reflected in the wide selection of underwear offered in the new department stores, some of which also issued their own illustrated mail order catalogues, where underclothes and hosiery were copiously represented. Other publications appeared which were aimed at those interested in the fetishist aspects of female underwear. In the 1870s in France the magazine *La Vie Parisienne* catered to the new underwear fetish while masquerading as a fashion magazine. In Britain 'home-grown titillation was provided by journals such as *The Englishwoman's Domestic Magazine* in which 'the correspondence on corsets and stays was so voluminous, that, like that of the domestic whipping of girls, it was republished separately.' (Hyde 1964: 149)

The influence of advertising and marketing, intentionally or not, were crucial to the perceived erotic allure of female underwear. Corsets, drawers and suspenders were still worn by both sexes, but by now they were markedly differentiated by the high degree of elaboration and the erotic appeal accorded female lingerie. In 1898 the French fashion historian Octave Uzanne noted that 'the most special characteristic of contemporary dress is the elaboration of the undergarments' (Steele 1985: 192). This is the period when sensuality and successful sex became identified with luxury undergarments. Lavish lingerie became an essential part of a bride's trousseau: 'Marguerite d'Aincourt, author of *Etudes Sur Le Costume* (1883), assumed that the bride would initially be too modest and shy to wear seductive lingerie and deshabille; but that they should still be part of her trousseau, because she would come to appreciate them, just as implicitly, she would come to enjoy sex.' (Steele 1985: 206)[18]

This elaboration of underwear and the recognition of its sensual elements was to result in the archetype for the erotic body in the twentieth century, when its full iconographic potential was to be developed. During the first decades that followed the First World War the covert symbolism became overt as a result of a combination of economic, social and cultural factors. The heavy garments of the pre-war period, including the underwear, were rejected as 'Victorian'. Corsetry and elaborate undergarments were replaced by lighter and more functional wear, and on the whole female underwear in the 1920s and 1930s had a highly visible profile. 'Unmentionables' were openly displayed, new printing techniques enabled sales catalogues to illustrate women's underwear in full colour, and (before the imposition of the Hayes Code) Hollywood contrived to expose its female stars in underclothes or night wear as often as it could. The advent of the suspender as a focus of eroticism seems to have coincided with the short skirt of the 1920s, when it was often, inadvertently or intentionally, revealed. Emphasizing the bare upper thigh, as it did, and connecting the stocking to the secret recesses where the underwear of the loins was hidden, the attraction of the suspender is fairly obvious.

While the garter remained in favour, the suspender belt achieved a fashionable as well as a functional status. The double dichotomy – functional/dysfunctional and pure/impure – and the implicit ambivalent status of the suspender belt as a functional artifice which disciplined the body, but at the same time did not cover the loins, was resolved to a degree by the introduction of the tampon. Meanwhile the media developed and reflected this dual status of functionality and fetishism and helped elevate the sexually symbolic value of the suspender belt. The association between sexuality and the suspender was reinforced in 1920s Hollywood when actresses 'had for the first time, in large numbers, put on rouge and lipstick, taken to short skirts and rayon stockings, and had abandoned the corset for the rubber "weight-reducing" girdle' (Featherstone 1995: 172). The fashion for short skirts allowed ample opportunities for an actress to display her suspenders above her stocking welt. 'The cinema offered the quickest route to high street interpretation when women were filled with the simple desire to emulate the glamour of a favourite female star' (ibid: 172). Consequently, the frequent undressing 'had the curious effect of immensely improving women's underwear in real life: the abandonment of linen and the substitution of real or artificial silk'.[19] Hollywood and the film industry generally has promoted images of consumerism by helping to 'create new standards of bodily presentation, bringing home to a mass audience the importance of looking good' (ibid: 179). The film industry has also created images of women which have taken them into new areas of popular mythology and collective fantasy, and helped formulate new erotic codes (Mulvey 1989).

The erotic ensemble of suspender belt and stockings was fixed by the 1950s. Since then the image of a semi-nude woman in a suspender belt and stockings, especially in a black suspender belt and black stockings, has become the most potent sexual icon of the latter half of the twentieth century. Instead of following and enhancing the contours of the female body, the belt, straps and stocking welts outline the area around the loins with horizontals and verticals, producing a discordant effect that is especially apparent when the archetypal black suspender belt and black stockings are worn against a white skin. The hard 'frame' created by the rectilinear lines also contradicts the soft and frilly underwear that often accompanies it, and concentrates the attention of the viewer firmly on the area of the female genitalia. This arrangement frankly disassociates the female pudenda from the rest of her anatomy in a way that would have been unthinkable at any previous period – it is a metaphorical invitation to treat the female loins as the totality of a woman's sexual attraction. When tights all but eclipsed the suspender belt and stockings for everyday wear in the later 1960s, the supposedly obsolete garments survived in 'men's magazines' and fashion outlets specializing in erotic wear, and the revival of the suspender belt in the 1990s was greeted with claims that its popularity was attributable to male demand.

Patterns and erotic narratives

There are identifiable patterns in the assimilation of female underwear. A new garment is often introduced as practical children's wear (drawers, tights and bodies), then, having been tested on this sartorially less controversial group, the garment is adopted by adults – usually with appeal to practicality, hygiene or health – to counteract adverse criticism. By this process the functional aspect of the item of underwear is safely and gradually accepted by consumers. When the garment has become everyday wear it is finally accorded sexual innuendoes and elaborated to express its sensual qualities, and, implicitly, those of the wearer. In the Victorian period the body was elaborately packaged to suggest an index of social behaviour. Eroticism was a part of this package, and to achieve this status female underwear was the ideal medium (Craik 1994: 119).

A related trend that applied to all undergarments, was that of increasing elaboration. This was made possible by technological innovation as well as public acceptance of the undergarment. Whereas the first drawers were made of simple fabrics such as cotton, flannel and calico (Carter 1992: 56), the later models became more sophisticated in design and materials used (silk and satin) (Pearsall 1981: 12). While the prototypes were plain, knee-length and divided, the later models were shortened with closed crotches. Both design and materials reflected the tendency of the manufacturer to play safe with the product, and only to elaborate it once the need for such elaboration had been established by his customers decorating their purchases at home with brocade and ribbons.

Though articles of underclothing had sometimes been worn previously, and the garter had been accorded erotic status in the eighteenth century, it was only in the nineteenth century that they became sufficiently defined and ubiquitous for other erotic stereotypes to develop. The intentional sexualization of female underclothes has been partly due to the mechanics of advertising, which emphasizes their sexual categorization and packages them with insistent sexual signals (recreational, scanty, frothy, frivolous and colourful). Barthes maintains that 'a narrative is never made up of anything other than functions: in different degrees, everything in it signifies'.[20] These narratives derive from tradition, and their impact is both social and individual: 'these culturally embedded forms furnish a repertoire of sense making devices'.[21] The most visible narratives and codes related to underwear are evident in advertising, whose messages constitute narratives. They describe and prescribe patterns of social presentability which include personal habits as well as appearance. They modify the self and the body by initiating and reinforcing social norms. Thus underwear advertising has been influential in creating, maintaining, and modifying feminine stereotypes. However, it has not been the only factor in this complex process.

The Victorians might have found the body as framed by the suspender belt easy to understand. Gilman observes that in the nineteenth century female sexuality came to be seen as pathological. Its central element, the female genitalia, 'came to define female for the 19th century' (1985: 215). The Victorians, he claims, had a 'fascination with the buttocks as a displacement of the genitalia'. In this context we can understand the appeal and the success of the suspender belt today. It is an artefact and a commodity which frames, ornaments and draws attention to the genitalia, helping to package female sexuality – a primitive, deviant and irrational element – for presentation and consumption. It is not surprising that the resulting image of the genitalia was initially perceived only as an illicit representation of femininity which belonged primarily to a woman who was herself perceived as deviant – the prostitute.

The symbolism of the black suspender belt and black lingerie has been for most of this century associated with cheapness and prostitution. The colour black has retained its symbolism and reinforced the iconographic function of the suspender belt – which has come to symbolize available sex in the twentieth century. Gabor (1972) records that *Penthouse* magazine, an up-market soft-core publication, created a stir by promoting female lingerie (especially black garments) in its illustrations in the 1960s, thus giving it a degree of social respectability. Since then the suspender belt has emerged as a symbol of a 'knowledgeable' female sexuality and has achieved a fetishist status. Its iconography implies knowledge, pleasure, desire and willingness. It accords its wearer an aura of sexual sophistication and presents her as a sexually active agent.

Conclusions

Sexual iconography is related not only to the body but also to the artefacts surrounding it. The artefacts which have been developed in the last 150 years have played an important role in the creation of images, texts and other cultural practices reflecting the sexualized body. A deeper understanding of the sexual symbolism surrounding the female body can be gained from the study of the material and ideological construction, production and development of these artefacts. The important factors in their emergence (the shame frontier, consumerism and middle-class ideologies) have been interrelated and articulated at various practical and discursive levels, and can be viewed as a complex process within the emergence of modernity.

Through their material nature, the artefacts had to achieve a functional status before they were loaded with symbolic connotations and came to stand for specific cultural practices. In the case of the suspender belt this transition from functionality to symbolism is reflected in some of the ideologies related to the body and sexuality. The media and technological innovations have not only assisted the process of transition, but they also modelled and changed the cultural practices created by this transition through the mechanisms of consumerism. This is a complex and interactive process in which ideologies of the body and popular images reinforce and transform each other, promoting novel ways of perceiving and understanding the female body and its representations.

In the nineteenth century the body was regarded as 'an organic machine' and a 'productive agent'.[22] By the end of the century three axis of reference for the female body had been articulated: the medically normal or abnormal body (which embraced theories of sexuality); the aesthetic body and its artistic representation (which sublimated the female appearance); and the disguised leisurely body (engineered with clothes, make-up and coiffure). The latter was promoted by advertisements which often alluded to the other two and whose influence has come to surpass that of either in their unadulterated form. This conglomerate body has become the aspiration of contemporary culture. It has become the 'body beautiful, openly sexual and associated with hedonism, leisure and display' (Featherstone 1995: 171). It is a desirable and pleasurable body; a metaphor for eroticism, aestheticism and consumerist display. As intimacy has given way in our contemporary culture to public display, so have its accessories and, intrinsically, the sexualized body.

Not only has the sexualized body become marketable, but it has also generated spheres of sexually related consumption – the 'consumer love-maps' (Gould 1991). These include 'aspects of the more general love-map which involves consumption, that is the purchase and use of products in the process of attracting a mate, engaging in sexual activity and maintaining sexual love relationships' (381). The suspender belt and erotic lingerie generally are thus central elements in the consumer love-maps, and paradigmatic for the development of the pleasurable body.

The emergence of the pleasurable body has been reflected in the development of underwear – an intricate process which has been coloured by aesthetic norms, fashionable standards, precepts of health and hygiene and erotic values – and generally in the success of a consumerist culture based on 'its ability to harness and channel genuine bodily needs and desires' (Featherstone 1995: 193). The proliferation of female underwear and the promotion of its image via advertising and marketing have articulated these genuine bodily needs. It has also created new forms of desire and cultural standards which have created a new discipline of the body. Modern underwear echoes the Foucauldian disciplined body, being another aspect of the 'body's mania for consumption' (Baudrillard 1988), but whereas in the nineteenth century the corseted body was externally disciplined, nowadays the focus of discipline has shifted. Now it is internally controlled and centred on a body ideology that requires that it appear equally attractive dressed and undressed. It is an ideology of self-surveillance and sexual aesthetics, which incorporates the use and display of artefacts like the suspender belt, and reinforces its symbolic values through them. In this process artefact, body and sexuality are almost interchangeable.

Notes

1. See for example Betterton, 1987 and Itzin, 1992.
2. The evolution and use of underwear reflect 'the whole training of the female body' in the 'rules of coquetry' (Freadman in Craik, 1994: 115).
3. Foucault documents the organic given to the body with the beginning of the nineteenth century noticing that 'the flesh was brought down to the level of the organism' (1990: 117) and accordingly 'the technology of sex was ordered in relation to the medical institution, the exigency of normality, and – instead of the question of death and everlasting punishment – the problem of life and illness' (ibid).
4. Bryan S. Turner in Featherstone (1995: 24).
5. 'In 1841, *The Handbook of the Toilet* recommended them as a fashion already adopted in France: "drawers are of incalculable advantage to women preventing many of the disorders and indispositions to which the British females are subject". The very severe winters of the 1840s may have precipitated their use'. (Carter 1992: 46). A more impartial view is that 'The development of swaying crinoline-cage in mid-century may have led to a more general acceptance of feminine underpants, as the immodesty of female trousers began to be outweighed by the danger of being exposed without

them. L'inexpressible became termed L'indispensable. (Although drawers were open up the inside of the legs, a yard or so of chemise was tucked into the drawers, thus shielding the thighs from view.) Doctors also argued that reasons of hygiene (such as the dangers of cold and germs) necessitated the use of drawers, in addition to the chemise and petticoat(s)'. (Steele 1985: 198)

6. Another source is a French article of 1890, 'De l'Adultere; Conseils Pratiques' in the magazine *Gil Blas* which presented a negative picture of drawers – from the point of view of an old voyeur: 'in my youth ... women did not wear drawers ... our imagination climbed the length of their stockings and seduced us into ecstasies toward those regions as intimate as they are delicious. We did not see, but we knew we could see, should the occasion arise. ... But today ... we know that our view would be irremediably arrested by an obstacle, that our suggestive voyage would end at a hollow of batiste and we come to a stop at the base of the wall.' (in Steele 1985: 199).

7. For example, David Kunzle (1982) and Valerie Steele (1985).

8. 'In the seventeenth century the custom of tight-lacing reached such a pitch that many a young virgin of high status would not be satisfied until she could encircle her own waist with her hands. Writing in 1654, Thomas Bulwer was horrified at the damage caused by the practice, complaining that when they "shut up their waists in a Whale-bone prison ... they open the door to Consumption, and a withering rottenness".' (in Morris 1985: 189)

9. Tight corsets had become so much a part of polite fashion that to appear without them was tantamount to having started to undress in public.

10. 'Due to the erotic associations attached to underwear, variants of these garments formed the basis of the wardrobe of prostitutes and showgirls.' (Craik 1994: 127)

11. A fetish is to be understood throughout as an object or article of clothing that heightens the sexual allure of the possessor.

12. Finch in Craik (1994: 121).

13. 'The seed of the idea for separating bust and hip-controlling corsetry had come in 1889 from the legendary contribution of the Parisian boutique owner Mme Herminie Cadolle, who decided to cut the midriff out of the full length corset to allow more movement from the waist. Her invention was first termed "corselet-ceinture" then "corselet-gorge".' (Carter 1992: 69,70)

14. The appearance of the brassiere in 1913 almost coincided with that of the suspender belt. It consisted simply of two soft triangles. The idea was bought by Warner, a famous manufacturer of lingerie for $1500 (Carter 1992). Previously the garment 'had always been long, coming over the corset, and it was boned and rigid. Caresse Crosby introduced the modern concept of a brief style which was free of bones and left the midriff free.' (Ewing 1978: 115)

15. 'The marketing of disposable pads with acknowledgement of the "hygienic handicap" and "the days a woman used to lose" (these quotes are from a full-page advertisement for Kotex that appeared in the elegant front section of *Vogue* in 1926) coincided not accidentally with such changes in fashion as the abandonment of the full corset, the shortening and slimming of skirts and a new, eager interest in trousers.' (Brownmiller 1984: 193)

16. 'An area of considerable expansion was in elastic materials after the development in about 1930, by the Dunlop Rubber Company, of elastic thread. In 1934, lastex batiste, hand knitted elastic and chiffon lastex yarn are all mentioned in catalogues kept by the manufacturing company Berlei, followed in 1935 by satin lastex, French lastex-yarn lace and aeroknit elastic panels – and so on to woven elastics in 1939.' (Carter 1992: 100,101) Nylon was a spin-off from a research programme initiated by Du Pont in 1927. Du Pont spent 11 years and $27 million developing the product, before launching the first ever nylon stockings at the New York World Fair in 1938.
17. In 1844 T. Hancock in the UK and Charles Goodyear in the USA patent 'vulcanised' rubber – a heat and stretch resilient form of latex. In the same year vulcanized rubber garters go on sale in the United Kingdom. With the invention of a chemical dye developed from aniline salts by Morley's in 1887, colours could be made fade-resistant and fast. This was instrumental in the popularity of black stockings that followed.
18. 'Do not describe [the conjugal chemise] to young girls; one should respect the exquisite and a little inordinate modesty of these seraphims, but have it placed in their bridal trousseau. They will not wear it at first, but after some time, they will understand the value of this Orient silk or batiste . . . [with] insertions of lace, all quivering with the Valenciennes which decorates it in flounces at the helm. They will get used to this transparent web, which, in front – from the start of the throat to the waist – reveals the charming graces of a young and supple bust.' (Steele 1985: 206)
19. James Laver, 1969, *Modesty in Dress: An Enquiry into the Fundamentals of Fashion*, Heinemann: London, quoted in Wilson (1985: 104).
20. In 'Introduction to the Structural Analysis of the Narrative' (1977: 89), in Barthes, R., *Image–Music–Text*, 1977, London: Fontana.
21. Mary M. Gergen (1988: 96) in *Analysing Everyday Explanation. A Casebook of Methods*.
22. J.M. Berthelot in Featherstone, 1995.

Bibliography

ANTAKI, C. (ed.) (1988) *Analysing Everyday Explanation: A Casebook of Methods.* London: Sage Publications.
BAUDRILLARD, J. (1988) *Selected Writings.* Cambridge MASS.: Cambridge University Press.
BELL, Q. (1976) *Of Human Finery.* New York: Schocken.
BERGER, J. (1973) *Ways of Seeing.* New York: Viking.
BROWNMILLER, S. (1984) *Femininity.* London: Hamish Hamilton.
BETTERTON, R. (ed.) (1987) *Looking On: Images of Femininity in the Visual Arts and Media.* London: Pandora.
CARTER, A. (1992) *Underwear. The Fashion History.* London: B.T. Batsford Ltd.
CRAIK, J. (1994) *The Face of Fashion. Cultural Studies in Fashion.* London and New York: Routledge.
ELIAS, N. (1978) *The Civilising Process.* Oxford: Basil Blackwell.
EWING, E. (1978) *Dress and Undress.* London: B.T. Batsford Ltd.
FARRELL, J. (1992) *Socks and Stockings.* London: Butler and Tanner.

FAUST, B. (1981) *Women, Sex and Pornography.* London: Penguin.

FEATHERSTONE, M. (ed.) (1995) *The Body: Social Processes and Cultural Theory.* London: Sage Publication.

FINCH, C. (1991) *Hooked and Buttoned Together. Victorian Underwear and Representation.* in Victorian Studies, vol. 34: no. 3: 337–63.

FOUCAULT, M. (1990) *A History of Sexuality. Volume 1.* New York: Vintage Books.

GABOR, M. (1972) *The Pin-up. A Modest History.* London: Pan Books.

GERGEN, M. (1988) *Analysing Everyday Explanation. A Casebook of Methods.* New York and London: New York University Press.

GILMAN, S. (1985) *Black Bodies, White Bodies: Towards an Iconography of Female Sexuality in the Late 19th Century Art, Medicine and Literature, in Critical Inquiry.* vol. 12: 1985, no. 1, pp.204–44.

GOULD, S. (1991) *'Towards a Theory of Sexuality and Consumption: The Consumer Love Maps',* in *Advances in Consumer Research,* vol. 18, pp.381–3.

HAWTHORNE, R. (1993) *Stockings and Suspenders.* London: Souvenir Press.

HOLLANDER, A. (1978) *Seeing through Clothes.* New York: Viking Press.

HYDE, H.M. (1964) *A History of Pornography.* London: Heineman.

ITZIN, C. (ed.) (1992) *Pornography, Women, Violence and Civil Liberties,* New York: Oxford University Press.

JORDANOVA, L. (1989) *Sexual Visions.* New York and London: Harvester Wheatsheaf.

KUNZLE, D. (1982) *Fashion and Fetishism.* Ottowa and New Jersey: Rowman and Littlefield.

LEVITT, S. (1986) *Victorians Unbuttoned. Registered Designs for Clothing, Their Makers and Wearers. 1839–1900.* London: George Allen & Unwin.

MARCUS, S. (1974) *The Other Victorians.* New York: Basic Books.

MOREL, J. (1976) *Lingerie Parisienne.* London and New York: Academy Editions, St. Martin's Press – now Palgrave.

MORRIS, D. (1985) *Bodywatching.* London: Jonathan Cape.

MUKERJI, C. (1983) *From Graven Images: Patterns of Modern Materialism.* New York: Columbia University Press.

MULVEY, L. (1989) *Visual and Other Pleasures.* London: Macmillan Press – now Palgrave.

PEARSALL, R. (1981) *Tell Me Pretty Maiden.* Exeter: Web & Bower.

SAINT-LAURENT, C. (1968) *A History of Ladies Underwear.* London: Michael Joseph.

STEELE, V. (1985) *Fashion and Eroticism.* Oxford and New York: Oxford University Press.

TURNER, B. (1991) *'Recent Developments in the Theory of the Body',* in M. Featherstone, M. Hepwarth and B.S. Turner (eds) (1991) *The Body Social Processes and Cultural Theory.* Sage London: Publications.

WILSON, E. (1985) *Adorned in Dreams.* London. Virago Press.

Part III

The Moral and Medical Regulation of Sex, Sexualities and Gender

9

From 'Peter Andre's six pack' to 'I do knees' – the Body in Young People's Moral Discourse

Rachel Thomson, Sheena McGrellis, Janet Holland,
Sheila Henderson and Sue Sharpe

Introduction

The body can be understood as inherently moral, playing an important role in the creation of moral boundaries and discourse. Mary Douglas has shown how the body becomes a metaphor for a society, with ideas of dirt, disease, purity and danger serving to map moral boundaries of acceptability (Douglas 1966). While Douglas's approach treats the body as a natural metaphor for moral order, more recent commentators have observed that the body is increasingly divorced from nature, and drawn into the realm of choice, modification and commodification. What Featherstone (1991) has called the 'secular' body, Shilling (1993) the 'unfinished' body, Fiske (1989) the 'aestheticized body' and Bordo (1993) the 'plastic' body, becomes part of the reflexive project of the self, subject to choice, aestheticizing and body-reflexive practices (Connell 1995: 59).

The disengagement of the body from nature does not mean that it no longer mediates the moral. Featherstone has argued that in becoming subject to choice and transformation, the body becomes moralized in a new way, 'with appearance being taken as a reflex of the self, the penalties of bodily neglect are a lowering of one's acceptability as a person, as well as an indication of laziness, low self esteem and even moral failure' (1991: 86). The further the body moves from nature into culture, into the orbit of individual control, choice and practices, the more moralized the body becomes.

Most of these theorists are concerned with the status and the meaning of the adult body. And while many of the metaphors that they employ to explore the unfinished nature of the body, draw on the experience of childhood, the bodies of children rarely feature in their discussions.

The embodiment of morality is experienced particularly by the child and the young person and modern practices of child rearing can be understood in terms of a 'civilizing process' where social relations are drawn into the body through practices of hygiene and etiquette (Elias 1982). This relationship between the embodiment of moral competence and the achievement of moral integrity has been explored by Giddens who argues that 'regularised control of the body is a fundamental means whereby a biography of self-identity is maintained; yet at the same time the self is also more or less on display to others in terms of its embodiment.' (1991: 57–8). He illustrates the point by quoting Goffman's discussion of the everyday work of maintaining a competent self through reference to the intense experiences of incompetence of childhood.

> almost any activity that an individual performs easily now was at some time for him something that required anxious mobilization of effort. To walk, to cross a road, to utter a complete sentence, to wear long pants, to tie one's own shoes, to add a column of figures – all these routines that allow the individual unthinking competent performance were attained through an acquisition process whose early stages were negotiated in a cold sweat. A series of formal tests is likely to have been involved and solo trials, that is, distantly supervised practice under real, and hence fateful, conditions (Goffman, 1971: 248)

Studies of children's perceptions of the body and of physical development confirm that bodily difference is an important signifier of identity, with ideas of 'normal development' based on the adult body providing a standard against which young people judge their own and others' progress (James 1993, Prendergast 1992). But this developmental route has been blurred by the process of commodification of the body, through which its meanings are divorced from their material markers, and as Featherstone argues 'the closer the actual body approximates the idealized images of youth, health, fitness and beauty, the higher its exchange value' (1991: 177). Just as youth becomes available to those who have the time, money or inclination to produce or consume it, the markers of adulthood become increasingly dispersed, uncertain and contradictory (Chisholm and Hurrelman 1995). In the context of this questioning of youth and adulthood, and of an ever more intensive scrutiny of the intersection of discourse and the material in relation to the adult body, the place of the body in young people's moral discourse becomes of increasing interest (James, Jenks and Prout, 1998).

The embodiment of morality needs also to be understood in terms of the construction of gender. Feminist commentators have observed that the aestheticizing of the body is a feature of femininity. From an early age women are taught to banish nature from the surfaces of their bodies in the form of hair, blood and fat (Bordo 1988: Martin, 1989). By 'letting their bodies go' women are likely to disrupt moral categories of social and sexual respectability (Skeggs, 1997). Young women must manage tensions between public appearance and private realities during menstruation at school (Prendergast 1992), and between the demands of a feminine and a sexual body (Holland *et al.* 1998). Some commentators question the view that the body is now subject to choice. Bordo argues that the unfinished body is not moral but moralistic. Although it appears we now can have 'any body', not just any body will do, nor is just any body possible. The discourse of choice, diversity and self improvement serves to camouflage the suffocation of actual bodily diversity through the tyranny of the norm of perfection. It is only in recent years that representations of the male body have begun to conform to some of the same aesthetic standards of tone and hairlessness. It is far from clear whether the bodies of all men are subject to the moral pressure communicated by these images.

In this chapter we explore the relationship between the body and morality in young people's moral discourse. First we examine young people's accounts of becoming moral agents, of being able to make and to be accountable for their own choices, a process of maturation in which moral and physical competence are entwined. We suggest that this story of maturity is highly differentiated by gender and contributes to the construction of masculine and feminine identities in a context of normative heterosexuality. We go on to consider the way that the body features in young people's moral discourse, what they think is acceptable to do with a body and what is not. This discussion returns us to tensions between the notions of choice and nature that inform their understandings of maturity. Yet here the values are reversed. In this context choice and control are perceived less positively and ideas of nature and authenticity are valued. Again these moral distinctions are made sense of in terms of gender and the relative authenticity of a 'natural' masculinity in contrast to an 'unnatural' femininity. In conclusion we draw together the main themes of the paper and reflect on their implications for theories of the body.

Youth values: identity, diversity and social change

The material on which this chapter is based is drawn from the study *Youth values: Identity, diversity and social change.*[1] The research was conducted in eight schools located in five distinct areas in the UK and involved young people aged 11–16.[2] A range of methods was employed (questionnaires (1730), focus group discussions (56), individual interviews (46), and classroom activities and exercises). The data used in this chapter are from a number of the focus group discussions and detailed field notes of those discussions. Group participants were asked to give their position on a continuum from strongly agree to strongly disagree on a number of value statements, and the statements and their positions were then discussed.[3] Each focus group was composed of between four and six volunteers drawn from a single school year group, a facilitator and an observer/note-taker. Some groups were mixed and some single sex, and participants knew each other but not necessarily well. Sessions were usually one hour in length, with time spent setting ground rules, making introductions and clarifying expectations. An average of six statements were discussed in each session, and the full set of 85 statements were developed from pilot work with young people and the findings of the questionnaire. Statements for each group were selected to enable some comparison across groups, as well as in response to particular concerns related to age, gender and locality identified through the questionnaire. Group discussions were recorded, transcribed and coded using NUD*IST.

Becoming a moral agent: a gendered route to maturity

The integration of moral and physical competence

In their discussions of the process of growing up, the young people in the study tended to sketch a continuum of development from the young child, who is unaware of the difference between right and wrong and needs to be shown by another, to that of the morally competent young person, who is able to make their own choices, having internalized the rules of socially appropriate behaviour. This process of internalization of rules from outside the body (or from a social or interrelational context) to inside the body in the form of a conscience, or personal beliefs and choice, was generally seen as taking place over time and through mediating practices such as physical punishments and rewards, and increasingly, social approval and disapproval.

Int: what age do you think children start knowing what's right and wrong?[4]

Polly: It depends how someone else – like if you do something wrong when you're little like knock a big china vase over or something when you're really tiny, you get told off and you think 'Oh no, I just got told off, I don't want to do that any more (laughs) – I'd rather have – do something right and get a sweet or something or get a piece of fruit or something', and then you work it out from there.

Int: With really young children, at what age do you think that they really know and at what age do they have to be told?

Polly: They really know when they start primary school, because that's when you're in a bigger

Ella: You have to have more independence and sort of make your own decisions about what you do and what you don't, what you can do and what you can't. [female fg, year 12, school 8][5]

Chris: At the age of 15 you are not expected to get a reward and so you are used to not getting a reward at that age, so its like natural, if you are mature enough you just suss it, you don't get a reward every time you are good. [young man, yr 8, school 7]

Moral competence (the ability to make choices and in doing so, to make distinctions between right from wrong) was described by the young people as developing in tandem with physical competence (the ability to do things yourself). In a subsequent discussion of the legal age of criminal responsibility, Polly makes this equation explicit:

Int: In terms of the law around this sort of thing, there's a law of criminal responsibility which says that under the age of 13 people don't have criminal responsibility – if you break the law under the age of 13 you aren't actually responsible for what you do? What's your opinion on that?

Polly: You're responsible because you did it (laughter) I mean, if you knew how to do it then you must know how to take responsibility for it – you must be able to 'cos you knew how to do it – knew how to do the thing that was wrong. [female fg, year 12, school 8]

Young people described different parenting practices and expressed different preferences and beliefs about the relative acceptability and efficacy of physical punishment, shouting, talking and bribery. From these discussions a dominant conception of the ideal process of moral development emerged – a relatively linear progression from dependent and unsocialized (natural) childhood to autonomous adulthood where the ability to make one's own choices brings with it moral competence. While discursively dominant, this is also a relatively unstable ideal. In practice young people describe this passage as complicated by a range of domestic and wider social and cultural factors that thwart, complicate or accelerate the direction and pace of development (see also Holland *et al.* 2000). In this context, it is interesting to consider the ways in which young people talk about the process of development and in particular how they negotiate the notion of 'maturity'. The clearest line of conflict over the meaning and desirability of maturity was drawn between the genders.

Gender and maturity

The widely made observation that girls mature more rapidly than boys, while drawing on notions of bodily change, is not wholly determined by it. Variations in levels of physical development will be familiar to anyone working in schools. From the ages of 12–15 it is possible to find bodies spanning the full range from childhood to adulthood as defined by sexualized boundaries of puberty and reproductive potential. But, while young people are highly sensitive to differences in physical development – particularly those who are either trailblazing or trailing behind – their discussions of maturity concentrate less on levels of physical development than on a notion of maturity which entails *control* of the body.

> *Lara*: Still in our year they muck around.
> *Shelly*: Like they make up stupid words in my class
> *Lara*: They all go round shouting it out, playing across the tables and everything –
> *Shelly*: Jumping on tables, screaming it out.
> *Lara*: Yeah, bad behaviour, fighting and stuff in class.
> *Shelly*: Yeah, and they think it's so hysterical
> *Jenny*: If someone farts or burps they just start laughing – its stupid
> [female fg, year 9, school 6]

In response to a statement that 'women are stronger than men' one young man, who was considerably smaller than his classmates, joked that it 'depends if you're about two foot tall', leading to the following discussion of the desirability of maturity:

David: Women are a lot stronger like than men, ahead than men I'd say
James: Yeah, but then you are talking about maturity aren't you
Kate: Yeah, women mature quicker than men
James: That's definitely true
David: Because we, us, I don't know if its just me and James, but me and James we like mess around and stuff
James: Yeah, we mess around a lot
David: And the girls think, Oh God they're just like primary school kids, but we're just like having fun.
James: So who cares yeah . . . what's the point in growing up quickly . . . [mixed fg, year 9, school 8]

A young man in another group explained to the girls that boys would take the charge of immaturity as 'a compliment'.

Kath: Boys are more immature than girls
Mary: When they get to 17 they are alright
Jason: When you say that boys are more immature, a lot of boys would take that as a compliment. They want to be more immature, that's what makes them popular. Lots of boys want to get low marks.
Rick: Act the whack
Mary: very few fellas would be bothered about getting good grades in class.
Kath: They get branded a stew
Elaine: But even though the progress is slow, they are always maturing. [mixed fg, year 10, school 2]

The switch from a discussion of maturity to that of achievement in a school environment can be understood as a method of translating the meaning of boys behaviour into a different value system. While 'acting the whack' may produce status with friends in the 'here and now', it may also result in poor examination results and jeopardize future achievement and status. James notes a contradiction between achievement in the future and in the present, explaining boys' approach to school as a result of their reliance on a certain future, a future which he observes to be disappearing:

James: This isn't sort of as true anymore, but I suppose a lot of boys think we are going to walk out of here and get a job but it's not true anymore is it? A lot of boys do think it but its not right any more. [mixed fg, year 9, school 8]

Accelerated femininity

The desirability of maturity may be shaped in part by the desirability and availability of adult identities. While young men seemed in little hurry to relinquish the freedoms of childhood, young women saw themselves as racing towards adulthood, if with some uncertainty:

> *Int*: Do you think that girls are in more of a hurry to grow up than boys?
> *Mary*: We want to grow up
> *Elaine*: Yeah, supermodels and we all rush out to get the micro-mini and the boob tube
> *Kath*: And there are more relationships where the girl is younger than the boy,
> *Jason*: They think if they are older that they can have so much fun.
> *Mary*: Maybe that's true
> *Elaine*: But they also sometimes want to be younger and to be looked after and protected. My Mum says 'I don't know whether you want to be older or younger'. [mixed group, year 10, school 2]

On a number of occasions young women described ways in which the embodiment of femininity serves to accelerate the development process. Sexuality, filtered through the project of femininity, plays an important part in young women's definitions of adulthood, with markers of physical development such as menstruation holding symbolic importance. It is in young women's discussions of magazines that the scrutiny of physical and personal development can be seen most clearly.

The common practice described by young women of reading beyond your age group, implicates them in knowledge about what happens to older girls and women as well what is 'normal' and what is 'not' for their age group. Clare finds this useful as support and information, and has availed herself of problems page advice:

> *Clare*: I read the problem pages, and it's nice to know that you're not the only one with problems, because most of the time, cos I'm not like big like most girls, and there's always like problems, like I haven't started things, I haven't started growing properly, I read about other people's problems and it makes me feel, well, yes, I'm not the only one. . . . About two years ago I had my story in a problem page and

apparently lots of people read it. It was just aꜝ
lems and that, and it kind of made me thin.
think about what I'm going to do when I'm oldeɪ,
I've grown up I think my life has changed just through ᵣ.
reading other people's problems. . . . [female fg, year 8, schoᴜ.

Although young women defend magazines as a valued source of entertainment, information, advice and support, they also express some
ambivalence about the way in which 'reading beyond' one's age can
result in a frightening process of acceleration, and they may resist the
final destination of femininity.

> *Helen*: You've learnt the basic stuff so why do you have to learn about
> everything else that we can learn when we are more old and that –
> you know, people are asking things, you know, 'How do I do this?'
> and you say, why can't they just learn that when I'm older, and you
> know, 'I can do it'.
> *Emma*: Cross that bridge when I come to it.
> *Maria*: Yeah, you know, it's people or things are too old or are too
> complex for people that are reading – the ages – the people who are
> reading the magazines. [young women, year 8, school 7]

In Helen's words there is a sense that in consuming such magazines she
is also engaging in a collective project of femininity that has its own
dynamic and which culminates in active heterosexuality.[6] Returning to
the equation of physical and moral competence, she worries about
'knowing it' before she can 'do it'.[7]

In becoming 'mature' young women are also becoming feminine, a
task that requires labour, skill and the discipline of the self and the body
(Smith 1988). While apparently similar to the process of becoming a
'civilized' moral agent which demands the internalization of external
rules in order to integrate moral and bodily competence, the process
of becoming feminine results in an effective disintegration of self and
body through the internalization of a gaze – learning to see oneself as
others see one, from the outside (Paechter, 1998). If the process of moral
development produces the body as self, then the process of feminization produces appearance as self – giving rise to a counter discourse of
'authenticity' which characterizes much of young people's moral discourse, particularly that of young women, for whom the tension
between the authentic and artificial self can be a source of resistance
and anger.

Iasculinity, femininity, emotion and control

Where the project of femininity leads girls into a process of reflexive and accelerated development, boys appear to experience or respond to the pressures of masculinity differently. While there are many possible versions of masculinity that young men may adopt or experiment with, not all are socially admired or rewarded. In this single sex group, female discussants made it very clear that boys who cannot control their emotions were not acceptable, while girls can control their feelings:

> *Evette*: Girls mature quicker than boys, it's surprising how many wimps there are around – I mean, well, our friend started crying because he thought his girlfriend was talking about him.
> *Clare*: And there's this boys in our class . . .
> *Evette*: Oh my God, he's such a wimp!
> *Jane*: He'd cry for anything.
> *Clare*: He'd just cry at anything – I mean we were in science last year and the teacher told him off and she was telling him to be quiet and he started crying.
> *Evette*: . . . I don't know, he – the boys are really weird – him and his twin brother – they don't really know how to express anger and so what they do is they just burst out crying and they completely lash out.
> *Int*: Would you say that girls are more controlled?
> *Jane*: Girls control their feelings. [female fg, year 8, school 7]

In another mixed group the gendered meanings of 'emotional strength' were explored, and the intolerance of wimps was questioned by both girls and boys:

> *Anne*: . . . men don't cry in front of women
> *James*: Yeah, but we just hold it back – its not that we're not feeling that . . .
> *David*: Women cry but men don't, hardly ever
> *Anne*: We just let our feelings out and go 'who cares!'
> *James*: But that's just in front of the girls' cos you do wind up seeming like a you're a wimp. But if something like really bad has happened and you're with your mates and I think you do, and you like trust them that they're not going to say anything that's going to make you sound like a real wimp and that.

David: But if any girl saw a bloke crying they'd just think, Oh God, what a wimp.

Anne: No, I don't think so, you've got to be quite strong to do it for other people.

James: But, a lot of girls would agree with that.

Anne: Boys show their emotions in different ways to us anyway

James: Anger

Anne: Yeah – anger

James: Frustration

Anne: I think boys do show their emotion just as much as we do but we just don't realise that we're doing it because we do it in a different way . . . I think boys have got a strength in showing it differently, in holding it back. We've got the strength in letting it out.

David: Yeah, but you can sort of sit there crying or something and blame it on your periods, but we haven't got an excuse have we? [mixed fg, year 10, school 8]

These two discussions contain, in a condensed form, the contradictions of 'acceptable' masculinity and femininity in control and expression of emotion and the importance of the collusive nature of the construction of these expressions. The accelerated physical maturity of girls must be matched with increasing control of their bodies and appearance, and of the appropriate expression of emotion. For girls to physically fight as an expression of anger, although some do, is less acceptable than for boys; for boys to cry, although some do, is less acceptable than for girls. The male twins are weird in Evette's view because they do not know how to express anger and frustration in an appropriate way, they cry, they lash out. And her expectations are reflected in David's view that *girls* would regard a crying bloke as a wimp, with which James concurs. But Anne and James question the expectations, for James it is safe to cry in the bosom of your male peers if something really bad has happened, as long as you can trust them to preserve your image, and not to say anything that will reveal you as a wimp. This indicates a more supportive side to the male peer group than is usually apparent, as well as the importance of image. Anne thinks that boys do express emotion, just differently than girls, and that the strength of each gender lies in the way in which they express or control emotions. In the responses in our study, girls' emotional maturity is linked to a culture of femininity which includes the negotiation of problems and relationships and the appropriate control over the expression of feelings.[8] The emotional development of boys was seen as stunted by the demands of masculinity to contain their feelings. Paradoxically then, it is boys who are seen to be emotionally out of control (and immature) and girls who are seen to be emotionally disciplined through the appropriate expression and public display of feeling. The eruptions of uncontrolled feelings and rages (as with the immoderate twins) stem from the conventions of masculinities which prevent boys from developing the skills which appropriate femininity demands of girls. The following exchange indicates the degree of control favoured by the female peer group:

> *Kay*: Some girls actually can't handle some issues – they just start crying all the time and it's like, there are two girls in my class, one cries at everything . . .
> *Int*: Do you think that's bad to cry, to lose it?
> *Kay*: If you can't handle it then you can't handle it, but you should really try and, you know, cope with it. Because you can't sit there all day crying about nothing.
> *Paula*: If you cry it makes everyone else annoyed cos they have to come and be nice to you when you cry – they all come and go 'don't worry, don't worry' and their break time gets ruined and then you think 'Well, I could have – you know, I could have waited you know'.
> [female fg, year 8, school 7]

We have argued that becoming feminine is not quite like becoming a 'civilized' moral agent which produces the body as self, because of the need for the internalization of a gaze, learning to see oneself as others see one. There is in this sense a permeability to the boundaries of the female body and self, which extends to relational and emotional work (Gilligan, 1995; Hochschild, 1983). In contrast, the requirements of masculinity can be understood in terms of the maintenance of boundaries, an impermeability between the self and wider social relations. This challenge of maintaining an integrity of the 'self' and the perception of the self, can be seen in the importance of image to young men, and particularly of the 'hard' image. It is largely girls in the study who draw attention to this aspect of masculinity.[9] Anne and Vicky here also provide interpretations which emphasize the importance of the process of containment of emotion and exteriorization in maintaining image:

> *Anne*: I think men are really worried about what everyone else thinks and of what everyone thinks of them if they cry or they're upset or if they're sad or something, they are worried about their reputation.
> [mixed fg, year 10, school 8]

Int: What kind of boys get respect?
Gordon: Hard men
Vicky: Hard men are usually softish, they don't want things that are wrong with them pointed out to them, so they pick on people. [mixed fg, year 11, school 4]

Northern Ireland, a location in our study, provides an illustration of a situation in which taking violent physical revenge can be an important part of a reputation as a 'hard man':

Int: Do you think girls attitudes on this [revenge] are different than boys, or women's attitudes different than men?
Jane: mm, yeah
Clare: Men are stronger than women, more reluctant to come to a compromise. It's their image.
Int: What, a man is more tied to his image as a fighter?
Clare: If someone would say something bad about them, that would change their image and they would have to try and get that image back. [female fg, year 8, school 7]

The statement in our title 'I do knees' was made by a young man in response to a question on the questionnaire asking what kind of voluntary work, if any, he undertook. It casts another light on the violence which has been very much a part of life in areas of Northern Ireland, where the practice of kneecapping, or the fear of having your knees 'done' was a reality for a minority of young people. This extreme form of physical punishment can be seen as a revisitation of the processes of punishment and reward that young people regarded as being part of the child's early moral learning. While young people were generally accepting of this in early childhood they are less clear about the legitimacy or effectiveness of physical punishment in adulthood. There is evidence, however, that some young people, growing up in an environment where such beatings are fairly regular occurrences, do accept this level of 'morally arbitrated' violence on the body as a suitable form of punishment or future deterrent. One young man believed that he himself deserved such a punishment in the past: 'I think if I deserve it I should get it' (Dermot, yr 9).

For others the discussion of the legitimacy of such a form of punishment was coloured by considerations of the nature of the crime, lack of confidence in forces of law and order, and an inherent belief that 'nobody's got a right to hit anybody':

Int: Do you agree with people getting beat up or punishment beatings or that, as a way of stopping . . .

Kitty: It depends what they done.

Gail: Naw not really. People haven't got a right to run about doing that to people – doing people's knees and all.

Ciaran: There's some boys that need it but – like druggies –.

Gail: Aye, people need – people need it . . .

Ciaran: – paedophiles and all.

Gail: Alright, – if they're going to go round – to people.

Kitty: Aye, there's no right for it like, but if that's the only way like they're going to get punished.

Gail: Aye if it's the only way they're going to get sorted out it's alright but they've no right to do it.

Ciaran: Nobody's got a right to hit anybody but if it's the only way to sort it out.

Kitty: But if the police aren't going to do nothing, somebody needs to. [mixed fg, year 12, school 3]

Although young women, in Northern Ireland and elsewhere in our study, regretted such violent masculinities, hard men could gain respect, and in at least one of our sites there were young women who aspired to and were prepared to fight for such an image for themselves.

The moral in bodily discourse: tensions between 'choice' and 'nature'

While it is impossible to look at the way in which children and young people talk about becoming moral without also hearing about their bodies, it is impossible to consider the way in which young people talk about their bodies without also hearing about morality. Authenticity, as expressed through tensions between the 'true' or 'natural self' and between 'images' or appearances were central to young people's moral discourse. Genuine and natural people, those who saw the 'real you' and not just the surface, could be trusted. Those who wanted you because of your appearance or because of your reputation, 'what they have heard about you', while desired, could not necessarily be trusted.

The distinction between the true self and self as representation becomes particularly clear when young people talk about negative icons in popular culture. In a discussion of Pamela Anderson and the ethics of plastic surgery, the true self and the self as appearance are not only understood to be distinct but to exist at the expense of each other.

Ella: Barbie Girl!
Int: What don't you like about her
Paula: She's just too full of herself
Kay: She's a tart
Int: She's a tart, she's too full of herself, what does that mean – 'too full of herself'?
Paula: Well, she kind of loves herself
Ella: She wants people to – men mainly, you know, just look at her and go wow! But there's nothing there to go wow.
Kay: It's plastic
Paula: Exactly, it's disgusting . . . [female fg, year 8, school 7]

From the perspective of these young women, to be 'full of yourself' is to exist entirely on the surface, to be available to the gaze of men, not in control of your image and thus so untrustworthy and unnatural. Natural beauty then becomes hidden from this gaze and distinguished from the body as that which cannot be seen.

The body work of the pop icon Michael Jackson was also widely condemned by young people in the study.[10] While medical need was considered to be an acceptable reason for the use of plastic surgery, its use to transgress or transcend embodied categories of gender, race and age was not.

Paula: He's ruined his face
Jo: He looks like a woman
Kay: If he wants to look like that it's up to him
Paula: I think the same, but I also think he shouldn't need to like change himself.
Int: Why do you think he does want to change his body?
Paula: Didn't he want to change the colour of his skin.
Ella: He's made himself look too much like Janet now hasn't he? [laughter] He's made his face look exactly like they are twins. [female fg, year 8, school 7]

Young men's discussions of the ethics of body work and plastic surgery are interesting in the ways in which a concern with the body as representation is made consistent with masculinity through the moralized notions of work and personal endeavour. When asked to distinguish plastic surgery, body building and dieting, plastic surgery was described by a group of 16–17 year old men as 'the easy option' and 'a little bit more extreme'.

In body building – you could say that that's just natural, but its not really natural to have your face restructured just because you don't like the way you look . . . [male fg, year 12, school 7]

When asked whether it might also be connected with appearance, they agreed, but qualified the implications:

Dan: Yes of course it is
Paul: Its about image these days
Dan: You do it with your willpower instead of your wallet with body building . . .
Paul: Body building is about work isn't it. It's about personal achievement. You've obviously put your effort into it to achieve body building, whereas with plastic surgery it is all about money.
Dan: And if you get something that you don't deserve then you don't feel as happy about it as if you've worked for it, and you've got it, and you actually feel that you deserve it. [male fg, year 12, school 7]

The integrity of male bodies is under increasing pressure and their exemption from processes of commodification no longer assured. The incorporation of male bodies into consumer culture in advertising and pop culture was a source of both hilarity and hostility for young women. While Michael Jackson was considered to be 'weird' having undergone a literal feminization, jettisoning both his blackness and his masculinity, Peter Andre was seen as a less threatening figure, feminized by offering his 'hyper masculine' body to the consumer's gaze.[11]

Ella: Plastic pecks! . . .
Int: But why do you call them plastic pecks?
Kay: Cos they're like plastic, they're all shiny
Jane: I do think they are real
Paula: I don't think he needs plastic surgery, he just waxes his body [laughter]
Int: Do you think that's nice, do you think his body is nice?
Paula: No, I think it's disgusting . . . but he's a nice guy, I've heard him on the radio and he's really nice . . . but I don't see why he feels the need to take his shirt off and show his waxy . . . [laughter] [young women, year 8]

The young women suggest, that Peter 'shouldn't feel the need to'. They recognize that inside that plastic body is 'a nice guy', the authentic self within, yet they also show some excitement that he does 'take his shirt off and show his waxy . . .', offering what Angela McRobbie has described as a form of 'girls' camp' (1997:198).

Conclusion

We have explored the relationship between the body and morality in young people's discourse, drawing on focus group discussions of moral issues in the *Youth Values* study. Young people are clear that moral responsibility starts early and is related to physical competence; the relationship between physical capacity to be able to undertake an act and moral responsibility for its enactment recurs in their comments. The morally competent young person makes the appropriate choice of action. We have characterized this as a progression from nature to culture, in which the place and meaning of choice is valued by young people. The role of adults is to facilitate the process of moral development, if necessary and when the child is young, through physical chastisement. But for them the process of internalization of the appropriate moral precepts should be based on negotiation and consent, and increasingly social approval and disapproval, as the child grows. The young people in the study see then a relatively linear progression from youth to maturity, from a lack of moral competence to becoming a moral agent, although the route may be strewn with domestic, social and cultural factors which can complicate progress. The route to maturity, and in particular to appropriate control over body and emotions, and their presentation, is also highly gendered and embodied.

We have examined the young people's understanding of maturity and found ambivalence about its acquisition. Young women seem to experience an accelerated femininity, particularly in relation to the body, which some of them seek, and towards which others are less favourably disposed. We have seen that the media, youth culture and its commodification, play an important part in developing their understanding of the normative requirements of femininity and the female 'self'. Teenage magazines are carefully age specific, and young women engage in reading beyond their age, which gives them access to an imagined future self, which can be both enticing and terrifying. Young women worry about bodily practices, particularly those related to normative heterosexuality and the sexually active woman, and knowing about these before they can 'do it'. The disjunction between knowing and bodily enactment complicates the integration of moral and embodied competence for these young women.

Young men, generally regarded as less mature and maturing more slowly than young women, can sometimes prize that state. That very physicality, fighting, farting, burping, messing around, which young women deride, can provide satisfaction, male peer status and a badge of group membership. An important part of the collusive construction of gender in the teenage years is the deployment of the body, and many of the practices of the school both formal and informal, for example, are directed towards its constraint and control, channelling it along gendered routes (Gordon *et al.*, 2000). Our data from this study point to the importance of the collusive construction of appropriately gendered control and constraint of the body and its emotions from the perspective of the young people. It would appear that big boys do not cry because they do not want to be considered wimps by girls.

The physical maturity of the girls is matched by an emotional and relational maturity, in which control of the emotions is an important element. But the requirements of femininity which at one level could be seen as the ultimate reflexive project of self, are other directed and require the internalization of the gaze of the other (Holland *et al.*, 1998; Bordo, 1988). This very permeability can lead to fears of inauthenticity, and a tension between the 'natural self' and image or appearance, which was important in the young people's moral discourse. This tension appeared most clearly in the analysis of their responses to physical bodily changes on the part of popular icons, taking up the option of the self improvement and transformation. While the bodily recreation undertaken by Michael Jackson for example could be interpreted as a magical solution to the social divisions of age, gender and 'race' (Willis, 1990:87–8), these young people reject *his* rejection of his masculinity and skin colour. And Pamela Anderson's emphasized (or enhanced – Connell, 1987:183) femininity, a genuinely inauthentic representation of self, is 'plastic . . . disgusting'. Peter Andre's fabled six pack provokes similar responses from the young men, although they regard the hard work of body building as possibly more 'natural' than employing the skills of the plastic surgeon through the power of the wallet.

Current theories of the body emphasize the plasticity of the body, arguing that it is and can be part of a reflexive project of self, and that this increase in control and choice over the body is taking place within a broader framework of a society in which traditional expectations can no longer necessarily be realized. It is in children and young people's bodies that this plasticity is most apparent and where the social meaning of choice and control can be seen at play. Children and young people's bodies are physically unfinished, in process, relative. In forging their identities they must work with not only their own and their peers' constantly changing bodies, but the changing societal and institutional meanings given to these bodies and changes (James *et al.*, 1998). Young people can be seen, and can see themselves, as in our data, as 'unfinished', simultaneously in both modernist narratives of development, and post or late modern narratives of self improvement and choice. But running through their moral discourse of the body are themes of natural and unnatural, choice and authenticity which delineate their moral resistance to the dominance of appearance (or surface) over essence (or depth).

Notes

1. Funded by the ESRC as part of the Childhood 5–16 Programme: L129251020.
2. The research was undertaken through eight schools located in five different areas which can be described as follows. In Northern Ireland: school 1, an inner city area with a predominantly working-class and mixed religious catchment; school 2, a suburban area with a mixed class and religious catchment (integrated); school 3, an inner city area with a working-class and religiously homogeneous catchment (Catholic); and school 4, an inner city area with a working-class and religiously homogeneous catchment (Protestant). In England: school 5, a large housing estate with a working-class and ethnically homogeneous catchment; school 6, an inner city area with a, largely working-class and ethnically diverse catchment; school 7, a commuter belt area with a largely middle-class and ethnically homogeneous catchment; and school 8, a rural village with a mixed class and ethnically homogeneous catchment.
3. See Lenderyou (1994) for a description of the 'values clarification game' adapted here. Examples of statements used in the study are: 'It is wrong to have a child unless you can support it'; 'If a girl says no to sex she doesn't really mean it'.
4. The terms right and wrong were taken from the vocabularies of the young people in the pilot study and were used in the development of research instruments.
5. Focus groups from which quotes are taken are designated by single sex (specified) or mixed, and school year (year 7 = age 11/12; 8 = 12/13; 9 = 13/14; 10 = 14/15; 11 = 15/16; 12 = 16/17).
6. Myers (1986) cited in Lury (1996) describes this contradiction of being simultaneously the objects and the audience of commodity exchange as a form of 'cannibalism'.
7. This concern about being 'physically ready' also characterized young people's discussions of changes to the legal age of sexual consent. See Thomson 2000.
8. Catherine Lutz (1996) makes this point. Through a discourse analysis of men and women's emotional talk, she challenges the traditional association of men with emotional control and women with the loss or lack of emotional control.
9. In the analysis so far it is young women commenting on young men, rather than the young men themselves. Differences in the ways young people talk about and construct gender will be analyzed in detail in later papers.

10. Michael Jackson was cited as a villain by many of young people in the study, the most common reasons given were that he had changed his skin colour, and was not appropriately masculine, 'he would rather look like a gaylord than being black'.
11. While Pamela Anderson was cited regularly by young women as a villain, young men regularly cited Peter Andre. He too was considered to be 'full of himself', and was condemned for 'wanting all the girls to look at him', being 'big headed and thinks he is gorgeous'.

Bibliography

BORDO, S. (1988) '*Anorexia Nervosa*: Psychopathology as crystallization of culture', in I. Diamond and L. Quinby *Feminism and Foucault: Reflections on Resistance*. Boston: Northwestern University Press.

BORDO, S. (1993) *Unbearable Weight: Feminism, Western Culture and the Body*. UCLA Press.

CHISHOLM, L. and K. HURRELMAN (1995) 'Adolescence in modern Europe. Pluralized transition patterns and their implications for personal and social risks'. *Journal of Aolescence*, 18:129–58.

CONNELL, R.W. (1987) *Gender, Power and Society: the Person and Sexual Politics*. Cambridge: Polity Press.

CONNELL, R.W. (1995) *Masculinities*. Cambridge: Polity Press.

DOUGLAS, M. (1966) *Purity and Danger*. London: Routledge & Kegan Paul.

ELIAS, N. (1982) *The Civilizing Process, Vol. 1: The History of Manners*. Oxford: Blackwell.

FEATHERSTONE, M. (1991) 'The body in consumer culture', in M. Featherstone, M. Hepworth and B. Turner (eds) (1991) *The Body: Social Processes and Cultural Theory*. London: Sage.

FISKE, J. (1989) *Reading the Popular*. London: Routledge.

GIDDENS, A. (1991) *Modernity and Self Identity: Self and Society in the Late Modern Age*. Cambridge: Polity Press.

GILLIGAN, C. (1995) 'The centrality of relationship in psychological development: A puzzle, some evidence, and a theory', in M. Blair and J. Holland (with S. Sheldon) *Identity and Diversity: Gender and the Experience of Education*. Clevedon: Multilingual Matters in association with The Open University.

GOFFMAN, I. (1971) *Relations in Public*. London: Penguin.

GORDON, T., J. HOLLAND and E. LAHELMA (2000) 'Moving bodies/still bodies: Embodiment and agency in schools', in L. McKie and N. Watson (eds) *Organising Bodies*. London: Macmillan Press – now Palgrave.

HOLLAND, J., R. THOMSON, S. HENDERSON, S. MCGRELLIS and S. SHARPE (2000) 'Catching on, wising up and learning from your mistakes: young people's accounts of moral development', *International Journal of Children's Rights*, 8, 3.

HOLLAND, J., C. RAMAZANOGLU, S. SHARPE and R. THOMSON (1998) *The Male in the Head: Young people, Heterosexuality and Power*. London: the Tufnell Press.

HOCHSCHILD, A. (1983) *The Managed Heart: Commercialisation of Human Feeling*. Berkeley: University of California Press.

JAMES, A. (1993) *Childhood Identities: Self and Social Relationships in the Experience of the Child*. Edinburgh: Edinburgh University Press.

JAMES, A., C. JENKS and A. PROUT (1998) *Theorizing Childhood*. Cambridge: Polity Press.

LENDERYOU, G. (1994) *Sex Education, Values and Morality*. London: Health Education Authority.

LURY, C. (1998) *Prosthetic Culture: Photography, Memory and Identity*. London: Routledge.

LUTZ, C. (1996) 'Engendered emotion: Gender, power and the rhetoric of emotional control in American discourse', in R. Harre and W. Parrott (eds) *The Emotions: Social, Cultural and Biological Dimensions*. London: Sage.

MARTIN, E. (1989) *The Woman in the Body*. Milton Keynes: Open University Press.

MCROBBIE, A. (1997) 'More! New sexualities in girls' and womens' magazines', in A. McRobbie (ed.) *Back to Reality: Social Experience and Cultural Studies*. Manchester: Manchester University Press.

PAECHTER, C. (1998) *Educating the Other: Gender, Power and Schooling*. London: Falmer Press.

PRENDERGAST, S. (1992) *This is the Time to Grow Up: Girls' Experiences of Menstruation in School*. Cambridge: Health Promotion Trust.

SHILLING, C. (1993) *The Body and Social Theory*. London: Sage.

SKEGGS, B. (1997) *Formations of Class and Gender: Becoming Respectable*. London: Sage.

SMITH, D.E. (1988) 'Femininity as discourse', in L. Roman, L.K. Christian Smith and E. Ellsworth (eds) *Becoming Feminine: The Politics of Popular Culture*. Lewes: Falmer Press.

THOMSON, R. (2000) 'Legal, protected and timely: young people's reflections on the age of heterosexual cousent' in D. Monk and J. Bridgeman (eds) *Feminist Perspectives on Child Law*. London: Cavendish Press.

WILLIS, S. (1990) 'I want the black one: Is there a place for Afro-American culture in a commodity culture'. *New Formations* 10:77–97.

10
The Intersexual Body and the Medical Regulation of Gender
Myra J. Hird and Jenz Germon

Introduction

> Do we truly need a true sex? With a persistence that borders on stub-
> bornness, modern Western societies have answered in the affirma-
> tive. They have obstinately brought into play this question of a 'true
> sex' in an order of things where one might have imagined that
> all that counted was the reality of the body and the intensity of its
> pleasures (Foucault 1980: vii).

The intersexed[1] individual has never constituted a free form absent
from discipline.[2] Contemporary analyses posit that shifts in societal
responses to intersexuality should be understood in terms of incre-
mental increases in negative disciplining. Social historians note, for
instance, that the intersexual first began to be medicalized in the sixteenth century (Foucault 1980; Epstein 1990; Hausman 1995). Ambroise
Parel declared in 1573 that physicians should have the authority to
determine the appropriate gender for the intersexual. His writing ger-
minates the idea that cultural gender-appropriate behaviour should
carry equal weight with genital appearance in decisions about gender
(re)assignment (Epstein 1990: 108). During the eighteenth century
modern medicine challenged the doctrine of humours. At the same time
the first drawings of sexualized human skeletons appeared, and from
this point research into sex differences accelerated (Schiebinger 1989).
The division of human bodies into male and female suited 'the economic needs of heterosexuality [lending] a naturalistic gloss to the institution of heterosexuality' (Butler 1990: 112). The social conditions of
intersexuals were not immediately affected by the curiosity of medical
science. In fact they remained much the same 'until the availability of

surgical and pharmacological interventions [that] could control or create a public sexual identity for them' (Epstein 1990: 106).

But it is not the case that the intersex body was *free* before medicalization. Instead what we find is a major shift over several centuries in the juridical disciplining of intersexual bodies. During the Middle Ages and the Renaissance, the Courts recognized intersexuals through the granting of legal standing. At issue was the intersexual's civil status rather than any concern about anatomical structures *per se*. The ritualized gendering of an infant at birth served (as it does to this day) a variety of functions, all of which can be regarded as mechanisms of the social organization of patrilineage: marriage, property, and inheritance rights.[3] The law assumed an unequivocal opposition between the sexes, which explains why intersexuals were subject to legal imputations of fraud. Such charges arose from the threat of *usurpation*. That is, gaining access to those privileges and powers to which they were not entitled, and indeed were meant to be denied.[4] (Epstein 1990) However intersexuals, upon entering adulthood were given the legal option of deciding their own sex although a medical examination was necessary to confirm the legitimacy of that choice. Once categorized, the decision could not be reversed[5] (Fausto-Sterling 1993; Foucault 1980).

In this paper we want to suggest that the modern regulatory technique of medical surgery radically disciplines the physical intersexual body. As well, it raises serious questions about the possibilities for, and limits of, transgression. In this paper we hope to explicate this shift in the disciplining of the intersexual body. As such this paper focuses more on societal responses to the intersexed body, rather than intersexuality as a subjectivity. Through this analysis we focus on the ways in which certain developments in medical technologies during the twentieth century led to changes in the way in which the body was encoded by medical science. These particular configurations of knowledge have enabled the deployment of a variety of technologies in the 'treatment' of intersexuals, which has led to the creation of new subject positions in the latter part of the twentieth century.

We begin by examining the variety of ways in which intersexuality was positioned within discourse from the Middle Ages to the nineteenth century. We further delineate three phases that occurred during the Classical Age, which necessitated a series of epistemological and ontological shifts. The first phase understood the intersexual as *two sexes in one body*. One of these sexes dominated and gender assignment was based on this *natural* domination. Phase two considered there to be *one true sex*, decipherable only by physicians. Gender assignment was based on the physician's expert declaration of the individual's *true* sex. In the most recent phase physicians and the psychiatric community conjoin *expertise* to uncover the *best sex* appropriate to morphology, psychology and, as we will argue, expediency. Through this medical and psychiatric configuration, the *material signifiers* of the body are altered to conform to a binary gender code.

Because social boundaries rely upon difference and hierarchy (Epstein 1990), the intersexual threatens to disrupt and blur the boundaries of 'everyday social relations', by the potential to 'profit from their anatomical oddities' (Foucault 1980: ix). Materially forbidden to exist today, intersexuals have been erased historically by the enforced *choice* of one gender or the other. Throughout the paper, we argue that the intersexual potentially threatens the stability of a naturalized gender order because intersexuals are essentially *(a)non* in such a system. We conclude by signalling some recent strategies that have been suggested for the conceptualization of the body in a way that opens up possibilities for the legitimization of an intersexual subjectivity. While these strategies appear to open spaces for a radical reinterpretation of gender, upon closer examination we propose that these strategies may be dependent upon the very gender order they seek to disrupt.

Monsters and society

> Madness only exists in society. It does not exist outside of the forms of sensibility that isolate it, and the forms of repulsion that expel it or capture it. Thus one can say that from the Middle Ages up to the Renaissance madness was present within the social horizon as an aesthetic and mundane fact; then in the seventeenth century ... madness underwent a period of silence, of exclusion. It lost the function of manifestation, of revelation, that it had had in the age of Shakespeare and Cervantes ... it becomes laughable, delusory. (Foucault 1989: 8–9).

According to Foucault, insanity is the creation of society. Or, in other words, it is not the individual who is insane, but society that deems her/him so. To yoke together the mad and the intersexual would seem, at first glance, to misrepresent the latter. Worse, it would appear to reinforce the modern perception which politicized intersexuality groups wish to confound. However, we wish to suggest that such an approximation is useful in understanding the shifting societal responses to intersexuality and we entreat a certain forbearance to make this claim.

The history of madness demonstrates that the classification of the variety of individuals we now consider 'insane' is a relatively recent invention.[6] It follows that the ways in which society interacts with madness is historically dependent. Up until the end of the Middle Ages, the 'insane' walked relatively freely among the 'sane'. Although the subject of comedy and ridicule, society 'just as often emphasized the tragic aspect of madness' (Barchilon in Foucault 1965: v). This tragic aspect was closely bound up with the association of insanity with death.[7] The mad person was seen to take the 'absolute limit of death' and turn it inward 'in a continuous irony' (Foucault 1965: 16). The insane, in effect, guarded the secrets of death and the human spirit. In a similar way, the intersexual may be seen as guarding the secrets of sexuality. In ancient times anatomical differences between men and women were used to ground the social development of individuals based on sex. The intersexual confounded such bifurcation. During this time, the intersexual was included in the loose classification of 'human monster' (Braidotti 1994; Foucault 1997). These beings were considered a double violation of the natural order: half-human and half-animal, they were the subject of particular trepidation as they 'combined the impossible and forbidden' (Foucault 1997: 51). There is evidence to suggest that those individuals who were explicitly identified as intersexual were considered to be *special* in some way, able to sense and partake of the joys and secrets of both sexes.[8] However, by the end of the Middle Ages and the emergence of the Renaissance we begin to see a shift in approach to the insane and the intersexual within this classification.[9] The mad were separated off, 'confined in the centre of social relations within a set of institutions which segregate unreason from reason' (Turner 1987: 64).

> [The] humanist praise of folly thus inaugurates a long tradition that will seek to define, control, and ultimately confiscate the experience of madness. This tradition tries to make of madness an experience in which the human being is constantly confronted with his [sic] moral truth, revealing the rules proper to his [sic] nature (Miller 1993: 102).

Medicine and psychiatry provided key sites for such regulation. Punishment was replaced by other forms of regulation (Turner 1987). From the Renaissance to modern society, this continued regulation has taken on a myriad of forms through classification, internment (in prisons and later mental institutions) and *cure*.[10] The increasing regulation within medicine and psychiatry also partially disqualified the individual as a legal subject[11] (Szasz 1970; Zola 1972; Foucault 1997). The intersexual 'monster' became less powerful; a figure more to be pitied than respected. This provided a discourse with which to pastorally regulate the intersexual through medicine and psychiatry. For the intersexual, as we discuss later in the paper, developments in surgical techniques have had a profound effect on their regulation.

Rendering them harmless: the development of medicine and the reconstitution of monsters

By the late Classical period, medical science understood that sex determination was an enormously complex mechanism that resulted in a wide variation of 'sexual types'. This variation stretched far beyond the two mutually exclusive categories of male and female. In spite of this, the notion that the intersexual constituted a combination of two sexes in the one body became supplanted by an understanding of a single *true* sex disguised within an ambiguous body. The invention of microscopy, along with increasingly sophisticated surgical techniques enabled an examination of gonadal tissue in live patients. Developments in anaesthesia and medical hygiene reduced the risks involved with laparotomy, and it was within this context that Klebs classified *true* intersexuality as the existence of both testicular and ovarian gonadal tissue (Hausman 1995: 78). Thus, the *pseudo*-intersexual came into being. The *pseudo*-intersexual was defined as a person with determinate gonads of either one sex or the other, but ambiguous genitalia. For instance, the female *pseudo*-intersexual is characterized by having ovaries and 'masculinised' genitals (Epstein 1990; Kessler 1990; Hausman 1995). This terminology necessarily presupposed the existence of a single dominant sex *in* the body.

This epistemological shift affected the intersexual body profoundly, for the delineation of a 'true' sex always underneath the surface waiting to be unshackled from the trickeries of nature, foreclosed the option of choosing a sex. The emergence of a *one sex* per body model created the role of expert for physicians via the medical examination: the ritual employed to decipher a *true* sex. Thus physicians positioned themselves as the *doubly inscribed*: both discoverer and determiner (Kessler 1990), entering into a mutually reinforcing relationship with the law to regulate the intersexual body.

Medicine, psychiatry and new forms of discipline

The mid nineteenth century witnessed the emergence of new ways of being as a result of a number of factors including the birth of the modern nation, colonization and industrialization. The emergent bureaucratic and administrative controls – those regulatory modes necessary to capitalist economy – were unfolding as Freud was developing his theory of the unconscious. The birth of psychoanalysis as a discipline, in unison with an increasing medicalization of the body, provided new regulatory techniques or mechanisms for the management of the modern subject. The modern regulation of sexuality was only possible once sexuality as a concept had come into being. Those early attempts to discover the *true* sex of the intersexual were part of a larger project to unravel the mysteries of the newly created subjectivity called 'sexuality', in an attempt to 'identify, classify, and characterize the different types of perversions. [Such] investigations dealt with the problem of sexual anomalies in [both] the individual and the race.' (Foucault 1980: xii)

The 'discovery' of hormones at the turn of the twentieth century heralded the birth of a new strand of medical science: endocrinology. The ability of the endocrinologist to 'fix nature's mistakes'[12] represented a 'victory for the ideal of humanity, victories for normality' (Hausman 1995: 26). Endocrinology gained significant ground as a cultural discourse in the first-half of the twentieth century, enabling endocrinologists to partake in the management of the intersexed body. Much of the medical literature of the day concerning intersexuality argued that *treatment* needed to equate with what would later be referred to as the 'sex of assignment'. Evident in this literature is a consolidation of the notion of 'psychosexual identity', later coined by John Money as 'gender identity' (Hausman 1995). But the physician's role would remain to some extent circumscribed until genital surgical techniques reached a certain level of sophistication. The rapid acceleration in the development of medical and surgical techniques, along with the emergence of new understandings of subjectivity, prepared the ground for a gradual shift in discourses around sex and sexuality. This shift would have a profound effect on the modern western intersexual.

The modern regulation of intersexuals may be characterized by the epistemological shift from the notion of a 'true' sex that determined one's sexed 'destiny', to that of *best* sex. That is, the sex deemed most appropriate or advantageous given genital morphology and psychological and social environment. Such a shift was only possible because of the advances in medical science and the development of the 'psy' disciplines[13] which made the notion of a sex change operation conceptually possible. Once this conceptual shift was made, medical technology enabled physicians to invoke a binary gender through the material production of sex (Hausman 1995). It must be noted, however, that this shift was not all encompassing. While *best* sex may underpin the rationale behind contemporary medical procedures, physicians continue to imply to parents that they are able to discover the child's *true* sex.

Since the 1950s, protocols for the treatment of infants born with ambiguous genitalia have been developed from the work of John Money. Money's work is central to understanding the development of modern medical discourses on intersexuality. Indeed, we would argue that the concept of gender identity has had a profound effect on the medical management of intersexuals. Borrowing the term from philology, Money defined 'gender' as the 'internal representations' of what it is to be a male or a female (identity), in unison with socially prescribed modes of conduct for that identity (role). The appropriation of this terminology was a result of Money's perceived need for:

> [a] terminology that would permit me to write about their [intersexual's] sexual and procreative lives as male or female, *despite the handicap* of having been born with a *birth defect of the sex organs* and *despite the relative success or failure* of attempted surgical *repair of the defect* (1985: 280 emphasis added).

It was not long before the term entered medical discourse, particularly with regard to homosexuals and intersexuals. While gender *role* rapidly came to represent the socially expressive component of the original definition[14] Money remained committed to the idea that these two referents (role and identity) constituted a synthesis and should not be separated.[15] His theory of gender development was thus premised on the notion of the acquisition of a *core* gender identity which occurs during the first two years of life and is considered to be a critical developmental period for the 'differentiation and establishment of gender identity and gender role' (1976: 51). A core gender identity results from the child's interactions with parents; the child's perception of her/his genitals; as well as some mysterious kind of 'biologic force' (1985: 282). This core identity builds upon itself as a result of cumulative experience. The critical period is said to cement an earlier in-utero period, where hormonal activation of the brain sets the direction of neural pathways in preparation for the reception of 'post-natal social gender identity signals' (Raymond 1994: 47). Using these concepts, Money was able to provide the rationale for the imperative to intervene as soon after birth as possible, *for the child's psycho-social well-being.*

Protocols for intersexual infants recommend that decisions regarding sex of assignment are based primarily on the presentation of external genitalia. Delays resulting from indecision may well result in the child failing to establish a gender identity in an unambiguous manner. Sex assignment then, is privileged over hormones, chromosomes, gonads, internal reproductive structures, indeed sometimes over external genital morphology (Hausman 1995). Surgical and hormonal treatment interventions are deployed in an attempt to ensure that the subject's body conforms to the assigned gender (Hausman 1995; Raymond 1994). Money's theory is highly contradictory. On the one hand, his theory clearly privileges socialization, to the point where socialization becomes destiny. As a result, his work promotes the inscription of the social (a gender) onto the biological (the intersexed body). On the other hand, the primacy of the appearance of the genitalia reveals a quite crude recourse to the primacy of the biological body, as the following discussion indicates.

The arrival of a new-born with ambiguous genitalia is considered a medical emergency (Pagon 1987). Referring to Money's protocol, gender reassignment surgery is carried out as soon as possible after birth. Decisions about whether to assign the infant as male or female have less to do with chromosomal or gonadal sex than with genitalia. That is, the size of the penis or phallic structure ultimately dictates whether the child is constructed as male or female (Dewhurst and Gordon 1969; Pagon 1987; Griffin and Wilson 1992). Consequently, it is common for XY type males to be assigned and raised as female. Chromosome tests *are* used to determine the genetic make-up of the child: if they reveal a genetic female, genital surgery is performed without delay. (Kessler 1990). An example of the level of expediency involved in surgical intervention is illustrated in the following quote by two key British surgeons:

> The clitoris may be reduced in size in various ways. The simplest and probably the most satisfactory is to remove it by amputation . . . the dorsal [erotic] nerve of the clitoris runs within the sheath of the corpora cavernosa and it does not seem that its dissection and preservation are practicable. Whilst in theory preservation of the glans has something to commend it, the results of *amputation appear satisfactory* (Dewhurst and Gordon 1969: 41 emphasis added).

Where tests indicate the presence of a Y chromosome, surgery may be delayed while tests are performed to determine the responsiveness of phallic tissue to androgen treatment. Such treatment serves to enlarge the penile structure to the point where it can pass as a *real* penis (Kessler 1990):

> Since . . . reproduction may be disregarded, the most important single consideration is the child's subsequent [hetero] sexual life. . . . If there is little or no penile growth the male sex will be out of the question and the female sex should be chosen; with good penile development the male sex may be appropriate' (Dewhurst and Gordon 1969: 45).

Surgeons consider the *condition* of a micro-penis so detrimental to a male's morale that reassignment as female is justified on this basis alone. The implication here then, is that *male* is not only or most importantly defined–contrary to common understandings–by the genetic condition of having one Y and one X chromosome, nor by the ability to produce sperm. Rather gender is determined by the aesthetics of an *appropriately sized* penis (Kessler 1990):

> If the subject has an inadequate phallus, the individual should be reared as female, regardless of the results of diagnostic tests. In the patient with an adequate phallus, however, as much information as possible should be obtained before a decision is made (Griffin and Wilson 1992: 1536).

Chromosomes are somehow more meaningful for girls than they are for boys, as illustrated by the way that test results indicating the presence of two X chromosomes provide an immediate mandate for removal of the phallic tissue. Implicit in the medical literature and the treatment protocols is a privileging of male-ness, and an undervaluing of female-ness. Delays in 'corrective' surgery to reduce (or remove) the phallic tissue of a 46XY infant beyond the neonatal period is to invite 'traumatic memories of having been castrated' (Kessler 1990: 8). This concern does not extend to 46XX infants. Clitoroplasty is undertaken when the child is anywhere between seven months[16] and four years of age. Vaginal construction may be delayed until adolescence, yet there is no concern evident in the medical literature for trauma resulting from such late intervention. Further, little attention is paid to aesthetics in the creation of a vagina as there is with penile construction. The only requirement is that it is able to accommodate a penis in spite of numerous problems associated with constructed vaginas. Scar tissue is often extremely hypersensitive resulting in extreme pain during intercourse. Because of the lack of elasticity in scar tissue, a daily regime of dilating the vagina is required to prevent the vagina from closing. Bowel tissue is often the material chosen to construct the vagina which lubricates in response to digestion rather than arousal (Laurent in Burke 1996).

As Pagon (1987) notes, in those instances where it is possible to 'make the genitalia conform satisfactorily to either sex' (Dewhurst and Gordon 1969: 45), the parent's desire to have either a male or female child will serve as the determinant in assigning a sex. Medical explanations to families of intersex infants focus on the idea of a *continuum of sexual differentiation*, pointing to the bipotentiality of early *neutral gonads*, through the use of terms like 'variation' rather than 'abnormality' (Epstein 1990):

> Knowing the proper terminology and understanding that genital ambiguity results from *normal developmental processes* helps to allay anxiety and provide a basis for understanding the type of evaluation necessary' (Pagon 1987: 1020).

Defining the 'truth'

The modern medico-psychiatric response to intersexuality reflects a particular power–knowledge relationship. That is, 'when scientists look to nature, they [ultimately] bring with them their sociopolitical beliefs about what is natural' (Spanier 1991: 330). This produces a self-referential process: creating, reflecting and reinscribing. This reinscription, or regulation, is an attempt to

> bring into discourse the very things that seem to escape discursivity, what poststructuralists have come to call 'the real'. Therefore, the codes created by scientific endeavour have a different relation to 'the real' than other kinds of codes (Hausman 1995: 24).

In other words, science has historically recognized the diversity inherent in sexual differentiation across many animal and plant species, including humans.[17] Despite this, modern discourses produce a specific knowledge about what is *natural* about gender. That is, gender consists of two mutually exclusive typologies: female and male. This sociopolitical belief 'is maintained and perpetuated by the medical community in the face of overwhelming physical evidence that this taxonomy is not mandated by biology' (Hausman 1995: 25). While physicians dealing with intersex infants are willing to partially accept the idea of plural sex, they continue to subscribe to a binary notion of gender as *the* necessary code. Doctors 'are willing to uphold binary gender by producing binary sex, . . . [and use] technology to enforce binary gender by making males and females out of intersexuals' (77). It becomes clear then, that the *authenticity* of gender resides not on, nor in the body, but rather results from a particular nexus of power, knowledge and truth. Experts come to *define* the *truth* by virtue of having *knowledge*. Those experts then proceed to *discover* the *truth,* again, produced by a particular relation to *knowledge* (Foucault 1980). In doing so they are doubly inscribed, as discoverer and as determiner. Indeed, these *experts* have been able to produce a discourse that:

> became powerful both as a justification for medical practices and as a generalised discourse available to the culture at large for identifying, describing, and regulating social behaviours. . . . If you weren't born into a sex you can always become one through being a gender. (Hausman 1995: 107).[18]

That something as 'natural' as gender can be, or indeed needs to be, produced artificially is a paradox that appears to have escaped the medical fraternity (Kessler 1990).[19] If it is possible to *become* a gender, then surely there can be no such thing as a natural gender. By what means does gender resist exposure as the 'constrained production' that it obviously is? A post-structuralist analysis would suggest that the body is not gendered in any significant way prior to being qualified within a discourse.[20] Through this modern discourse, gender has come to be naturalized on the body, masquerading as essence. The chimera of binary gender is achieved by performance. Repeated performance produces the illusion of some type of internal essence:

> but produce[s] this on the *surface* of the body. . . . As in other ritual social dramas, the action of gender requires a performance that is repeated. This repetition is at once a re-enactment and re-experiencing of a set of meanings already socially established; and it is the mundane and ritualized form of their legitimation (Butler 1990: 136,140).

The medical obsession with constructing *pseudo*-male and female bodies from intersexed bodies is driven by a heterosexual imperative. If we are to understand that gender serves as a regulatory mechanism of heterosexuality, then by extension, it is clear that heterosexuality is itself a regulatory mechanism: of reproduction. Paradoxically, medical *experts* will often sacrifice reproduction in the interests of heterosexuality in the *management* of intersexuals. By doing so, they indeed lend a naturalistic gloss to the normative institution of heterosexuality.

Resisting the medical machine

Given the network of techniques brought to bear on the intersexual body through modern medical discourses, how might we begin to conceptualize the body in a way that ratifies an intersexual subjectivity? A number of political intersexual organizations, such as The Intersex Society of Aotearoa/New Zealand (ISNZ) and Intersexual Society of North America (ISNA), are increasingly articulating a counter-discourse. These organizations' primary political objective is the abolition of unnecessary genital surgery. Both organizations believe that since the 'authenticity of gender seems only to reside in the proclamation of the expert, then the power to proclaim an alternative is equally available' (Kessler 1990: 25).

Given the pervasiveness of modern medical discourses, it is not surprising that political intersexual organizations have resisted through a politics of inclusion. The *freedom* accorded to the intersexual in ancient times consisted of the legal right to choose which sex to *be*. Such a *choice* is reified in modern political movements. According to the ISNZ, most genital surgery is *cosmetic*, and must, therefore, be deferred until the individual concerned is able to make an informed decision and provide informed consent. What is at stake here is 'the right of each individual to make decisions about our own bodies, and to define ourselves' (Feinberg 1996: 105). However, such choice does little more than reify the bifurcation of gender categories. The subjectivity of the intersexual exists only within the socio-historical discourses of sexuality. The idea that there exists some essential relationship between sex and truth remains intact.

Sandy Stone, for instance, offers a strategy whereby intersexuals become conceptualized 'as a *genre*–a set of embodied texts whose potential for *productive* disruption of structured sexualities and spectra of desire has yet to be explored' (1991: 296). However, there is nothing in this textual interpretation that determines that intersexuality will challenge the available categories of sex other than present the possibility of a 'third' sex, for instance. Indeed this is evidenced by the suggestion of an intersexual advocate that the intersexed child be assigned a gender during infancy and given the option of surgery upon reaching some unspecified age of consent (Wilton 1997: 91). Another example of an attempt to consider gender possibilities with regard to intersexuality is that of Fausto-Sterling (1993), who argues for the expansion of gender categories in order to delineate wide-ranging variation within the 'catch-all' term of intersex. She identifies three sub-groupings, attributing to each the following terms: *herms* are those in possession of one testis and one ovary; *merms* comprise those with testes and some elements of female genitalia, but no ovaries; and finally, *ferms* who have ovaries and some degree of masculinized genitalia, but no testes. These sub-categories are each deserving of consideration as a sex in their own right according to Fausto-Sterling. However as critics point out, such categorizing is something of a poison chalice given the uncritical acceptance of the concepts *true* and *pseudo* intersexuality,[21] which does little to seriously undermine the dominant gender order.

The intersexual body itself may yet prove a site to explore the power–knowledge *truth* of gender. As Hausman suggests, 'we . . . need to recognize the body as a system that asserts a certain resistance to (or constraint upon) the ideology system regulating it' (1995: 14). The resistance of the intersexed body to the enforced regulation of gender is clearly evidenced by the ongoing problems that surgeons face in their attempts at successful penile construction, and the (repetitively) routine complications of vaginoplasty, not to speak of the long-term effects of consuming huge doses of sex hormones:

> In this sense we can read the body's resistance to 'gender' . . . as suggesting that in a critical return to 'sex' we may find a way to destabilise 'gender' as a normal-ising narrative in the twentieth century. (Hausman 1995: 200)

A *critical* return to *sex* does perhaps hold disruptive potential for the relation of the expert to the subject. If the transgression of the *uncorrected* intersexual brings any truth to society, it is in how our common sense understanding of sexual meaning is constructed. For,

> as much as a culture strenuously tried to outlaw the limit-experience impulse, it could only be fettered, never transcended. In dreams we confront our own truth in all of its raw daemonic purity; in eroticism we glimpse the happy world of desire prior to its tragic division into normal and abnormal acts; in madness he [*sic*] confronts the nothingness of existence. (Foucault in Miller 1993: 105)

And in the intersexual we confront the possibility of our own sexuality. However, we know this transgression to be tenuous. The subject is never free of regulation: as one form is transgressed, another is imagined.

Notes

1. The term 'intersexuality' was coined in 1920. Before this time, hermaphroditism was more commonly used.
2. For example, the ancient Jewish books of law (the Talmud and the Tosefta), contain extensive lists of regulations directed at intersexuals. These include sanctions against inheriting property; shaving; serving as witnesses in legal trials; and entering the priesthood, among others (Fausto-Sterling 1993: 23).
3. These included the prevention of fraud; the regulation and maintenance of differential privilege between males and females; and the regulation of morality and reproductive family life.
4. Voting, for example, was the prerogative of (white) men–as citizens. Women and '*others*' were not citizens and were thereby prohibited from voting. Where persons of indeterminate gender marry, the sanctity of heterosexual marriage is threatened because such bonds carry the spectre of homosexuality. If one partner's gender is ambiguous, then 'the sex of both partners may be the same or ambiguous and therefore potentially the same' (Epstein 1990: 129).
5. Harsh legal penalties were metered out to those caught transgressing. Legal injunctions targeted the outward manifestations of gender as a means of regulating the social behaviour of intersexuals (Epstein 1990; Foucault 1980; Kessler 1990; Butler 1993).
6. In ancient times, the 'insane' served as an umbrella under which all sorts of individuals, including transients and intersexuals, stood.
7. Death is viewed as human's ultimate preoccupation by such philosophers as Heidegger, Nietzsche and Husserl.
8. This is not to make the claim that this is how intersexuals experienced themselves, only to posit reasons for their relative autonomy in society at that time.
9. The age of confinement, and the exclusion of the unreasoned, corresponded with a philosophical shift in the work of Descartes whereby madness (unreason) was excluded from the domain of philosophy (Brown 1985).
10. One of the most interesting and revealing developments in the psychiatric classification system was the classification of the homosexual as mentally ill.
11. Szasz (1970) argues that the concept of insanity has provided the judicial system with a useful device for dealing with criminal offenders, providing the basis for stripping the subject of legal status. Furthermore, the term insane was (and is still) used to justify non-consensual medical intervention.
12. Endocrinology is concerned with disease occurring *within* the human organism: produced *by* the body rather than by external contagions.
13. Nicolas Rose (1996) coined the term 'psy' to describe the regulating disciplines of psychiatry, psychology and psychoanalysis.

14. The term 'gender identity' was adopted by clinical psychology to represent 'a psychodynamic state of being' (Money 1985: 282).
15. This is made explicit in the provocatively entitled article, 'The conceptual neutering of gender and the criminalisation of sex' (Money 1985).
16. Despite increased risks of stenosis or injury that accompany early vaginal construction, some physicians 'prefer' to complete all surgical procedures before the child reaches 18 months of age. See Perlmutter and Reitelman (1992).
17. In spite of the multitude of physical and physiological problems that arise from the (re)construction of intersexual flesh, 'scientific dogma persists with the assumption that intersexuals are doomed to a life of misery without medical intervention' (Fausto-Sterling 1993: 23).
18. However, evident in the emergent counter-discourse of medically-mediated intersexuals is that the *source* of the trauma is not the experience of inhabiting an intersexed body but rather, from the experience of medical interventions. (See Burke 1996; Holmes 1995; Triea 1996; Bodeker 1997).
19. Stone draws attention to the way that medical discourses around trans-sexuality bear startling similarities to elements of colonial discourse. We would suggest that this analysis also extends to intersexuality. In this account both discourses share a 'fascination with the exotic', which then extends to 'professional investigations'. In addition, a 'denial of subjectivity' inevitably results in a 'lack of access to the dominant discourse', which is 'followed by a species of rehabilitation' (1991: 293).
20. In *The History of Sexuality* (1979) Foucault inverts the traditional understanding of the relationship between sexuality and sex. 'Sex' has been understood as the root cause of the structure and meaning of desire (including sexuality). For Foucault, the body does not respond to some form of essential sex, creating desires, pleasures and sexuality. It is sexuality, invested by power relations that 'produces' sex.
21. The INSA has expressed concern at the uncritical acceptance of Victorian classifications by Anne Fausto-Sterling. 'We call those ones pseudo-intersexuals, . . . because that is how we fool ourselves that the world is not full of intersexuals' (Chase in Burke 1996: 225).

Bibliography

BARCHILON, J. (1965) 'Introduction', in M. Foucault (ed.) *Madness and Civilisation: A History of Insanity in the Age of Reason*. London: Tavistock.
BODEKER, H. (1997) 'Portrait of the Artist as a Young Herm': http://www.qis.net/~triea/hieke.html.
BRAIDOTTI, R. (1994) *Nomadic Subjects: Embodiment and Sexual Difference in Contemporary Feminist Theory*. New York: Columbia University Press.
BROWN, T.M. (1985) 'Descartes, Dualism, and Psychosomatic Medicine' in W.F. Bynum, R. Porter and M. Shepherd (eds) *The Anatomy of Madness, Essays in the History of Psychiatry*. London and New York: Tavistock.
BURKE, P. (1996) *Gender Shock: Exploding the Myths of Male and Female*. New York: Anchor Books.
BUTLER, J. (1990) *Gender Trouble: Feminism and the Subversion of Identity*. New York: Routledge.

BUTLER, J. (1993) *Bodies That Matter: On the Discursive Limits of 'Sex'*. New York: Routledge.

DEWHURST, C. and R. GORDON (1969) *The Intersexual Disorders*. London: Balliere, Tindall and Cassell.

EHRHARDT, A.A. (1985) 'Sexual Orientation After Prenatal Exposure To Exogenous Estrogen'. *Archives of Sexual Behaviour*. 14:57–77.

EPSTEIN, J. (1990) 'Either/Or – Neither/Both: Sexual Ambiguity and the Ideology of Gender'. *Genders*. 7:19–25.

FAUSTO-STERLING, A. (1993) 'The Five Sexes: Why Male and Female Are Not Enough'. *The Sciences*. March/April:20–24.

FEINBERG, L. (1996) Transgender Warriors. Boston: Beacon Press.

FOUCAULT, M. (ed.) (1965) *Madness and Civilisation: A History of Insanity in the Age of Reason*. London: Tavistock.

FOUCAULT, M. (1979) *The History of Sexuality: An Introduction. Vol.1*. New York: Vintage.

FOUCAULT, M. (1980) *Herculine Barbin: Being the Recently Discovered Memoirs of a 19th century French Intersexual*. New York: Pantheon.

FOUCAULT, M. (1989) *Foucault Live. Collected Interviews, 1961–1984*. S. Lotringer (ed) New York: Semiotext|e|.

FOUCAULT, M. (1997) 'The Abnormals' in P. Rabinow (ed.) *Ethics Subjectivity and Truth. The Essential Works of Michel Foucault*, 1954–1984; vol.1. 51–57. New York: The New Press.

GRIFFIN, J.E. and J.D. WILSON (1992) 'Disorders of Sexual Differentiation' in P.C. Walsh, A.B. Retik, T.A. Stamey and E.D. Vaughan (eds) *Campbells Urology*. Philadelphia: Saunders.

HAUSMAN, B. (1995) *Changing Sex: Transsexualism, Technology and the Idea of Gender*. Durham: Duke University Press.

HOLMES, M. (1995) 'Queer Cut Bodies: Intersexuality and Homophobia in Medical Practice':
http://cwis.use.edu/Library/QF/queer/papers/holmes.long.html.

KESSLER, S. 'The Medical Construction of Gender: Case Management of Intersexed Infants'. *Signs*. 16:3–26.

MILLER, J. (1993) *The Passion of Michel Foucault*. New York: Simon and Schuster.

MONEY, J. (1985) 'The Conceptual Neutering of Gender and the Criminalisation of Sex'. *Archives of Sexual Behaviour*. 14:279–291.

MONEY, J. and A.A. EHRHARDT (1972) *Man and Woman Boy and Girl: the Differentiation and Dimorphism of Gender Identity from Conception to Maturity*. Baltimore: Johns Hopkins University Press.

MONEY, J. and P. TUCKER (1976) *Sexual Signatures*. London: Harrap.

PAGON, R.A. (1987) 'Diagnostic Approach To The Newborn With Ambiguous Genitalia'. *Pediatric Clinics of North America*. 34:1019–1031.

PERLMUTTER, A.D. and M.D. REITELMAN (1992) 'Surgical Management of Intersexuality' in P.C. Walsh, A.B. Retik, T.A. Stamey and E.D. Vaughan (eds) *Campbell's Urology*. Philadelphia: Saunders.

RAYMOND, J. (1994) *The Transsexual Empire: The Making of the She-Male*. New York: Teachers College Press.

ROSE, N. (1996) *Inventing Ourselves*. Cambridge: Cambridge University Press.

SCHIEBINGER, L. (1988) *The Mind Has No Sex? Women in the Origins of Modern Science*. Cambridge, MASS: Harvard University Press.

SPANIER, B. (1991) ' "Lessons" from "Nature": Gender Ideology and Sexual Ambiguity in Biology' in J. Epstein and K. Straub (eds) *Body Guards: The Cultural Politics of Gender Ambiguity*. New York: Routledge.

STONE, S. (1991) 'The Empire Strikes Back: a Post-Transsexual Manifesto' in J. Epstein and K. Straub (eds) *Body Guards: The Cultural Politics of Gender Ambiguity*. New York: Routledge.

SZASZ, T. (1970) *The Manufacture of Madness*. New York: Harper and Row.

TRIEA, K. (1996) 'Untitled' : http: //www.qis.net/~triea/kira.html.

TURNER, B. (1987) *Medical Power and Social Knowledge*. London: Sage.

WILTON, K. (1997) 'The Third Sex'. *Next*. 54–58.

ZOLA, I.K. (1972) 'Medicine as an Institution of Social Control'. *Sociological Review*. 20:487–504.

11
Telling Body Transgendering Stories

Richard Ekins and Dave King

Introduction

This chapter re-frames our earlier work on cross-dressing and sex-changing in terms of the 'narrative turn' (Maines 1993; Maines and Ulmer 1993) in contemporary social science and cultural theory. Elsewhere, we have analyzed two decades of fieldwork, life history work, archival work and contact with several thousand cross-dressers and sex-changers in terms of a qualitative sociology and social psychology principally indebted to symbolic interactionism, historical analysis and grounded theory (for example, Ekins 1983; 1993; 1997; King 1981; 1993; Ekins and King 1996a; 1998). Here, we draw upon Plummer's work on 'sexual stories' (Plummer 1995; 1996) in order to consider contemporary transgender diversity in terms of a number of conceptually distinct 'narratives of transgendering' that we have discerned in our research into contemporary cross-dressing and sex-changing in Western Europe, North America, South Africa, Australia and New Zealand.

In Ekins (1997) it was found instructive to present a grounded theory of male cross-dressing and sex-changing in terms of the 'basic social process' of male femaling. Ekins argued that male femaling takes place in three major modes: those of body femaling, erotic femaling and gender femaling, and examined each mode and their interrelations, in terms of sex (the body), sexuality (genital feelings and responses), and gender (social and cultural accompaniments, like dress, posture, gesture, and speech style). He suggested, in some concluding comments to the book that 'systematic study of the particular relationship male femalers have with their bodies would provide valuable case material for the fast developing sociology of the body. There are signs that this is being grasped as regards "transsexuals" (Stone 1991; Lewins 1995). But what about other male femalers?' (Ekins 1997: 166). Anselm Strauss highlighted the point when in a foreword to *Male Femaling* he made the remark that 'not incidentally there are other implications in Ekins' work for the study of the human body, a topic on which a great many words, not all correct or profound, have been written in the last decade or so by psychologists and other behavioural scientists' (Ekins 1997: xiv–xv).

In this chapter, we seek to move forward some of the arguments about the human body introduced in *Male Femaling*. We do so in terms of, what in recent publications, we have referred to as 'transgendering' (Ekins and King 1996b; see also, Bolin 1994). The term 'transgender' has been used in four rather different senses. Virginia Prince pioneered the terms 'transgenderist' and 'transgenderal' to refer to people who lived full-time in the gender opposite to their biological sex, but did not seek sex/gender reassignment surgery (Prince 1976: 145). Richard Ekins established the Trans-Gender Archive in 1986. The term was chosen to provide an umbrella concept which avoided such medical categories as transsexual and transvestite; which included the widest possible range of transgender phenomena; and which took the sociological view that aspects of sex, sexuality and gender (not just gender), including the binary divide, all have socially constructed components. Not long afterwards, the 'transgender community' came to be used as an umbrella term to include transsexuals, transvestites, transgenderists, drag queens and so on, as well as (in some uses) to include their partners and friends and professional service providers.

Most recently, the term came to presuppose a radical edge – to refer to the transgressive nature of 'transgendering', as in Boswell's (1997: 54) view that, 'Transgender has to do with reinventing and realizing oneself more fully outside of the current systems of gender.' For us, now, 'transgendering' refers *both* to the idea of moving across (transferring) from one pre-existing gender category to the other (either temporarily or permanently), *and* to the idea of transcending or living 'beyond gender' altogether. This conceptualization has the advantage over that of 'male femaling', in that it may be seen as inclusive of both male femaling and 'female maling', and covers both those who transgender themselves and those who transgender others. Mindful of transgender diversities yet to be explored, we find Thom and More's (1998: 3) embracive and futuristic usage of 'transgender' particularly useful:

> 'Transgender' is used as a broad and inclusive term to describe the community of all self identified cross gender people whether intersex, transsexual men and women, cross dressers, drag kings and drag queens, transgenderists, androgynous, bi-gendered, third gendered or as yet unnamed gender gifted people.

Modes and processes of transgendering the body

As Shilling points out, the contemporary body is increasingly seen as 'a project which should be worked at and accomplished as part of an individual's self-identity' (1993: 5). With a relatively stable sense of being either a man or a woman, the gendered nature of the body is taken for granted and body projects will revolve around becoming and expressing oneself as a certain type of man or woman. For a number of people who are becoming increasingly vocal, however, the gendered nature of their body is not to be taken for granted and many embark on a project of transgendering it.

Drawing upon Plummer's work on sexual stories (1995), we focus in this paper on the various stories that are told of transgendering and particularly the role of the body in that process. Stories come in many forms but here our concern is with the personal narrative (as is Plummer's). A number of conceptually distinct contemporary transgendering body stories have emerged from our research. Here we group them into four main modes of body transgendering stories depending on their relationship to the male/female binary divide. In particular, we have categorized four types of body stories in terms of four modes of transgendering: 'migrating', 'oscillating', 'erasing' and 'transcending' – terms which reflect the core characteristics of each mode. Migrating body stories involve moving the body from one side of the binary divide to the other on a permanent basis (see also, Hirschauer 1997). Oscillating body stories are stories of moving backwards and forwards over the gender 'border', only temporarily resting on one side or the other. Erasing body stories are those in which the gender of the person erasing is expunged. Transcending body stories tell of moving beyond gender into a third space.

The nature of the binary gender divide is such that male and female bodies are deemed mutually exclusive. What ethnomethodologists refer to as the 'natural attitude' towards gender (Garfinkel 1967: 122–8; Kessler and McKenna 1978: 113–14) assumes that all human beings will belong to one of two discrete gender categories permanently determined on the basis of biologically ('naturally') given characteristics. This 'natural attitude' specifies that every body must be either male or female. A body cannot be both male and female, or neither. Not only are male and female held to be discrete categories, they are also held to be opposites.

Given the above, transgendering is a problematic process. Our data suggests that four core sub-processes are involved. The first sub-process involves 'substituting'. The person who is transgendering their body (with or without outside help) replaces the body parts (or the characteristics of those parts) which are associated with one gender, with those associated with the other. Thus a penis is replaced with a vagina; a flat chest is replaced with breasts; smooth skin replaces rough skin; no body hair replaces body hair; a short hair style is replaced with a long hair style and so on. The degree of substitution will depend on a number of factors such as the particular personal project of the individual, the personal circumstances, the availability and development of any technology and aids that may be used, and (where not covered by a relevant health care scheme) the financial resources to afford them. Where substituting is controlled in some way (that is, subject to medical or legal regulation), the question of a person's entitlement to the substitution may arise. An important dimension of substituting which we discuss further, in later sections, is the permanent or temporary nature of the substitution.

'Concealing', as the second sub-process, refers to the concealing or hiding of parts of the body which are seen to conflict with the intended gender display. It may involve hiding the Adam's apple; tucking the penis; binding the breasts. But this will depend on the actual bodily features; a male femaler with a prominent Adam's apple and heavy dark beard growth will have more concealing to do than a male femaler without these recognizably male characteristics. However, even male femalers with ideal body characteristics for their projects and who have undergone as much substitution as possible will remain chromosomally male and in some settings (for example, some sporting contests) this will require concealing.

For female malers, however, displaying male characteristics may be more important than concealing female ones if Kessler and McKenna (1978: 158–9) are right when they argue:

> In order for a female gender attribution to be made, there must be an absence of anything which can be construed as a 'male only' characteristic. In order for a male gender attribution to be made, the presence of at least one 'male' sign must be noticed, and one sign may be enough. This is because the basic categorizing 'schema is: *See someone as female only when you cannot see them as male*' (Kessler and McKenna 1978: 158).

In addition to concealing and displaying, body transgendering may involve 'implying' certain body parts. Because the body is usually apprehended in social interaction in its clothed form, it is possible to imply the gendered form of the body beneath. So, for example, males can wear breast forms inside a bra, or hip pads inside a panty girdle; females may place something in their underpants to imply the possession of a penis. Implying may be the only sub-process involved in the case of what Turkle (1997) calls 'virtual gender swapping' on internet discussion lists or, indeed, in any situation where interaction is not face to face such as that involving the telephone or written communication.

The fourth sub-process is 'redefining'. Whereas the meanings of substituting, concealing and implying are relatively easily grasped, particularly in relation to the acceptance of the binary divide, redefining is more subtle and multi-layered. At one level, the nature of the body and its parts may be redefined. The male to female transsexual may redefine her beard growth as facial hair. The penis may be redefined as a 'growth between the legs', as in 'I was a woman who had needed some corrective surgery. The growth was gone and my labia, clitoris and vagina were free' (Spry 1997: 152). More subtly, the self may be redefined, and insofar as the self is an embodied self, body transgendering will be coterminous with this self redefining. Finally, these kinds of self and body redefinitions may involve redefining the classificatory systems of gender. The transcending body story, for instance, seeks to subvert and/or move beyond the binary divide. In the process of this redefining, the selves, bodies and body parts within the redefined system of classification will take on new meanings.

We turn now to develop our mapping of contemporary transgender diversity in terms of the four major body transgendering stories, and their attendant sub-processes.

Migrating body stories

The Concise Oxford Dictionary (1995) defines migrating as 'moving from one place of abode to another especially in a different country'. In migrating body stories the 'place of abode' is the body and the reference to a different country suggests a move of some considerable significance. Many body migrants speak of starting a new life or of being reborn. While return may be possible, at its inception the journey is seen as one way; it is not expected that there will be any turning back. Migrating stories may be seen as part of a broader category of 'modernist tales'. Plummer (1995: 49–50) outlines the main elements of one major type of modernist story. It begins with tales of pain and suffering, usually in silence and secrecy. There follows a crucial turning point, a new understanding, and a perceived need for action which, in turn, leads to a transformation, a victory and triumph over suffering. Typical plots (forms) involve journeys, searches or quests to establish a home (finding oneself). Many of these elements are to be found in transsexual autobiographies and are clearly evident in the titles of some of them, as in *April Ashley's Odyssey* (Fallowell and Ashley 1982) and *What took you so long: a Girl's Journey to Manhood* (Thompson 1995). Prosser could be echoing Plummer when he writes: 'Reproduced in autobiography, transsexuality emerges as an archetypal story structured around shared tropes and fulfilling a particular narrative organization of consecutive stages: suffering and confusion; the epiphany of self-discovery; corporeal and social transformation/conversion; and finally the arrival "home" – the reassignment.' (Prosser 1998: 101)

In migrating body stories, the prominent sub-process of body transgendering is that of substituting, which may be variously progressive, problematic, rapid and extensive. Complete substitution (transformation) however is not possible except in fantasy. Modern medical interventions can accomplish a great deal especially if administered early in the life of the body. Even so, chromosomal and gonadal substitutions are not possible and after puberty certain aspects of the body such as height or skeletal shape may be beyond substitution. Therefore, transgendering the body will always involve other sub-processes. To varying degrees, depending on the individual's personal project, their physique and the particular setting, the sub-processes of concealing, implying and redefining will be in play. The following extracts give us an insight into some of the variations in the nature, pacing, extent and limitations of body substituting. Stella finds the effect of hormones on her developing bust to be unremarkable, until she stops taking them. Following her genital surgery, her body substituting proceeds more swiftly. As Stella puts it:

> I thought my bust wasn't developing very much until I was due to go into hospital and had to stop taking the hormones. And then I noticed that the reverse on my bust was very quick. I noticed that it did not disappear and that, I suppose, was the first time I realized just how much it had developed. I've been back on the hormones now for three weeks and its amazing how my bust has developed as much in those three weeks as it had in the three years before. Looking at myself in the nude, I think my body looks reasonably like a woman's body. I wouldn't say it looks like a Marilyn Monroe type of woman's body but I would say that it looks more like a

woman's body than a man's which is what matters. (Research interview)

Body substituting is altogether more speedy and dramatic, however, in the following account (written by Mark Rees for Ekins and King 1996a):

> The action of the hormones was almost immediate. A couple of weeks later I had my last period and within a month or so people began to notice a change in my voice. . . . Although the growth of my facial hair took much longer, I was surprised by the rapidity of the changes generally. . . . My superficial veins especially in the forearms became more obvious as the subcutaneous fat decreased. The decrease was most obvious around the breasts, hips and thighs. There was an increase in muscle development with a corresponding weight increase, redistribution and increase in body hair and clitoral enlargement. After six months I was able to live as a man. . . . I had been living as a man for nearly three years before undergoing a bilateral mastectomy. This was straightforward and relatively painless. . . . The hysterectomy and oophorectomy (removal of the ovaries) a year later was less easy; I developed a massive haematoma which necessitated blood transfusions. . . . A phalloplasty (the construction of a penis) is probably what most female-to-male transsexuals yearn for more than anything else, yet it is a most difficult, risky and unsatisfactory procedure. . . . Other areas of the body have to be mutilated in order to acquire tissue for the construction. Rather than enter the fraught area of phalloplasties, a number of female-to-male transsexuals have equipped themselves with very realistic looking prostheses, which enable them to urinate in a male fashion if desired. I would not use one myself – they are expensive and add bother to life, both in the fixing and in the cleaning.

We can discern three major variations of the migrating body story depending on the nature of the relationship between the 'gendered body' and the 'gendered mind': 'simple-matching migrating', where the migrator seeks to acquire a new body to fit his/her mind, which is thought of as being located in the 'wrong body'; 'coterminous migrating' where, to varying degrees, a new mind and new body emerge simultaneously; and, finally, 'mix-matching migrating', where the new body is sought, but the mind remains of the opposite sex to the new body.

The 'classic' transsexual story is a good example of the 'simple-matching' variation. Following is a recent example from the autobiography of Raymond Thompson (1995):

> The first time I was born, it was in a body which was other than male. By some cosmic mistake, as a budding human being I had somehow chosen the wrong body, or the wrong body had chosen me. I am a transsexual person, a man really. It took me more than thirty years to reach a stage where my body started to fit my identity as a man, but now there is no doubt about it. Here I am, well and truly the male that I have always known myself to be.

Coterminous migrating may have the same end result, but here the mind migrates with the body. An interview excerpt from Ekins (1997: 21–2) is illustrative:

> *Maria*: There are two sorts of transsexual. There are those like Helen, who see their appendage as an accident. They see themselves as women, who have some mistake as regards their bodies. And then there are the other sort, who know they are men, but still want to be women.
> *Researcher*: Isn't that a bid odd? Going through the change, but still thinking you're male?
> *Maria*: Well, I don't know. As I keep on with this, I find that I'm like stripping away what I have learned in being male. It's like peeling away the layers of an onion.
> *Researcher*: So, what is underneath?
> *Maria*: I don't know, but I'm finding out. All I can say is that whenever I act the female role, I feel more like myself. It might be that underneath all the layers is a female identity.

A final, and so far little discussed, variant, is where the body migrates from one sex to another, but the mind remains in its original sex (mix-matching migrating). Ronnie did not like living as a man. He underwent electrolysis on his facial and body hair. He ingested female hormones and had breast implant surgery. He adopted feminine intonation in his voice. After such body and gender transgendering he became 'Carole' and was able to 'pass' as a woman in most settings. Indeed, providing he 'tucked' his penis, he was able to share a bed with 'other' females without them suspecting he was other than the female he appeared. He did, however, retain his penis, and notwithstanding his extensive use of female hormones was able to maintain an erection and experience male orgasm. He made attachments to a number of lesbian women and once he felt that they would not be put off by his disclosure, he told them of what he referred to as his 'she-male' identity. By no means were all the self-identified lesbian women put off sexual relations with him by his disclosure. A number of Ronnie's lesbian partners engaged in penetrative intercourse with him, with Ronnie taking the 'masculine' active and aggressive role. In his/her identification as a 'she male', Ronnie/Carole did not regard him/herself as either a woman with a penis (a phallic woman), or a male to female transsexual. Rather, he/she perceived of him/herself as 'a man in a woman's body'. (Research interview)

There is no necessary congruity between sex, sexuality and gender in body migrating stories. Many body migrators identify as gay or lesbian. Some do not display in the clothes of their new 'sex'. However, where maximum substituting takes place sexuality and gender substituting will variously precede, accompany, or follow the body migrating, and the migrating will be permanent. The story of Gail Hill (see Ekins 1997: 146–54), a coterminous migrator, is illustrative. Gail identifies as a 'transsexual/new woman'. Post-surgically, she views herself as having a female body to match her female identity. She has a steady boyfriend with whom she has regular sexual intercourse (sexuality). Her presentation of self is as an attractive woman in her 30s (gender display). Having been post-operative for a number of years, we asked her to write about how she experienced her body. Her response illustrates the maximum substituting, migrating body story, and is not dissimilar to many stories that we might have been given by many genetic women who accept unproblematically the binary divide, and the congruity between sex, sexuality and gender. She writes:

Like many women, there are areas that I would wish to be improved on. I could do with a bit more fat on my hips and a bit less around my waist, though my 38–29–35 figure is more than acceptable. My hair is long and curly, not quite natural blonde, and I wish it were a little straighter, though some women with straight hair wish theirs was more like mine. My skin, though fairly smooth is beginning to show my thirty nine and a bit years. Perhaps I should be sterner and not smile or laugh so much. The lines round my eyes give it all away. By far the hardest aspect that I struggle to cope with is the continued need for some electrolysis to facial hair, the only remaining physical reminder of my previous life. Moving rapidly on from the least favourable bit of me to some more enjoyable areas. My breasts, though enhanced with a few ounces of silicone, evidenced by the two almost imperceptible lines under the curve of each, are much more pleasing. (Personal communication 1998)

Oscillating body stories

While migrating body stories for the most part entail a one-way journey, oscillating body stories, in contrast, entail moving to and fro between male and female polarities, across and between the binary divide. The oscillator has a return ticket although the frequency of the journey and the length of stay can vary, depending on the transgenderer's social cir-cumstances and his/her personal projects. Some may spend a few hours every week on the other side of the divide; others may only manage the journey every few months but they might be able to stay for a week or more; still others may spend their working day as male and the rest of the time as female. There are oscillators who oscillate (largely in fantasy) minute to minute, even second to second. Some may, like the couples who retire to their favourite holiday destination, eventually decide to buy a one way ticket and migrate. Like migrating stories, oscillating stories may be seen as modernist tales. In oscillating stories there are elements of silent suffering, discovery and coming to terms with being different; but these elements are less evident than in the migrating stories. In oscillating stories, we find less material on 'being' – on iden-tity and relationships; and more detail about 'doing' – on excursions 'over the gender border'. As with migrating stories the binary divide is accepted. Medical help is not enlisted, although other people may play a part in facilitating the excursions.

The main sub-processes involved in oscillating body stories are imply-ing, concealing and redefining. Except in fantasy, substituting is mainly, but not entirely, restricted to reversible substitutions and to those which can be concealed such as, in males, removing body hair. Oscillating body stories will typically involve much implying: the wearing of wigs, the use of padded bras and padded girdles; the wearing of false moustaches and beards and something in the underpants to imply the possession of a penis.

One common oscillating story is that of the male transvestite. Unlike the migrating story, it is rare to find these in commercially published autobiographies (Pepper 1982, provides one exception). Often found in older medical case reports and occasionally in magazine feature articles, the most detailed published stories are found in the newsletters of transvestite organizations such as the Beaumont Society. The following examples (Pauline, Brenda, Helena, John and Peter) from research interviews illustrate some of the variation.

Pauline is 41, divorced and living alone. She has a well paid job and lives in a very private, moderately expensive flat. She never cross-dresses in public, so Pauline spends as much time as she can in her flat, dressed as a woman, only leaving it for necessary work or shopping trips. She buys her large collection of women's clothes through mail order catalogues, and buys her wigs, padded girdles and silicone breasts from a specialist mail order transvestite supplier. Her body is kept free of hair by depilating, shaving or plucking. She was clean shaven at the time of interview, and was keenly experimenting with her new electrolysis machine.

Whereas Pauline's body transgendering is known only to herself, Brenda's wife knows and tolerates her husband's cross-dressing. Brenda (38) initiated her wife into her activities early in their marriage and was free to buy women's clothes or to borrow her wife's. Before the children were born and while they were small, there was also no lack of opportunity; if she was careful not to annoy her wife by cross-dressing every day. She could spend evenings (perhaps twice a week) cross-dressed, after the children were in bed. As the children grew up, however, this was no longer possible since neither partner wished the children to be aware of what was going on. Brenda's body femaling was limited to concealing and implying. Once, when her wife spent a fortnight with the children at the grandparents' house, Brenda had shaved off her body hair but although she would have liked to do this more often she did not do so as she thought it would upset her wife.

Helena, on the other hand, participates in a number of social worlds within which she wishes to present different aspects of her body femaling, while presenting a male body in other settings. Helena is 35, single and living alone. She advertises her services as a transvestite prostitute in contact magazines and for these engagements presents as a lookalike of 1940s movie stars. She maintains an hourglass figure with the use of a corset and a padded bra placed over her chest carefully taped to create cleavage. Helena is also a member of a transvestite group that meets to cross-dress, principally in leather fetish gear. For this group, she adopts a punk image and redefines her slim male body as an anorexic girl's body. As a male, Helena works as a teacher in a boys' secondary school, involving herself in cricket coaching in the summer months. The extent of her body substituting is limited, primarily by her need to avoid possible detection in this work setting. In consequence, she never removes the hair from her hands and that on the first two inches of her forearm and throughout the cricket season leaves all her arm hair intact so that she can roll up her sleeves while bowling. In her cross-dressing, she makes a virtue out of necessity and extols the virtues of gloves – 1940s and elegant-style for her work as a prostitute; 1980s and fetish-style for her punk look, and, in both cases, elbow length for the summer months.

In the above examples, substituting is limited by the need to return to the male side of the divide at some point. Pauline appears as a man in the relatively impersonal public world of work and is, therefore, able to substitute in intimate ways which will not be outwardly visible. Brenda, however, also has to be a man in the private intimate relationship with her wife and her body is therefore more open to scrutiny. Helena substitutes differently according to the setting and time of the year. All, in different settings, are needing or wanting to present as men but also as masculine, heterosexual non-transvestite men. Where this is not the case, substituting is likely to be more extensive and visible, as, for instance, where the oscillator is known to be a drag queen prominent in gay and transvestite settings.

Fantasy rapid oscillating body transgendering provides particularly illuminating illustrative material on the complex interrelations between sex, sexuality and gender. John lives and works as a male. At home, he lives with his female partner who sees herself as heterosexual. Before John joins his partner in bed at night, he applies a toner and a hormone bust enlargement cream to his nipples (preparatory substituting). He is not sure that the cream is leading to breast development, but it is making his nipples more sensitive. Occasionally he supplements this regimen with a course of hormone pills that he has acquired from a prostitute he visits. These do lead to breast tissue enlargement and sensitivity (embryonic substituting). He joins his wife in bed. As he touches her body he feels heterosexually aroused and with his penis erect enters his wife. For this period he identifies as a man with a man's body. In due time his wife climaxes. To maintain his erection, he now oscillates into female mode. He disavows his male body and 'his' penis becomes his wife's. He now has his wife's vagina (fantasy substituting). When he climaxes, it is, he feels, a female orgasm. His pre-come is 'her' lubrication. His ejaculatory fluid is his wife's. With intercourse over, his male self slowly re-emerges.

In John's case his body transgendering leads to what he fantasizes are female sexual responses. Indeed, his fantasy body transgendering is a pre-condition of sustained sexual arousal and ejaculation. For others, like Peter, gender femaling (that is, actual cross-dressing) is a precondition of sexual arousal and ejaculation. Peter can only make love with his partner when he is cross-dressed (gender femaling), and although his partner does not encourage Peter's cross-dressing, she goes along with it rather than lose him. Peter identifies as a transvestite with transsexual leanings. He has never had contact with medical professionals. Rather, his exploration of cross-dressing sub-cultures has led him to the view that his 'oscillating' lifestyle is his best compromise. He has no interest in politicizing his position, and he keeps as private as possible his transgendering practices and aspirations: an oscillation between the boundaried dual worlds separated by the binary divide.

Erasing body stories

Migrating body stories are commonplace in the medical literature. They have been supplemented by a steady stream of migrating autobiographies. Oscillating body stories are commonplace in the sub-cultural literature; rather less so in the medical literature and infrequent in mainstream literature. The acknowledgement of what we are terming 'erasing' stories is in its infancy, however. In the medical, social sciences and mainstream literature it is an almost entirely hidden story.

Those with male bodies seek to expunge their maleness and eliminate in themselves the existence of a binary divide. Similarly, but conversely, with female erasers.[1] There is, of course, a literature on the eunuch: the castrated man. Our research to date, however, has focused on contemporary Western erasing, in particular, on stories of contemporary male femaling 'sissies' and, most recently, on life history work with 'third gender' 'gender-freeing' writer and activist, Christie Elan-Cane. There are two principal variants of the erasing story depending on the position of the eraser in relation to the traditional version of the binary male/female divide. In one variant, erasing self-consciously buttresses the traditional version of the binary male/female divide for all males and females who are not erasing/being erased. In the other variant, the eraser considers the binary divide a source of oppression and seeks a modification of the binary gender system which will enable those 'without gender' to live 'gender-free' lives.

Illustrative of the first variant are the writings of Debra Rose (1993a; 1993b; 1994; 1995). Rose's writings are a blend of fact and fiction. They do, however, provide a particularly systematic account of one major sissy maid lifestyle and a lifestyle that has a considerable following. Many of our sissy informants tell us that her journal *Sissy Maid*

Quarterly (SMQ: 1994–1996) 'plugs into' their innermost thoughts, fantasies and wishes with astonishing insight and accuracy. We know of at least one sissy who educated his mistress into the SMQ vision by sending her each copy as it came out. Between them, mistress and maid then set about systematic sissification. In Rose's world, being male involves being active, virile and – by virtue of maleness – attracted to females; being female involves being attractive to males and finding males attractive because of their virility. However, Rose's view of the binary divide is given the modern twist that recognizes that women are increasingly successful in the world of work and, in consequence are ill-suited – and, in any event, have no time – for housework and the traditional role of the housewife. It is here that the sissy maid comes into his own. He is an ineffectual male quite unable to compete for a female's affections in the conventional way. Rather, he is best fitted to take on the role of the housemaid and do the work previously done by the traditional housewife, and before that, by the various maids in service. To be best fitted for this role, his already weak maleness must be systematically expunged (erased). To effect this, the maid must be 'trained' – most usually, by a training mistress, prior to service; or, less frequently, the training will occur in-service. Alternatively, the trainee may be sent to a Training Academy.

While the details of the trainings vary, the *sine qua non* of all of them is systematic erasing. There is much concealing (of attributes of masculinity). There is much redefining (sissies dress in effeminate and feminine attire *not* in order to cross the binary divide, but to further their emasculating). Such substituting and implying as there is, is co-opted in the service of erasing. The following is a typical trajectory. We will highlight major phases, with particular reference to body erasing, and the interrelations between sex, sexuality and gender.

Phase 1 – Initial body erasing: the sissy's body will be stripped of his body hair, including his pubic hair, giving him a pre-pubescent look. He will be made to wear a gaff – 'a small, tight, panty-like item whose sole purpose is to firmly pin a sissy's genitals back between his legs under his bottom, where they belong' (Rose 1994: 36). 'When properly gaffed, a sissy's front exhibits the smooth, girlish appearance one expects from a sissy' (Rose 1994: 36).

Phase 2 – Initial gender erasing: his male body image now erased, the sissy must wear gender neutral attire. To erase masculinity, these clothes will be variously effeminate or feminine. In particular, his now shaven body will be introduced to feminine and sensual fabrics designed to give him sensual pleasure (re-direction of sexuality to himself – solitary narcissism). The clothes are designed to erase his masculinity, *not* to create a sense of himself as a woman, as in oscillation.

Phase 3 – Becoming a maid: the sissy will now be issued with clothing – a maid's uniform designed to cement his role as a maid in service to his mistress. Not only is he being increasingly neutered, but his passivity and subservience is being reinforced. He will be initiated into the tasks of keeping house: cleaning, polishing and cooking, and taking care of his mistress's personal wardrobe and boudoir.

Phase 4 – Erasing sexuality: the sissy's tightly fitted gaff will make erections impossible. However, the sissy will be permitted to masturbate when in his bed alone at night (re-direction of sexuality). His single-bed will be fitted with (preferably pink) rubber sheets. They are easy to clean, a constant reminder of his sissiness, and are fitted with the intended outcome that eventually the sissy will, in effect, be having a sexual relationship with his sheets, as in: 'I always get "in the mood" by rubbing myself against my rubber bottom sheet. Although I sometimes think of my cute gym instructor when I do it, more and more I don't really think of anyone at all. Rather than think about a girl, I like to concentrate on how great the slick, wet rubber sheet feels!' (Rose 1993b: 42)

Phase 5 – Mistress's little helper: with all semblance of masculinity fast evaporating, the sissy now gains pleasure from being the 'perfect little helper': 'My world is now a gentle, soft, and scented one in which my duties are perfectly and strictly defined. And I am proud of my growing abilities as a cook, seamstress, housekeeper, and personal maid-servant. The approval of my mistress means much to me now, and I bask in any small compliment or favor she bestows upon me.' (Sissy Jennie 1994: 21)

Phase 6 – Vicarious living: with his sexuality redirected and his initiation into worlds of female sex, sexuality and gender maximized by his personal relationship with his mistress, the sissy is now prepared for a life which is lived vicariously through his mistress. He becomes privy to the intimacies of her relationships and will eventually act as a maid to her boyfriends, and later, if appropriate, her husband.

Phase 7 – Consolidating erasing: many mistresses put their sissies on a light dose of female hormones. With constant gaffing, the re-direction of sexuality, and reduced libido, the sissy's sexuality becomes increasingly diffused over his entire body. The pleasure he obtains from serving his mistress, living vicariously through her and feeling the fit and texture of his feminine clothing all come to compensate for, and, indeed, be preferred to, any lingering regrets at his lost masculinity. In due course, he may cease to masturbate. He becomes an increasingly asexual 'neither male nor female' maid in service.

In marked contrast to Rose's vision of erasing is that of writer and activist Christie Elan-Cane. Christie is the first to pioneer publicly 'per'[2] particular 'third gender' body erasing. Christie, a biological female, felt 'in the wrong body' from per earliest days. With the onset of puberty, per development of breasts and menstruation was particularly distressing. As Christie (Elan-Cane 1997: 1) puts it: 'I was never able to come to terms with "womanhood"'. I had the body of a woman and therefore I was considered by everyone to be a woman and I was repelled. I was disgusted by the physical changes to my body when I started to develop at puberty.' Never identifying as transsexual, Christie eventually found a surgeon who would remove per breasts and, some years later, per womb. Now at ease with per body, Christie began to identify as 'neither male, nor female': 'a third gender person'. Although open to the possibility of further body erasing – having per ovaries removed, for instance, for Christie, 'everything fell into place' once surgery was completed. Whereas Christie had flirted with a lesbian identity prior to surgery, now Christie found perself attracted to men, provided they saw per as being a third gender person. Per sexual partner is now a male who relates to per as third gender – neither male, nor female. Christie wears androgynous 'gender-free' clothes – mostly black 'neither male, nor female' 'shirts'; black trouser suits – a sort of contemporary Chairman Mao suit, and keeps per head meticulously shaven – all appropriate to per 'third gender' identification, following per body erasing. Having erased all undesired vestiges of per femaleness and femininity, Christie has no need of further concealing, redefining, substituting or implying.

Secure in per personal erasing, Christie has increasingly turned per attention to publicizing per position, with the intention of enabling a space to be provided within a bi-polarized gender system, for 'third genders' like perself. Initial steps include campaigning for the use of a non-gender specific form of address ('per' – derived from person; Pr as a title to replace Mr or Mrs), and the inclusion of the gender-free in equal rights legislation (Elan-Cane 1997;1998). In Christie's view: 'there is no reason why there should be two diametrically opposed genders nor is there any reason why gender should exist at all' (Elan-Cane 1998: 7) and, in these senses, per position might be seen as a subversive one.

However, it is not per present intention to seek to undermine the binary divide, an approach which Christie regards as both unrealistic and impracticable. Rather, Christie seeks social legitimacy for perself and others like per (Personal communication 1998).

Transcending body stories

In recent years there have emerged a number of body stories which we focus on here under the general title of 'transcending body stories'. Despite her chapter title 'Transcending and Transgendering: Male-to-Female Transsexuals, Dichotomy and Diversity', Bolin (1994) does not discuss the meaning of the word 'transcending'. We have chosen the term because of its idea of 'going beyond'. In these stories, while the body may be transgendered by means of substituting, concealing and implying, as in the other modes, the meaning of this is fundamentally redefined. They are, in Stone's (1991: 295) words, 'disruptive to the accepted discourses of gender'. In these stories, the whole process of transgendering is radically redefined by rendering problematic the binary gender divide. Further, these stories go beyond the framing of transgendering within the medical categories of transvestism and transsexualism.

Transcending body stories are stories whose time has come. They are a part of what Plummer calls 'the rise of the "late modernist sexual story"' (1995: 133) and they share their characteristics with stories in other fields. These stories are not replacing modernist ones but rather coexist with them. Plummer identifies three main attributes of late modern stories: first, stories of authority give way to participant stories; second, stories of essence and truth are giving way to stories of difference; and third stories of the 'categorically clear' give way to stories of deconstruction. We can discern these elements in transcending stories as medical authority is questioned, diversity is celebrated and the certainty of sex and gender categories is called into question.

The style of the transcending story is also very different from the other three major modes. Transcending body stories are not chronological personal narratives. The cover 'blurb' for perhaps the best known transcending story, Kate Bornstein's *Gender Outlaw* (1994) describes it as 'a manifesto, a memoir and a performance all rolled into one'. In fact the memoirs are principally used as a vehicle to make questionable our 'common sense' assumptions about what it means to be a man or a woman. Similarly, in *Transgender Warrior* (1996), Leslie Feinberg uses his own personal experiences to lead us through a transgender history and to outline his political philosophy. In *Read My Lips* (1997), Wilchins mixes together personal experiences with current gender theories and transgender politics. The linearity of the modern story is replaced by 'a little bit from here, a little bit from there. Sort of a cut-and-paste thing.' (Bornstein 1994: 3)

In contrast to migrating stories – modernist tales of suffering and survival – these transcending stories tell bold tales of 'transgender warriors' fighting a war against an enemy and for a people. The enemy is seen as our cultural rules concerning gender, such as those discerned by Garfinkel (1967) in his study of Agnes. The people who are being fought for are the members of a broadly defined transgender community. A noteworthy feature of the new transcending personal narratives is that they convey a strong sense of being a part of a community, a movement organized around political action. In earlier migrating narratives the uniqueness of the story is often emphasized, as for instance, in Cowell (1954) and Morris (1975). When previous 'body migrants' are mentioned in these stories, they are depicted as 'remarkable', rare and isolated individuals (Cowell 1954: 122–31).

Interwoven with this is the emergence of a trans identity which is both permanent and 'out' (Bolin 1994: 472–3). In migrating body stories, successfully claiming transsexual status is necessary in order to become entitled to hormonal and surgical body change, but it hardly functions as a central and permanent identity. The identity is female or male: transsexual denotes a temporary status in which the body is out of line with the identity. In oscillating body stories, 'transvestite' may be a self-defined, more or less permanent identity, but it has largely been a secret one and its pathological connotations hardly a source of pride.

In the 1990s transgender has emerged as an identity in itself, an alternative to an unambiguous male or female identity and one of which to be proud. As Bolin (1994: 473) puts it: 'it is akin to a new kind of ethnicity'. So now, for some people, 'the experience of crossed or transposed gender is a strong part of their gender identity; being out of the closet is part of that expression' (Nataf 1996: 16).

These stories then tell of battles against violence and discrimination and for various rights. The 1995 International Bill of Gender Rights (reprinted in Feinberg 1996: 171–5) claims that 'all human beings have the right to define their own gender identity . . . to free expression of their self-defined gender identity (and) to change their bodies cosmetically, chemically, or surgically, so as to express a self-defined gender identity' (1996: 172–3). This is, of course, contrary to the dominant view that the chemical and surgical alteration of the body is not a person's right but is only to be undertaken if authorized by an appropriate medical professional. The Harry Benjamin International Gender Dysphoria Association (1998), for instance, states in its *The Standards of Care for Gender Identity Disorder* that, 'Hormones are not to be administered simply because patients demand them' (33) and 'Surgical treatment for a person with a gender identity disorder [GID] is not merely another elective procedure. Typical elective procedures only involve a private mutually consenting contract between a suffering person and a technically competent surgeon. Surgeries for GID are to be undertaken only after a comprehensive evaluation by a qualified mental health professional' (1998: 37).

In migrating body stories, a 'pathological state' (gender dysphoria) is dealt with by means of a medically assisted and controlled migration across the gender divide. Transcending body stories question the idea of pathology in a manner analogous to the way in which gays challenged the disease status of homosexuality. If there is no disease, then genital surgery and other body gender alterations may be a matter of personal choice. As Califia (1997: 224) puts it: 'transsexuals are becoming informed consumers of medical service'. She draws a parallel with the S/M view on body modification writing of the 'individual's right to own his or her own body, and make whatever temporary or permanent changes to that body the individual pleases. . . . A new sort of transgendered person has emerged, one who approaches sex reassignment with the same mindset that they would obtaining a piercing or a tattoo.'

That some doctors may be prepared to see themselves as providing a service for their transgendered clients rather than diagnosing and treating them is evident in the work by Bockting and Coleman (1992). They use the term 'gender dysphoric client' rather than patient throughout. Such clients they claim 'often have a more ambiguous gender identity and are more ambivalent about a gender role transition than they initially admit' (1992: 143). Their treatment programme, they say, allows their clients to 'discover and express their unique identity' (1992: 143) and 'allows for individuals to identify as neither man nor woman, but as someone whose identity transcends the culturally sanctioned dichotomy' (1992: 144).

The idea of the 'gender outlaw' shifts our attention to another way in which transcending stories go beyond our conventional understandings. This idea points to the position of trans people as located somewhere outside the spaces customarily offered to men and women, as people who are beyond the laws of gender. So the assumption that there are only two (opposite) genders is opened up to scrutiny. Instead, it is suggested that there is the possibility of a 'third' space outside the gender dichotomy. Stone (1991: 295) argues that the transsexual speaks, 'from outside the boundaries of gender, beyond the constructed oppositional nodes which have been predefined as the only positions from which discourse is possible'. Gender, in this story becomes something which is much more complex than a dichotomy, a series of categories, or a continuum. Boswell (1997: 54) argues that the notion of transgender, 'refers to the transgressing of gender norms, or being freely gendered, or transcending gender altogether in order to become more fully human'.

Kate Bornstein advocates 'gender fluidity', which is 'the ability to freely and knowingly become one or many of a limitless number of genders, for any length of time, at any rate of change. Gender fluidity recognizes no borders or rules of gender' (Bornstein 1994: 52). There is an element of impermanence here similar to that in oscillating stories, although oscillating is not an appropriate term because it implies a movement between two given points which transcending stories question. The critique of the binary gender divide and the ideas of gender fluidity and impermanence would seem to rule out surgical and hormonal substituting because of their permanent and binary nature. Bornstein does indeed argue that the demand for surgery is largely a result of the 'cultural genital imperative' (1994: 119), although she does not advocate the withdrawal of surgical facilities.

Being 'out' is also important to this aspect of the transcending story. To the extent that the transvestite or transsexual passes as a person of the other gender, and to the extent that their transgendering remains a matter of 'closed awareness' (Glaser and Strauss 1964), the 'fact' of two invariant genders remains unquestioned. As Stone (1991: 295) puts it, 'authentic experience is replaced by a particular kind of story, one that supports the old constructed positions.'

A recent variant of the transcending story is being told by those people born with intersexed bodies. As Fausto-Sterling (1993) states, 'Hermaphrodites have unruly bodies. They do not fall naturally into a binary classification; only a surgical shoehorn can put them there.' And this is exactly what has happened: during this century, intersexed bodies have been surgically and hormonally fitted into one or the other gender category. Now, some people with intersexed bodies who were neither aware nor able to control such surgical and hormonal intervention, are questioning those practices and demanding the right to determine if, when and how their bodies should be altered. These intersex stories contain many of the elements of those transcending stories considered above: the emphasis on personal choice, the challenging of medical authority, the acceptance of bodies which are not unambiguously male or female.

So what this amounts to then is a recognition of a wide diversity of gender expression and of gendered bodies. As Denny (1995: 1) asserts:

> With the new way of looking at things, suddenly all sorts of options have opened up for transgendered people: living full-time without genital surgery, recreating in one gender role while working in another, identifying as neither gender, or both, blending character-istics of different genders in new and creative ways, identifying as genders and sexes heretofore undreamed of – even designer genitals do not seem beyond reason.

Conclusions and implications

In this chapter we have proposed a number of categorizations that might provide the foundations for a conceptual framework for a com-prehensive sociology of body transgendering stories. In particular, we have introduced four major modes, or styles, of body transgendering: those of migrating, oscillating, erasing and transcending, and presented them in terms of contemporary body transgendering stories. We con-sidered four major sub-processes of transgendering the body in terms of each story, with reference to a number of illustrations taken from diverse sources: our own field work, the sub-cultural literature, and the writings of contemporary cultural theorists. Throughout the chapter, our emphasis has been on illustrating the interrelations between the four sub-processes of body transgendering identified, and between sex, sexuality and gender, with particular reference to the binary male/ female divide.

In view of the infant state of the new interdisciplinary field of trans-gender studies, we considered it important to focus initially on personal narrative. However, even at the level of the personal narrative, much work remains to be done. We have introduced major variants within each mode of body transgendering. Many variants were ignored, however; some, only touched upon. Intersex stories, for instance, are stories that promise to be of increasing significance, both personally and politically. Much work remains to be done on fleshing out the dimensions and properties of the sub-processes introduced, and the full complexity of their interrelations.

As regards the binary divide, our categorizations may be used to illuminate the extent to which contemporary body transgendering styles tend to reinforce or subvert that divide. Migrating and oscillating tend to shore up the divide. Transcending tends to deconstruct the divide. Erasing is janus faced: it deconstructs insofar as it creates a 'third space' or 'gender-free' zone; it shores up, insofar as it buttresses the binary divide for all who are not personally erasing. Public visibility is clearly a major factor in potential subversion. Insofar as erasing body stories are largely private, hidden and neglected stories, they have yet to make an impact in the public domain. Similarly, to a large extent the same may be said of oscillating stories. Although much more widespread, they remain essentially confined to private practices, the sub-cultural literature, and the 'human interest' stories of women's magazines. Transcending body stories are becoming increasingly vociferous, sophisticated and politically astute. It remains to be seen to what extent they are harbingers of a new order, or simply the outpourings of a disenfranchized minority.

Acknowledgements

We wish to thank the many transgendered people who have so readily shared their time and thoughts with us, particularly those referred to in the text of this chapter. Thanks are due to the Sociology Research Unit of Assessment at the University of Ulster, for financial support. Special thanks go to Dr Wendy Saunderson for her constructive comment throughout the preparation of this chapter. Parts of this chapter appeared in R. Ekins and D. King, 'Towards a Sociology of Transgendered Bodies', *Sociological Review*, 47, 1999:580–602.

Notes

1. In a denser theorization, 'erasing' might be identified as a sub-process (eliminating aspects of maleness or femaleness, masculinity or femininity) variously present in all the modes of transgendering, but particularly prominent in what would then be termed 'negating', to denote the mode of transgendering in which those with male (or female) bodies seek both to nullify their maleness (or femaleness) and deny in themselves the existence of a binary divide.
2. For Christie Elan-Cane: 'To gain validity and social legitimacy it is imperative that the Third Gender has a proper title that is non-gender specific and a

correct form of address.' Christie's own preference rejects 'his' or 'her' for 'per', derived from 'person' (Elan-Cane 1998: 3–4).

Bibliography

BOCKTING, W.O. and E. COLEMAN (1992) 'A Comprehensive Approach to the Treatment of Gender Dysphoria', in W.O. Bockting and E. Coleman (eds) *Gender Dysphoria: Interdisciplinary Approaches in Clinical Management*. New York: Haworth Press.

BOLIN, A. (1994) 'Transcending and Transgendering: Male-to-Female Transsexuals, Dichtomy and Diversity', in G. Herdt (ed.) *Third Sex, Third Gender: Beyond Dimorphism in Culture and History*. New York: Zone Books.

BORNSTEIN, K. (1994) *Gender Outlaw: On Men, Women And The Rest Of Us*. London: Routledge.

BOSWELL, H. (1997) 'The Transgender Paradigm Shift Toward Free Expression', in B. Bullough, V.L. Bullough and J. Elias (eds) *Gender Blending*. New York: Prometheus Books.

CALIFIA, P. (1997) *Sex Changes: The Politics of Transgenderism*. San Francisco: Cleis Press.

Concise Oxford Dictionary of Current English, 9th edn (1995) Oxford: Oxford University Press.

COWELL, R. (1954) *Roberta Cowell's Story: An Autobiography*. London: Heinemann.

DENNY, D. (1995) 'The Paradigm Shift is Here'. *Aegis News*, 4:1.

EKINS, R. (1983) 'The Assignment of Motives as a Problem in the Double Hermeneutic: the Case of Transvestism and Transsexuality', paper for the Sociological Association of Ireland Conference, Wexford, Ireland.

EKINS, R. (1993) 'On Male Femaling: A Grounded Theory Approach to Cross-Dressing and Sex-Changing'. *Sociological Review*. 41:1–29.

EKINS, R. (1997) *Male Femaling: a Grounded Theory Approach to Cross-Dressing and Sex-Changing*. London: Routledge.

EKINS, R. and D. KING (eds) (1996a) *Blending Genders: Social Aspects of Cross-Dressing and Sex-Changing*. London: Routledge.

EKINS, R. and D. KING (1996b) 'Is the Future Transgendered?' in A. Purnell (ed.) *Proceedings of the 4th International Gender Dysphoria Conference*. London: Gender Trust, pp. 97–103.

EKINS, R. and D. KING (1998) 'Blending Genders: Contributions to the Emerging Field of Transgender Studies', in D. Denny (ed.) *Current Concepts in Transgender Identity*. New York: Garland Publishing.

ELAN-CANE, C. (1997) 'Prepared Speech for Cybergender Discussion', Transgender Film and Video Festival, London.

ELAN-CANE, C. (1998) 'A World Without Gender', talk for the Third International Congress on Sex and Gender, Exeter College, Oxford.

FALLOWELL, D. and A. ASHLEY (1982) *April Ashley's Odyssey*. London: Jonathan Cape.

FAUSTO-STERLING, A. (1993) 'The Five Sexes: Why Male And Female Are Not Enough'. *Sciences*, 33:2, 20–5.

FEINBERG, L. (1996) *Transgender Warriors: Making History from Joan of Arc to Dennis Rodman*. Boston: Beacon Press.

GARFINKEL, H. (1967) *Studies in Ethnomethodology.* Englewood Cliffs, NJ: Prentice Hall.

GLASER, B.G. and A.L. STRAUSS (1964) 'Awareness Contexts and Social Interaction'. *American Sociological Review*, 29, 669–79.

Harry Benjamin International Gender Dysphoria Assocation (1998) *The Standards of Care for Gender Identity Disorders – Fifth Version*, Dusseldorf: Symposion.

HIRSCHAUER, S. (1997) 'The Medicalization of Gender Migration'. *International Journal of Transgenderism*, 1,1, http//www.symposion.com/ijt/ijtc0104.htm

KESSLER, S.J. and W. MCKENNA (1978) *Gender: An Ethnomethodological Approach.* New York: Wiley.

KING, D. (1981) 'Gender Confusions: Psychological and Psychiatric Conceptions of Transvestism and Transsexuality', in K. Plummer (ed.) *The Making of the Modern Homosexual.* London: Hutchinson.

KING, D. (1993) *The Transvestite and the Transsexual: Public Categories and Private Identities.* Aldershot: Avebury.

LEWINS, F. (1995) *Transsexualism in Society: A Sociology of Male-To-Female Transsexuals*, Melbourne: Macmillan Press – now Palgrave.

MAINES, D.R. (1993) 'Narrative's Moment and Sociology's Phenomena: Toward a Narrative Sociology'. *Sociological Quarterly*, 34:17–38.

MAINES, D.R. and J.T. ULMER (1993) 'The Relevance of Narrative for Interactionist Thought', in N.K. Denzin (ed.) *Studies in Symbolic Interaction.* Vol. 14. Greenwich, Connecticut: JAI Press.

MORRIS, J. (1975) *Conundrum.* London: Coronet Books.

NATAF, Z.I. (1996) *Lesbians Talk Transgender.* London: Scarlet Press.

PEPPER, J. (1982) *A Man's Tale.* London: Quartet Books.

PLUMMER, K. (1995) *Telling Sexual Stories: Power, Change and Social Worlds.* London: Routledge.

PLUMMER, K. (1996) 'Intimate Citizenship and the Culture of Sexual Story Telling', in J. Weeks and J. Holland (eds) *Sexual Cultures: Communities, Values and Intimacy.* London: Macmillan Press – now Palgrave.

PRINCE, V. (1976) *Understanding Cross Dressing*, Box 35091, Los Angeles, CA 90036: Chevalier Publications.

PROSSER, J. (1998) *Second Skins: The Body Narratives of Transsexuality*, New York: Columbia University Press.

REES, M. (1996) 'Becoming a Man: the Personal Account of a Female-to-Male Transsexual', in R. Ekins and D. King (eds) *Blending Genders: Social Aspects of Cross-Dressing and Sex-Changing.* London: Routledge.

ROSE, D.R. (1993a) *Maid in Form 'A', 'B', and 'C'.* Capistrano Beach, CA: Sandy Thomas Adv.

ROSE, D.R. (1993b) *The Sissy Maid Academy, Vols 1 & 2.* Capistrano Beach, CA: Sandy Thomas Adv.

ROSE, D.R. (1994) 'Top Drawer', *Sissy Maid Quarterly*, 1:36–7.

ROSE, D.R. (1995) *Where the Sissies Come From.* Capistrano Beach, CA: Sandy Thomas Adv.

SHILLING, C. (1993) *The Body and Social Theory.* London: Sage.

SISSY, J. (1994) 'A Sissy's World', *Sissy Maid Quarterly*, 2:16–21.

Sissy Maid Quarterly, Nos 1–5, 1994–96 Capistrano Beach, CA: A Sandy Thomas Publication, produced in conjunction with Rose Productions.

STONE, S. (1991) 'The Empire Strikes Back: A Posttranssexual Manifesto', in J. Epstein and K. Straub (eds) *Bodyguards*. London: Routledge.

SPRY, J. (1997) *Orlando's Sleep – An Autobiography of Gender*. Norwich, VT: New Victoria Publishers.

THOM, B. and K. MORE (1998) 'Welcome to the Festival', in *The Second International Transgender Film and Video Festival*. London: Alchemy.

THOMPSON, R. and K. SEWELL (1995) *What Took You So Long: A Girl's Journey to Manhood*. London: Penguin.

TURKLE, S. (1997) 'Tinysex and Gender Trouble', in S. Kemp and J. Squires (eds) *Feminisms*. Oxford: Oxford University Press.

WILCHINS, R. (1997) *Read My Lips: Sexual Subversion and the End of Gender*. New York: Firebrand Books.

12
Double Damnation: Gay Disabled Men and the Negotiation of Masculinity

Terry O'Neill and Myra J. Hird

Introduction

In common with all males, gay disabled men regularly encounter diverse and conflicting claims about the 'essence' of their masculinity. Such claims, given that they often circulate explicitly contradictory accounts of both the characteristics and the project of masculinity, have had the sometimes unanticipated effect of exposing the lives of men as being relatively disunited and disparate. In this context, claims that there continues to exist a single coherent masculinity have been significantly discredited. Where once the assumption of unproblematic integration into collective gender identity guided understandings, there has emerged a new appreciation of the disquieting potential of masculinity. For marginalized males, and for those who choose to study their experiences, these new ways of understanding the complexity of masculinity, and the absence of coherence, are significant. The acknowledgement that there exists a plurality of differentially empowered masculinities substantiates what most gay disabled men have long known. Indeed, many such men may understand these advances less as theoretical innovation than as a validation of the extent and duration of their struggle. Few categories of male are so knowledgeable of the tentative nature, and fragility, of masculinity. Gay disabled men operate in the world with an awareness that the business of 'being a man' is a project of the self and others, which must be continually worked on and worked through. And so it is the case that masculine difference, for so long ignored or obscured in analyses of male gender, has acquired a tentative legitimacy.

By maintaining, after Bob Connell, a clear analytical distinction between hegemonic (dominant) and subordinate (alternative) masculinities (Chowdorow 1994), this chapter also centralizes the significance and implications of male difference. This provides an analytic space in which to locate and to explore some aspects of the ways in which gay disabled men interpret and structure their relations to the dominant male gender construct. It also facilitates the analysis of relations *between* marginalized male formations. Nevertheless, and notwithstanding emergent counter-claims from feminist, lesbian, gay and disabled discourses, it remains that differentiated interpretations such as this are, themselves, marginalized. The characteristics and the project of masculinity are most often situated within universal claims of male gender (Chowdorow 1994) which explicitly ignore the significant individual and cultural differences which exist among men themselves. At a minimum, alternative discourses suggest complexity where blithe over-simplification once governed analyses. Beyond this advance, the success of counter-discourses is often less easily measured. It remains the perception of many men, homosexual and heterosexual, disabled and able-bodied, that they must continue to comply with an array of key gender expectations. Over time, these elements have been configured into what, after Lyotard (Truett-Anderson 1996), might be described as a particular form of male metanarrative which functions to define the parameters of the 'dominant myth' (Ranciere, cited in Silverman 1992: 30) of masculinity. Commonly normative and normalizing in its substance and operation, the metanarrative of masculinity continues to provide the central discursive point of reference by which the lives and aspirations of individual males might be evaluated by themselves and others.

Given that the analysis of masculinity has most usually been predicated on a unified and unitary categorization of males, it remains that the subjective dimension of men's experience is generally overlooked or ignored (Burn 1996; Nencel 1996). Already marginalized in a hierarchized system of masculinities, it is therefore unsurprising that deep and particularized analytic silences have continued to envelop the lives of gay men who live with disability. This chapter is based on the narratives of 13 gay disabled men. These narratives provide the backdrop to an exploration and analysis of a form of marginalized subjectivity notable both for its evident complexities (Smith 1988) and its status as a subjective work-in-process for a number of the individuals involved. Like all subjects, the men in this study are explicitly gendered beings who provide highly individualized accounts and often markedly divergent interpretations of similar experiences and settings. Their voices describe convergence and conflict, commonality and contradiction.

There are common themes of social and emotional isolation. All too often, and providing a measure of their structural and analytical marginalization, the respondents expressed a degree of incredulity that we were interested in their stories. It became clear that for the majority of the participants, the study provided the first opportunity to speak about and to explore crucial aspects of their construction of masculinity.

Most of our respondents were relatively sensitive to the normalizing constraints implicit in those male gender metanarratives which ascribe to men collective attributes at the level of social structure. Consequently, a high proportion of these gay disabled men exhibited unusually nuanced understandings of the sometimes obscure relationships between the hegemonic gender construct and the variously configured marginalized formulations to which they variously ascribed as individuals. Although the hegemonic–marginalized relationship was usually understood to be explicitly dichotomous and often personally detrimental, the range of strategies employed by individuals made clear that this relationship can not be characterized as implacably oppositional. The respondents occupy complex zones of highly contested personal and political male difference. Their collective situation, to the limited extent that it can be generalized, markedly contrasts with the variety of their accounts and the scope of their interpretations.

This study does not, and could not, detail the long-awaited project of a reformed and reformist unitary voice of male difference and male marginality. Nor has it identified easy or 'natural' alliances between individuals or groups who inhabit the social terrain of difference. Instead, it details some of the evident tensions which exist between marginalized male formations and explores the possibility that new configurations of constraint have emerged to stifle many of the personal and political opportunities provided by the legitimation of male difference. Significantly, and in accord with Mullin's (1995) view that the modern insistence on a 'unified' self encourages subjects to prioritize certain subject positions while silencing others, almost all the respondents in this study articulated a prioritization of gay over disabled masculinity. Such a clear subordination of disability to sexuality may be seen to compromise some of the emancipatory claims articulated by the politics of male difference and to bring into question their more general utility with respect to the formulation of a coherent gay disabled subjectivity.

In formulating this critique we hope to engage with an elemental but sometimes relegated precondition of effective gender study. This requires the acknowledgement that difference(s) cannot be productively analyzed in social or theoretical isolation as an entity in and of itself. The internal and external complexity so characteristic of marginality and its analysis infer that its condition of emergence, its very conditioning, is heavily dependent upon a succession of hegemonic male gender constructs. In these circumstances a necessary first step towards the exploration of male difference begins with the dominant construct, and the complex of forces which it exerts upon both hegemonic and marginalized males in the matter of their gender.

Situating the marginalized male in discourse

Hegemonic masculinity maintains alliances with quite specific forms of male gender discourse and, in doing so, alternatively explicates and conceals its own highly refined relations with power and its operation. Among the more extravagant claims made by the dominant prevailing discourse of masculinity is that it can provide for all males a stable and coherent gender identity. By explicitly linking itself with common sense understandings, this discourse works to normalize diverse male subjects through the incorporation of doctrines of naturalism and essentialism, and, by holding out the promise of an unproblematic sense of gendered self based upon cultural and ideological assumptions that masculinity is singular rather than plural. For marginalized males, the evident distance between hegemonic description and their own lived experience may provide the reflective space in which counter-subjectivities are formulated and reformulated. If discourse has the power to enact what it names (Butler 1993), then, necessarily, marginalized subjectivities must strive to name the absences and silences implicit in hegemonic discourse. In these settings subjects are constituted not only by the substance but also by the deficit of discourse.

A number of theorists, including Foucault (1979) have described the possibility that the ways in which masculinity is represented within discourse is closely related to the production of power, the propagation of knowledge and claims of the validity of specific 'truths' concerning masculinity. In a male world of discernible variability and explicit difference, the hegemonic claim to the continued existence of a unitary and unifying male identity may be interpreted as the product of explicit discursive interests. Similarly, oppositional discourses which instead emphasize male variability must also be seen to attempt to integrate masculinity into very specific, albeit alternative, 'knowledges' and 'truths' of their own. Each discursive position, whether unitary or differential, articulates interests and formulates particularized, although contrasting, representations of both gender and power.

Few male groups are as conditioned to recognize the variety or the implications of male gender discourses as are gay men with disabilities. Accordingly, the majority of respondents in this study attributed their discursive knowledgeability directly to their experience of marginality, and to the particular subjectivities which marginalization was understood to encourage. These interpretations were often recognized by respondents as relatively insightful and especially so when discussed in relation to heterosexual able-bodied subjectivities. Thus, the alternative subject-positions maintained by respondents, although seen to be explicitly subordinated both discursively and structurally, were nevertheless viewed as incorporating a distinctive potentiality amid a range of inherently relational male gender discourses. Very clearly, impaired and/or homosexual male bodies retain, in the very conditions of their emergence and existence, the personal and political potential to destabilize the hegemonic discursive claim of a single and unproblematic male subjectivity.

Gay-disabled are both recipients and exponents of diverse discursive interests. Theirs is an alternative subject-position which is of interest to structures of masculinity and which, simultaneously, has discernible interests of its own. The sense of subjective absence or, at best, relegation, experienced by many gay disabled males has had a lengthy historical trajectory. Consequently, it is difficult, if not impossible, to conduct an analysis of these subjectivities without either cultural or geopolitical introspection (Anderson 1991), or without continued reference to the historical trajectory of the localized hegemonic construct of masculinity. In local contexts, any attempt to under-emphasize the linkages between prevailing representations of masculinity and hegemonic conceptualizations of national identity remains problematic. The ideological elements implicit in constructs of national identity are commonly heterosexist, most usually explicitly masculinized, and may be actively utilized by the state to functionally incorporate localized and exemplary male characteristics into the pursuit of state interests (Phillips 1987). Nevertheless, and seemingly paradoxically given the explicitly normalizing pressures which it customarily exerts upon masculinity, the state must maintain a simultaneous claim to its capacity to incorporate and manage (Skocpol 1985) diverse domestic male interests and representations. This apparent contradiction highlights the representation of masculinity by the state as a site of graduated inconsistency and contradiction. Furthermore, it problematizes the extent to which the state might effectively continue to maintain its very clear interests in the parameters and experience of masculinity.

Nowhere are the inconsistencies and conditionality of approaches by the state to masculinity more evident than in its responses, over time, to the marginalized masculinities within its domain. Functioning under an operational premise that all masculinities may be coherently structured under the normalizing rubric of a hegemonic construct, states have intervened to order the experience of both male homosexuality and male impairment. In a variety of ways, states have sought, periodically, to describe the terms and extent to which gay disabled subjectivity might be construed as a legitimate alternative by the alienated and disenfranchized males of its constituency. Always responsive to its social control objectives, and notwithstanding more recent challenges made by homosexual activism, the state has explicitly configured masculinity with marriage (Connell 1995), and thus, heterosexuality. Although legislative sanctions relating to homosexuality have relaxed, the state retains the capacity to superintend the boundaries of acceptable masculinity and so directs many of the circumstances of male homosexuality's integration. In its evasion of substantive commitments to the elimination of the continuing high levels of social antipathy and physical violence endured by many gay men, the state demonstrates its central complicity in the construction of the subjective experience of acceptable homosexuality as both tenuous and perennially conditional.

Even at the level of its more prosaic activities, the state demonstrates its predisposition towards selection and exclusion. National infrastructural and developmental objectives are often interpreted as being most effectively achieved by the labour exerted by an exemplary male physicality which is implicitly heterosexual and vigorously unimpaired. When viewed through the lens of state interest, it becomes clear that male exemplars are highly variable over time. There are close associations between the ways in which the state assesses its interests and the extent to which the male bodies under its control are interpreted as an expendable resource. For instance, the impairment of male bodies in the pursuit of state interests is reconstituted as exemplary while times of relative peace reinscribe impairment as a personal and social deficit. By retaining for itself a central role in the definition of exemplary masculinity the state necessarily plays an equivalent role in determining the setting and management of the conditions required for the acceptable emergence of both male homosexuality and disability.

Just as linkages may be seen to continue to exist between contemporary domestic male gender constructs and those existing in previous eras, it is clear that in quite specific ways gay disabled subjectivities are also imbued with the histories of nations' political structuring within the world system (Wallerstein 1991). These complex processes of macro-contextualization lend important dimensions to both the experience and analysis of marginalized masculinities and may make it more possible to explicate the tensions which structure their relations with the hegemonic formation. To the extent that it retains the capacity to reorder both its own and common sense understandings of acceptable masculinity, the role of the state remains central to the lived experience of gay disabled men. Its periodic interventions in the arena of male gender are seldom undertaken lightly or without heed to wider political consequences. For the men in this study, any opportunity to advance their political objectives is heavily contingent upon the state's prevailing assessment of political pragmatism and the extent to which it may safely accommodate contentious differences without adverse reactions in its electorate. Accommodations have been, and continue to be made, between state power and the politics of marginalized masculinities, but such *rapprochements* are often conditional and remain emblematic of the wider power relations still dominated by hegemonic masculinities.

> They [politicians] pay lip service to it. Like the Honourable Prime Minister who went to the Hero Parade [a local annual gay community event] but next week in the [Parliamentary] House went the other way. And this is typical. (Rob, age 54)

As a consequence, large numbers of gay-disabled men have judged their relationship to the state as being locked into a condition of structural imbalance which holds little potential for substantive change. For these men, the most viable alternative is seen to be a subjective affiliation with a politics of male difference.

Marginalized males and the dilemma of identity

Unavoidably, the extent and type of political response chosen by individual gay disabled men remains crucially influenced by the matrix of understandings and organizing principles derived from their status as men in society.

> I think being a man is wonderful because I can stand up on my two feet. I can stand up and I can. . . . make things happen for myself. (Warwick, age 33)

The men in this study frequently drew upon their background knowledge of the ways in which male structural power can operate, although they presented variable assessments of its range or characteristics in relation to their own experiences. It seemed clear, or at various times in the past had been made clear to many respondents by able-bodied heterosexual males, that their positioning in male structural power was at best conditional and, at worst, non-existent. As a result, most of the men were resistant to any unqualified attempt to associate their own experiences with either the operation or benefits of hegemonic male structural power. Nevertheless, and notwithstanding these reservations, it was also the case that the majority of the men questioned acknowledged that they derived, at the minimum, peripheral advantages arising from their status as men in society. In a number of ways, then, the respondents demonstrated a relatively complex and differentiated interpretation of male structural power in which power itself was understood as multi-layered and considerably more difficult to access or maintain by gay disabled bodies.

> I'm disabled and, you know, people have to make compensations and . . . that severely weakens my position in society. Umm, so I just don't tend to choose that option very often. (Michael, age 28)

In common with all men, gay disabled men acquire knowledge not only about power and its operation but also about the relationship of masculinity itself to power. This learning of masculinity involves not only the learning of one of the most fundamental binary oppositions upon which the social order rests – that of male–female – but also the learning of differential value and asymmetrical power and hierarchy (Chowdorow 1994) between masculinities. For gay disabled males, and the differences which they embody, these general processes have particular subjective relevance. They learn that male bodies may be cultivated in ways which encourage differential responses and, thus, that physical prowess is a key marker of masculinity. They learn to understand the male power of defining commonalities and differences, of what and who is 'natural' and 'unnatural', 'normal' and 'abnormal'; of being able to label (Prieur, 1996) or not to label, and the very particular significances of age, class, sexuality and subculture (Burn, 1996) to the exercise and relations of male power. Locally, gay disabled men come to understand the specificity of cultural meanings and the significance of local myths (Melhuss 1996) of male gender and national identity. For these men the learning of masculinity almost always involves complex and parallel processes of identifying both their differences and their commonalities in relation to males generally. At a generalized level, then, it is to attempt to accomplish a subjective accommodation with a hegemonic gender construct which is explicitly heterosexual, able-bodied, and therefore substantively unattainable.

As subjects of its selection and exclusion, gay-disabled males also learn to recognize the violences (Tierney 1997) implicit in the dominating, and unitary, model of male sexual character.

> I don't push my luck in terms of teasing straight men, which is something a lot of gay men do. (Ian, age 33)

> When I cross the street I tend to walk slightly higher, and I walk slightly faster, and I also enlarge the space around my body ... so that my arms are slightly out from my sides. Just an attitude of confidence, and that to me is to deter what would deter a lot of people. It seems to have worked so far. (Michael, age 28)

> With my friends, and we were walking along. One of my ex-partners, him and I was holding hands, walking the street. And there was this group [of straight men]. You know, [they] touched me, kicked me, and all stuff like that. But I just told them, you know, just leave us alone. You know, what right do they have to do that? What punishment do I deserve that? Because there's so much scars. They're filled up. But sometimes it just happens. (Tom, age 29)

> But what I mean, I mean, even then, I mean I didn't go to the police about it. Umm, I just like ... comes with the turf. The world has taught us that it will critique us. So we've learned to do it ourselves, before they do. Slap yourself in the face before they even decide they're not sure if they like you. (Sam, age 37)

In common with all men, they are made aware that normalization is still the dominant order of the day (Bordo 1993). Conditioned as both subjects and agents of a normalizing masculine ideology which often works to outlaw difference, gay-disabled men operate within the knowledge that possibilities for change are limited (Grant 1993). Generated by their experience of difference, and irrespective of their aspirations, such men are imbued with the certainty that the dominant discourse of masculinity continues to function as a tactical element (Foucault 1979) to support existing power relations in society. Nevertheless, it is also the case that the power objectives of hegemonic masculinity are not well served by any widespread impression that it is irredeemably monolithic and implacable. Marginalized male subjects must therefore be instilled, as a necessary component of their learning of masculinity, with an understanding that the constraining influences of the dominant construct might, under certain circumstances, be ameliorated.

Power, whether discursive, state or hegemonic male power, must reconfigure itself in order to ensure that existing relations of power might prevail. In short, hegemonic male power is only tolerable if it is seen to leave a measure of freedom (Foucault 1979), a space for dissent – however slight – which might encourage among gay disabled subjects a sense of their potential both to evade that power (Foucault 1979) and to assume a variety of subject positions (Grant 1993) in relation to it. The differences which such males embody must, therefore, be provided with restricted contexts in which marginalized masculinities might be produced in distinctive ways (Archetti 1996). In these settings, the counter-discourses formulated by gay disabled males represent explicitly oppositional, although contained, understandings of the heterogeneity of males as a social category. For the marginalized males who subscribe to them, such discourses are seen as effectively subversive of the fictional unity (Bailey 1993) and homogeneity which is asserted by the hegemonic male gender construct. Furthermore, these discourses are interpreted as an attempt to develop a more adequate language of representation which, in turn, might create the conditions where multiple male identities can be de-coupled from hegemonic male norms (Tierney 1997).

Such discourses may be a means by which marginalized individuals and groups attempt to gain control of their discourses and practices instead of being controlled (Cherryholmes 1988) or oppressed by them. By operating as sites of conflict concerning identity production they also indicate to all males that identities are always relational in that they only exist in relation to other potential identities (Weeks 1987). Here, identity is most definitely and politically differentiation; (Chauncey 1995; Tierney 1997) the active choice of identification with a particular social position and organizing sense of self which has implications for subject positions and subjectivities (Weeks 1987). To this extent, the politics of difference at least partially accommodate the oppositions and contradictions embodied by gay disabled males. They are arenas from which marginalized men might more effectively articulate and disseminate the distinctiveness of their experiences, and also provide an organizing locale for identity claims and for the contesting of resources generated by male structural power more generally.

Respondents in the study customarily interpreted the relative subordination of their subject position as an inevitable outcome of any intersection of homosexuality and impairment with hegemonic male power.
However, many men still maintained that an organized politics of male
difference had the potential to significantly curtail some of the negative influences of hegemonic masculinity. They understood that, given
the opportunity, the very particular and relatively unexploited potentials and powers of gay disabled bodies had distinct capacities to positively reconfigure the relations between hegemonic and marginalized
masculinities. Or, that they had important understandings gained from
their experiences which, if they could only be assimilated into hegemonic subjectivities, would deliver benefits to *all* men. In describing the
conditions necessary for such a profound *rapprochement*, however, none
of the respondents envisaged that either a dismantling or radical restruc-
turing of hegemonic masculinity would be a necessary prerequisite.
Almost exclusively, they cited the renovation of the dominant construct, but not its demolition, as the principle route by which an integrated and coherent gay disabled subjectivity might be achieved.

> In terms of power and money and prestige, and stuff like that, its
> more advantageous [to be a male in our society]. I've got more in
> common with him [a straight white businessman] than anything
> else. Well, we're both male, we're both white and, me being gay, I'm
> sort of in touch with my feminine side, and a lot of straight males,
> if you give them the opportunity and also the space for them to
> express their kind of feminine side, they're usually bloody grateful.
> Incredibly grateful but that, you know, it doesn't happen very often.
> (Michael, age 28)

Here, then, were complex subject positions which at once compre-
hended hegemonic masculinity in terms of both opportunity and
constraint. Respondents remained aware of the conditions of their marginality; that heterosexual and able-bodied males had, and would retain,
their ability to either confer or withdraw benefits. Thus, these gay disabled men also demonstrated an awareness of the delicate relationships
between their subjective aspirations and the on-going conditionality of
their access to male structural power.

For men such as these, this positioning of self in relation to hegemonic masculinity is fraught with difficulties arising from their embodiment of not one, but two distinct male differences. Nevertheless, and
unsurprisingly, all the respondents maintained that a key personal

objective was the formulation of a functional identity. As a group, they described the important connections between clear subject-positioning, identity, and their own and others' perception that male marginality does not mean, has never meant, either passivity or an inability to resist. To the extent that the opportunity to formulate a coherent marginalized identity was seen as both recent and tenuous, many respondents also described a sense of obligation to affiliate with an organizing politics upon which such an identity might be based. The facility to adopt an oppositional subject-position was accepted as a given in today's society, and the specific configuration of subject-position by any individual was considered to be a matter of personal preference in almost every respect. Thus, in the matter of constituting a preferred subject-position (gay *or* disabled), respondents very easily reinterpreted their enforced structural marginality as effective and knowledgeable personal identity choice.

Nevertheless, for these men in particular, the positioning of subjectivity and identity within the particular nexus of sexuality, the body, and gay and disabled discourses can present some very specific difficulties. Gay disabled men are now presented with markedly different, and sometimes divergent, possibilities around which they might organize their identities. Respectively, the politics of disability and gay politics articulate a variety of claims about the necessity and attainability of linkages between personal affiliation, emancipatory objectives and subjective coherence. The differences in political understanding and strategizing were also evident in the accounts provided by respondents. All the men questioned made distinctions between their homosexuality and their impairment when they described their perceptions of relative empowerment or disempowerment. Power in these circumstances was recognized as sensitive to, and differentially exploitative of, the inherent male bodily characteristics represented either by homosexuality or impairment. In their turn, these assessments were then integrated by individuals to underscore the rationality of their chosen subject-position. In the continued absence of a more coherent alternative, the gay disabled men in this study responded in a strikingly similar way. With alacrity, and in clear subordination of the alternative subject-position available to them, almost all the men interviewed very decisively expressed preference of a gay identity over a disabled identity.

I look upon myself as gay. I don't worry about the disabled part. It just doesn't enter into things. (Rob, age 54)

There's not really a disabled [identity]. Prioritise one identity? Well it would have to be the gay one first. And then all the others can just get in behind. (Michael, age 28)

I'm gay, and I'm also a New Zealander, but in particular I'm gay. Yes [I prioritize my gay identity] above everything. (Evan, age 60)

I'm most happy to be labelled as a gay man. I'm very comfortable as a gay man. The other part is still being worked on. Yes. Very much. (Craig, age 23)

[His homosexuality] Yes, well that's the paramount thing. (Roger, age 74)

For me its quite important that I'm identified as a gay man. (Ian, age 33)

All the respondents maintained that they had assumed a gay 'versus' a disabled identity primarily on the basis of their individual experience of homosexuality and impairment. Nevertheless, it was also clear that these personal understandings of this identity, and its potentials, were structured beyond actual lived experience by an array of discourses among which the dominant discourse of masculinity still featured prominently. Each man indicated that his own distinctively gendered body provided him with the key point of reference for his interpretation of power and its operation. Drawing upon their experience of *dis*empowerment arising both from their sexuality and their physical impairment, respondents made assessments of the ways in which marginalized bodies function as the site of a range of possible relationships between differentially empowered masculinities. While most clearly objects of hegemonic male power, these men also understood their bodies to be focal points for struggles over power (Bordo 1993), subjective coherence and access to structural resources. Crucially, respondents recognized that their bodies, although clearly marginalized among a hierarchy of masculinities, nevertheless incorporated certain potentials and interests which were derived from their status as *male* bodies in society. It is this understanding, we would argue, which continues to crucially influence the ways in which gay disabled males structure the terms of their engagement with their homosexuality or disability. By constructing an identity amalgam which explicitly subordinates disability to homosexuality, the respondents in this study signalled their assessment of the relative efficacy and potentials represented by the two identities available to them.

Within the confined subjective space conceded by the dominant gender construct, and responding to its periodic incitements to discourse, gay disabled males can be seen to replicate the complex hierarchization of masculinities enacted by hegemonic masculinity itself.[1] Similarly, the preferred oppositional subject-position which is permitted to emerge is also disposed towards the maintenance of its own *internal* differences and to confound the possibility of alliance even *within* subjectivity. These processes of internalized contention and relegation seldom bring into serious contention the power relations maintained by hegemonic masculinity. Instead, we would argue, hegemonic masculinity has formulated new and sometimes obscure responses to the challenges and contradictions inherent in homosexual and disabled male bodies. More plainly, the marginalized masculinity represented by the conjuncture between homosexuality and impairment in male bodies, is now regulated in much less discernible ways and most commonly at the level of subjectivity.

If, as this study argues, gay disabled men operate within explicitly conditioned and externally regulated subject positions, these men are unwittingly complicit in their own disempowerment. What, then, are the implications for their *em*powerment? Most of the men interviewed understood that power was principally achievable by means of political affiliation, integration and activism. To the extent that in their cases the process of establishing and maintaining subject positions entailed the incorporation of two marginalized subjectivities, the task is quantifiably more difficult and potentially conflicting. A number of dilemmas must be recognized and negotiated both by the marginalized individual and by the marginalized group with which he aspires to identify. Which discourse–identity should be prioritized, if any? Is it even possible to maintain an equitable subjective investment in two identities? If one identity is to be conferred with a higher status, then which is to be subordinated, and why? How then, are these relationships to be managed by the individual, or by the group? And if the individual does achieve a functional resonance with a prioritized discursive position, what are the implications for his relationship with the subordinated identity? Not the least of these dilemmas, as we have described above, is the distinct possibility that what may appear as agency in the matter of marginalized male gender identity may, instead, be a form of subjectedness (Foucault 1986).

I am disabled but I've been, throughout my life, I've been taught and I've learned, to minimise the effects of disability in my life. (Rob, age 54)

Conclusion

The men in this study, in a variety of ways, demonstrated great knowledgeability about the ways and extent to which their bodies are regulated in society by hegemonic masculinity. They described how these understandings had been accumulated both from their learning of hegemonic masculinity and also from insights generated by their experiences as distinctively *different* males. For them, marginality was seen to represent a series of tensions between their aspirations for a coherent gay-disabled subjectivity and their continued, if relegated, access to male structural power. Notwithstanding that deployments of hegemonic male power are directly connected to gay disabled bodies (Foucault 1979) and their social control, each of the respondents recognized the possibility for dissent. However, these men saw no real possibility of organizing their dissension under the rubric of a combined homosexual–disabled axis. More particularly, neither dissent nor its objective – the contestation of male structural power – was considered plausible if undertaken under the auspices of an identity which prioritized impairment over sexuality.

Each of the men in this study understood that he had made an active identity choice based upon his perceptions of the extent to which he might be able to counteract those power relations which seek the submission of his subjectivity (Foucault 1986). A number of respondents noted the absence of homosexuality with disability in discourse, and even more lamented the absence of a politics of difference which, they envisaged, would be more responsive to the very specific subjective requirements of their combined disability and homosexuality.

> My big problem, and it was a real problem, why am I disabled and gay? It seemed to be a two-fold judgement, in inverted commas, but, OK, I've worked through both of these now but it was a real struggle. I mean, what I've learned has been through my own reading or talking to others and nobody's been very helpful at all. I've had to learn it all myself and its been most interesting, actually, discovering what makes me tick and why. (Rob, age 54)

> So my knowledge of my body has come from myself, and from looking at it and touching it, and so on. (Evan, age 60)

> I was much more aware of my homosexuality than my disability. I'm learning about my disability now with reference to my gayness. I look to my gay experiences to teach me. (Evan, age 60)

Yeah, [a gay-disabled group would be] useful for self-esteem, awareness, things like that. Yes, it would. Yeah, if there was such a group
as that I would probably join it. That would be my first disabled
group. (Craig, age 23)

It's really quite hard for me. Sometimes I haven't got anyone to share
that fear with. Or that identity of disability in the body. For me it
has not been recognized for a very long time. (Warwick, age 33)

I'm a gay person, so that's that. But you think, just going through
the gay hearing world, it doesn't fit in. Not quite right. Nothing
much in common. (Tom, age 28).

However, and even if such a discourse were available, the differences
which it might articulate are not easily unified (Yates 1994; Biggart and
Furlong 1996). In the meantime, and almost without exception, respod-
ents very decisively prioritized their homosexuality. Even further, and
excepting those who perceived that their disability gave them no choice
in the matter, none of the males aspired to formulate an identity which
prioritized their disability as its organizing principle.

It remains that the nexus of sexuality, the impaired body and gay
'versus' disabled discourses in the constitution of subjectivity has been
only partially explored and the characteristics of a fully integrated gay
disabled masculinity only tentatively articulated. Although its immi-
nence sometimes seems to be in little doubt, the ways in which gay
disabled men already organize their identities suggest to us that their
responses to such an eventuality would be complex and difficult to
predict. In the interim, it is apparent that the marginalized males in this
study have uniformly decided that their homosexuality provides the key
to their identity. By explicitly prioritizing one of the two subject positions available to them, they have signalled their intention to organize
their gay-disabled subjectivities in a very specific way.

Having made this decision, for some the reconciliation of their differences under the auspices of a prioritized gay identity was often problematic. Many individuals found that their internal subordination of
disability was paralleled by similar responses to their disability from the
able-bodied gay community.

[Comparative acceptability of disability in the gay community] On
the balance of things, I'd say less than the wider community. Yeah,
simply because of that gay male kind of sort of thing where youth is
everything. Perfection. Perfect body and perfect kind of hair, and the

perfect lifestyle and the perfect everything. I'm not perfect, and I don't have the perfect body 'cause I don't have perfect hearing. (Michael, age 28)

I probably felt very insecure in the gay community at a very young age (Warwick, age 33)

The gay community, on a level of acceptance, they're just like the wider community. (Andrew, age 37)

When I first came out I expected that the gay community would be really accepting of me because I was, you know, part of a minority group. I felt the gay community would see me as, you know, different and therefore special and all that crap. And what I discovered was completely the opposite. That gay culture rejected me more than the heterosexual culture. (Ian, age 33)

[The gay community] Not good. I would, I would never have . . . no, I was, you're not part of the scene. You can't get involved in a way with the, umm, you're not physically attractive, in terms of their criteria. (Bill, age 78)

Nevertheless, and although a high proportion of men described a variety of negative experiences, the emancipatory discourses which had motivated their primary identification as gay men in the first instance still sufficed to maintain their affiliation. Generally, nothing in their experience of impairment had lead them to consider disability as a relevant primary identifier. To the contrary, and in emulation of society more generally, disability was most frequently described as irredeemable liability.

I find disability groups too, you know, too introspective. Yeah, I mean you can say the same thing about the gay community but we're forced into it by the attitudes of society. OK, we can stand up for ourselves so let's do it. (Rob, age 54)

Most respondents described on-going, and occasionally profound, tensions between their disability and their homosexuality. Given these outcomes, it is debatable that their subordination of disability to a homosexual identity has provided the individuals in this study with the relative subjective coherence to which they aspire. It is possible, we believe, that their most profitable strategy would be to avoid the internal hierachization and effective re-oppression of marginalized masculinities and, instead, to turn their attentions explicitly back to the hegemonic formation. It remains the case that hegemonic masculinity simultaneously formulates marginalized masculinities and also decides the extent and terms of the relations *between* these masculinities. Arguably, this is manifest in the extent to which the gay disabled men in this study subjectively hierarchize their differences and interpret them not as opportunities for alliances (Irigary 1987) or for self-actualization but, rather, in terms of their separation and isolation.

Gay-disabled subjectivities arise from, and are centrally concerned with, the twin projects of accommodating both external and internal diversity. Notwithstanding these commonalities, individual gay bodies exist and operate as unique physical, subjective, political and historical constructs. The multiplicity of ways in which they are conditioned lend such bodies an analytic significance which extends beyond their marginalization to draw attention to the locales of power in which their marginality is defined and maintained. Hegemonic masculinity continues, and sometimes in very diffuse ways, to regulate the actual heterogeneity (Miller 1993) of masculinity and to conceal the extent of the differences which exist between men. This project of homogenization, the very constitution of the significance of homogeneity to self, can be seen to have disquieting echoes in the ways and extent to which the men in this study have silenced (Mullin 1995) their impairment to their homosexuality. In this subjective context, the full extent of the possibilities arising from their internal diversity (Measor 1978; Laclau 1995; Mullin 1995) is effectively denied and the benefits of this relativization are almost exclusively accrued by the hegemonic construct. It is our view that, if a coherent gay-disabled subjectivity is to be fashioned, it will arise from the discursive space generated by the tensions and conflicts (Foucault 1980) caused by the current silencing of disability to homosexuality. In both its subjective and political contexts, gay disabled men must attempt to ensure that their differences become *less* manageable, not more manageable. In the interim, their damnation is indeed doubled. By conforming to a very specific and conditioned interpretation of the possibilities represented by their differences, they have succeeded in replicating the structures and rationales of their oppressors and, thus, to facilitate their continued marginalization.

Notes

1. This is not to imply that gay-disabled subjectivities in their current formulations represent a new variation on the old theme of the 'cultural dope'. The

men in this study, and their stories, serve to re-emphasis the structural impla-
cability of hegemonic male power as it is presently configured and to draw
renewed attention to the manifest obscurity of its operations. For marginalized males, these convergences and reductions simply serve to conflate
the spectrum of possible male gender practices into a disciplinary domain of
acceptable male attitudes and behaviours. These are the contexts in which
occur the complex and often debilitating regulation of the male differences
embodied by homosexuality and disability. It is also a context in which
diverse claims about the characteristics and extent of the power available to
gay disabled men collide with the interests arrayed against that eventuality.

Bibliography

ANDERSON, B. (1991) *Imagined Communities (revised edition)* London: Verso.
ARCHETTI, E.P. (1996) 'Playing Styles and Masculine Virtues in Argentine
    Football', in M. Melhuss and K.A. Stolen (eds) *Machos, Mistresses, Madonnas:
    Contesting the Power of Latin American Gender Imagery*. London and New York:
    Verso.
BAILEY, M. (1993) 'Foucauldian feminism contesting bodies, sexuality and iden-
    tity', in D. Ramazanoghu (ed.) *Up Against Foucault*. London: Routledge.
BIGGART, A. and A. FURLONG (1996) 'Educating "Discouraged Workers":
    Cultural Diversity in the Upper Secondary School' *British Journal of Sociology
    of Education* 17:253–66.
BORDO, S. (1993) 'Feminism, Foucault and the Politics of the Body', in
    C. Ramazanoghu (ed.) *Up Against Foucault*. London: Routledge.
BURN, S.M. (1996) *The Social Psychology of Gender*. New York: McGraw Hill.
BUTLER, J. (1993) Arguing with the Real, *Bodies that Matter*. London: Routledge.
CHAUNCEY, G. (1995) *Gay New York: The Making of the Gay Male World,
    1890–1940*. London: HarperCollins.
CHERRYHOLMES, C. (1988) *Power and Criticism: Poststructural Investigations in
    Education*. New York: Teachers' College Press.
CHOWDOROW, N.J. (1994) *Femininities, Masculinities, Sexualities*, Kentucky:
    University of Kentucky Press.
CONNELL, R.W. (1995) *Masculinities*. Australia: Allen & Unwin.
FOUCAULT, M. (1979) *History of Sexuality, Vol. 1, An Introduction*, London: Allen
    Lane.
FOUCAULT, M. (1980) 'Two Lectures', in C. Gordon (ed.) *Michel Foucault:
    Power/Knowledge: Selected Interviews and Other Writings, 1972–1977*. Brighton:
    Harvester Press.
FOUCAULT, M. (1986) 'The Subject and Power', in B. Wallis (ed.), *Art After
    Modernism: Rethinking Representation*. New York: New York Museum of Con-
    temporary Art.
GRANT, Barbara (1993) *Making University Students: The Construction of Student
    Subjectivities*. University of Auckland: unpublished MA Thesis.
IRIGARY, L. (1987) 'Sexual Difference', in T. Moi, *French Feminist Thought*. Oxford:
    Blackwells.
LACLAU, E. (1995) 'Subject of Politics, Politics of the Subject'. *Differences: A
    Journal of Feminist Cultural Studies* 7:146–64.

MEASOR, N. (1978) 'Persons, Indeterminacy and Responsibility'. *The Philosophical Review* LXXXVII: 414–22.

MELHUSS, M. (1996) 'Power, Value and the Ambiguous Meanings of Gender', in M. Melhuss and K.A. Stolen (eds) *Machos, Mistresses, Madonnas: Contesting the Power of Latin American Gender Imagery*. London and New York: Verso.

MELHUSS, M. (1996) 'Introduction', in M. Melhuss and K.A. Stolen (eds) *Machos, Mistresses, Madonnas: Contesting the Power of Latin American Gender Imagery*. London and New York: Verso.

MILLER, T. (1993) *The Well-Tempered Self: Citizenship, Culture, and the Post-modern Subject*. Baltimore: Johns Hopkins University Press.

MULLIN, A. (1995) 'Selves, diverse and divided: can feminists have diversity without multiplicity?', *Hypatia* 10:1–30.

NENCEL, L. (1996) 'Pacharachas, Putas and Chicas de su casa: Labelling, Femininity and Men's Sexual Selves in Lima, Peru', in M. Melhuss and K.A. Stolen (eds) *Machos, Mistresses, Madonnas: Contesting the Power of Latin American Gender Imagery*. London and New York: Verso.

PHILLIPS, J. (1987) *A Man's Country? The Image of the Pakeha Male – A History*. Auckland: Penguin.

PRIEUR, A. (1996) 'Domination and desire: Male Homosexuality and the Construction of Masculinity in Mexico', in M. Melhuss and K.A. Stolen (eds) *Machos, Mistresses, Madonnas: Contesting the Power of Latin American Gender Imagery*. London and New York: Verso.

SILVERMAN, K. (1992) *Male Subjectivity at the Margins*. New York and London: Routledge.

SKOCPOL, T. (1985) 'Bringing the State Back In: Strategies of Analysis in Current Research', in P. Evans, D. Rueschemeyer and T. Skocpol (eds) *Bringing the State Back In*. Cambridge: Cambridge University Press.

SMITH, B. (1988) 'Woman: The One and the Many', in E. Spelman (ed.) *Inessential Woman*. London: The Women's Press.

TIERNEY, W.G. (1997) *Academic Outlaws: Queer Theory and Cultural Studies in the Academy*. Thousand Oaks, California: Sage.

TRUETT-ANDERSON, W. (1996) (ed.) *The Fontana Postmodernism Reader*. London: Fontana.

WALLERSTEIN, I. (1991) 'The National and the Universal: Can There Be Such a Thing as World Culture?' in A.D. King (ed.) *Culture Globalisation and the World-System: Contemporary Conditions for the Representation of Identity*. Basingstoke: Macmillan Education.

WEEKS, J. (1987) 'Questions of Identity', in P. Caplan (ed.) *The Cultural Construction of Sexuality*. London: Tavistock.

YATES, L. (1994) 'A Feminist theory of Social Differentiation', in L. Nicholson (ed.) *Feminism/Postmodernism*. New York: Routledge.

13

A Break From the Norm: Exploring the Experiences of Queer Crips

Ruth Butler

Introduction: acknowledging difference

The London Gay Pride march is repeatedly led by the disability rights banner, but the disabled[1] contingent of the crowd are marginalized in the parties which follow it by 'the cult of "body beautiful" and celebration of glamour and glitz' (Corbett 1994: 345). In a dominantly able bodied gay 'community'[2] disability issues arc side lined, often given little more than tokenistic recognition. As a result many disabled lesbians, gay men and bisexual individuals (LGBs)[3] feel the need to attend Pride festivals, not to support gay rights, but to draw the LGB population's attention to their disabled members (Shakespeare *et al.* 1996).

Despite the human body taking an infinite array of shapes and sizes, and definitions of them in terms of their physical structure, social utility and symbolic value varying widely from place to place and time to time, society's narrow expectations of any particular body are usually closely allied to the crude images associated with the social classifications of gender, age, race, ability, class and sexuality into which they are placed. What is more, at any given time and place one such classification is usually taken as dominant over all others. Only recently has work on marginalized groups, through its flirtations with postmodernism, begun to draw attention to differences within populations which have formerly been considered to have a single unifying identity. The misleading and unhelpful nature of dichotomies such as those of male/female, black/white, homosexual/heterosexual and disabled/able bodied have been problematized by an awareness of the numerous social, economic and political axes – class, gender, race, age, sexuality and (dis)ability, among others – which cut across such simplistic binary divisions and are themselves fluid concepts.

This work has liberated knowledge and produced fruitful theoretical controversies about populations' identities and how they may be 'known' (Gibson-Graham 1996). An appreciation of the complexities of people's embodied experiences, and the forces of power and resistance which create and recreate such experiences have been brought to light. For individuals whose 'different' perspectives on the world have previously gone unheard in a society which often fails to acknowledge that social categories are not mutually exclusive, such work promises an acknowledgement of their existence and the possibility of their experiences and concerns being raised in broader debates. However, such developments in theoretical discourse have not always been taken on board by service providers or welcomed by political activists. Service providers still fail to meet the varying needs of all those who wish to take advantage of their facilities and there are fears in political circles that discussions of difference will bring about divisions and disunity, threatening political objectives. As a result many individuals remain marginalized from the 'communities', they at least in part, identify with.

This chapter explores these issues by drawing on literature about the experiences of disabled LGBs in Britain as a case study and falls into three main sections. First it considers the social structures within which individuals must function, drawing particular attention to the pressures on people to conform to the narrowly defined 'norms' expected of them. In this context the chapter secondly explores the implications of the expectation of a 'normal' able body among those frequenting the gay 'scene'[4] on disabled individuals' access to and acceptance in such spaces. Third, the strategies of resistance disabled LGBs are using in order to redress such negative experiences are outlined. The paper concludes by suggesting the need for further research in the area of different, multiple identities, pointing out some of its potential benefits.

Recognizing the influence of 'norms'

An individual's behaviour and presentation of self in public space results from a combination of firstly their awareness of what they know or believe themselves to be, and secondly how they believe others to view them and hence what they believe to be expected of them (Goffman 1963). On the one hand, having pride in oneself means self-confidence to express oneself and value ones identity (Corbett 1994). Recognition and acceptance of both their physiology and their sexuality is central to anyone's self-esteem, self-respect and a conscious sense of being a man or woman (Morris 1989). These are issues which gay pride and disability politics have both underlined. On the other hand, however, whatever pride in themselves disabled LGBs may have behind closed doors, they are distinctly aware of those around them's reactions towards them. The surveillance of others upon any individual's behaviour has strong implications for their 'performance' in different spaces.

These processes of surveillance function at two levels, what will be referred to here as the 'society' and the 'category'. First at the 'society' level, in a self defensive manner individuals tend to see themselves as 'normal', and hence socially acceptable, and those they view as 'other', as deviant (Shakespeare 1994b). In this way each person distances themselves from the undesirable margins of society and what these are believed to represent (Sibley 1995). Self defensive, distancing processes produce a social structure where people are measured against unspecified yet apparently desirable 'norms' according to that broad population's culture. Within such a social structure some categories of people are considered more 'normal' and hence desirable than others. For example, essentialist argument suggests that the biological instinct to reproduce means heterosexuality is 'normal'. Equally, an able body, is seemingly preferable to impairment, which often reminds individuals of their physicality, animality, human frailty and ultimate death. In ableist hetero-patriarchal society images of heterosexual, able bodied couples are represented as having the desirable lifestyle to which everyone should try to conform.

Constructionists have, more recently, argued that biological differences do not have any inherent meaning, but rather that characteristics and behaviours have been attributed to biological phenomena. However, what is common to both these arguments is the recognition of the impact of the society level 'norms' – of biological or social construction – which individuals recognize and accommodate in their self-presentation and behaviour in order to survive the social jungle. People's fear of marginalization, how it encourages them to recognize the categories society considers to be its 'norms' and build them into their own evaluation of their identity have been made clear by many authors (Goffman 1963, Young 1990). The existence of 'a persuasive social pressure to be "more normal" than we are' is widely recognized, as is many individuals' compliance with it (Corbett 1994: 346). Each individual is to some extent objectified by the gaze of others. Their efforts to shape their bodies into an image that both they and others are comfortable with, in a consumer culture, have made the fashion and beauty industries highly profitable. Foucault suggests that power is diffused throughout all levels of the social order from national and international government to individual bodies (McDowell 1995). There are many forms of control, surveillance and discipline focused on the body constantly forming and reforming what are considered to be the appropriate 'norms' of behaviour and presentation. However, it is self-surveillance and self-correction which has one of the strongest influences in perpetuating a social structure which functions around such 'norms'.

> There is no need for arms, physical violence, material constraints. Just a gaze, an inspecting gaze, a gaze which each individual under its weight will end by interiorizing to the point that he is his own overseer, each individual thus exercising this surveillance over, and against himself. (Foucault 1977: 155 cited in McDowell 1995: 78)

Policing of the self in this way, in an attempt to present an image of belonging to groups considered 'normal' by society, involves more than a recognition of the pecking order of social classifications. There is also a need to be aware of the more specific characteristics and behaviours, considered 'normal' of each specific category of people, that is the category level 'norms'. The social, economic and political categories that an individual is associated with by others at any one time will strongly affect the 'norms' with which others expect them to comply. Butler and Bowlby (1997: 420) note:

> In the case of women, reactions to their presence in public space will vary depending on whether they are behaving in ways that are seen currently as acceptable for women. . . . For example, a young woman pushing a pram down a street is less likely to suffer sexual harassment than the same woman walking alone down the street at night or mending her car in the street.

It is sometimes possible for an individual to hide their membership of a particular category from others. Where the 'normal' characteristics of a social category, such as those of disabled or LGB are mostly negative, this can be a desirable practice; an issue which will be returned too later. However, while some invisible impairments and an individual's sexuality need only be disclosed in certain circumstances and can be hidden at other times, some impairments, among other social variables, cannot. It is still open to debate to what extent people choose to decorate their bodies to their own tastes and to what extent they feel forced to do so (Baker 1984), but it is undeniable that:

Disabled men and women are encouraged by media representations of 'normal' bodies to obscure by dress and bodily decoration what are seen by others as bodily inadequacies. (Butler 1998: 86)

Their inability to do so on occasions means that many individuals have no alternative but to pay the price of obvious membership of the disabled population. Negative connotations of incompetence, dependence and asexuality, among other factors can create their own difficulties for an individual. For example:

Sexual confidence is so centrally about beauty, potency and independence that disabled women and men feel undermined. (Shakespeare 1996: 193)

What is more the negative images associated with marginalized groups such as those of disabled people and LGBs can play a damaging role in people's recognition of their identity and comfort with it. The 'norms' expected of a category of people can be alien to an individual's own experiences, or ones which they wish to distance themselves from. As a result they can cause them to fail to recognize their alliance with others who may in reality be able to sympathize with and support them (Jenness 1992).

These broad and wide ranging implications of both social and category level 'norms' are being increasingly widely researched, but such work still focuses mostly on a single variable at any one time and presumes it to be dominant in an individual's life. What still remains under-researched, even in the light of postmodern theory, is the impact of an individual's membership of more than one category and how those categories interrelationships impacts on their lives.

The gay community is, like society as a whole, predominantly able bodied. The sexual and emotional acts which are seen by society as defining its membership are equally seen as able bodied acts, by both other LGBs and more distant onlookers. These ableist assumptions can impact heavily on disabled LGBs lives.

The false promises of the gay 'scene'

Fears of marginalization, due to a lack of conformity with society 'norms', mean that the need to know that one is not alone in one's circumstances is important for any individual. This is a feeling recognized by Polio (1994) who recalls her efforts as an isolated, lesbian, disabled mother to contact others who might be in a similar position for support. Having places where LGBs can be open about their sexuality and enjoy the company of others with similar experiences is of great importance (Bell 1991). The gay 'scene' can offer space to meet for support, companionship, to form relationships and to build a personal identity (Valentine 1993a). The 'scene' is particularly important to, and indeed dominated by, younger individuals who have not yet built up broader support and friendship networks. The lack of such spaces has been recognized as a problem facing LGBs in isolated rural areas (D'Augelli and Hart 1987, Bell and Valentine 1995b). It is true that many LGBs upon recognizing their sexuality suffer from loneliness and depression as isolated individuals outside the gay 'scene' (Valentine 1993a). There is a high attempted suicide rate among young people who have identified themselves as homosexual, but do not have the relevant knowledge or support to be able to deal with it (Valentine 1995). It should equally be noted that problems of low income and discrimination in the housing market for some LGBs (as well as disabled people (Barnes 1991)) mean that the probability of home ownership and access to private space in which to express themselves is reduced (Bell 1991).

However, while its value should not be underestimated in this way, it should nevertheless be acknowledged that the support the gay 'scene' can offer to LGBs is limited, as these spaces only allow them to express their sexuality under the gaze of a dominant able bodied majority and within their particular expectations of their category's 'norms' of behaviour and appearance. Valentine (1993a) suggests that experiences of homophobia unites individuals across class, age and other social divisions, as mutual support fosters a sense of 'community'. All social backgrounds frequent the gay 'scene' it is argued, resulting in broad friendship groups, supportive of each others' common experiences. Whether the 'scene' is quite so tolerant in reality is questionable. It must in particular, be asked whether this 'united community' is inclusive of disability.

Expressions of ableism

There have been many similarities between the oppression faced by disabled people, regardless of sexuality, and LGBs, regardless of corporeality. For example, both populations have been discriminated against on the basis of 'medical diagnosis'[5] and both couples with disabled members and same sex couples are met with social disapproval (Shakespeare 1996). In recent years the issues of HIV and AIDS have arguably increased the potential convergence of disability and gay politics (Hearn 1991, Corbett 1994). Yet the 'gay scene' is not as understanding as may be expected (Corbett 1994). While safe sex and the raising of funds for AIDS charities have relatively high profiles, access to gay venues for people with AIDS showing visible impairments is heavily restricted (Shakespeare 1996). The common experiences and needs of people with HIV/AIDS and people with other disabilities have not been recognized. HIV/AIDS is both a disability issue (Shakespeare 1994a, Campbell 1995) and a gay issue which could potentially unite the two overlapping 'communities' in their common struggles over oppression. There is little evidence to date to suggest that this is the case.

Strong foci in the gay men's 'community', as alluded to in the opening paragraph of this chapter, are the 'body beautiful', glamour, dancing and recreational drugs in which it is not always possible or desirable for disabled people to participate (Corbett 1994, Shakespeare 1996). Participants in Shakespeare's (1996; 201) research into disabled people's sexuality also reported a growing 'body fetishism' in the lesbian 'community'. It is acknowledged that many lesbians have chosen to challenge the social pressures for women to conform to male requirements of female bodily presentation, but it is equally noted that they can pay heavily for doing so. It is hard for anyone to meet the narrow ideals of physical beauty which exist in Western culture, yet the cost of marginalization for those who deviate too far from the dream is as high in the gay 'community' as elsewhere (Shakespeare 1996).

'Ugliness' and 'deviance' are often seen as 'normal' for the category of disabled people. Treated as a single, homogenous group in spite of their varying circumstances in terms of both their individual impairments and their social, economic and political circumstances there is a common assumption that disabled people are asexual (Greengross 1976, Oliver 1983, Morris 1989, 1991, Corbett 1994, Shakespeare 1996, Shakespeare *et al.* 1996). It is an idea which the media establishment has been both influenced by and helped to reinforce (Shakespeare 1996). At times, images of sexual expression by disabled people have consciously been censored from public gaze. A case in hand was the attempted censorship by Westminster Council of the film *Crash*. Among the reasons for their desire to withdraw the film was a love scene involving a disabled woman (Norman 1996).

Fears of hereditary disease and images of incapable, weak and generally undesirable impaired bodies, make disability and asexuality seem synonymous in ableist, hetero-patriarchal society. The idea of disabled people as sexual beings is generally a source of either horror or amusement (Greengross 1976). Despite long-running telephone sex lines and more recently the development of cyber sex, sexual activity is still seen as a very physical, embodied experience which 'deviant' bodies cannot participate in satisfactorily. Homosexual activity has equally been questioned on the basis of physiology due to homosexual couples lacking the ability to have 'intercourse', in heterosexual terms and hence, what is considered a meaningful relationship. This arguably suggests more about heterosexual and/or able bodied people's fears of inadequacy than it does about disabled LGBs' assumed inabilities. It may be expected, as with the AIDS issue, that LGBs may be more understanding, in this case, of disabled people's sexual needs and desires. However, ableist views exist in both gay and heterosexual space and the pressures on disabled people to conform to the asexual role expected of them persist.

Underlining this, as a disabled lesbian, Field (1993: 18) notes that she and others are sometimes 'not "invited" to be part of our own gay community'. She suggests that other LGBs often assume disabled LGBs do not exist and can certainly not conceive of having a relationship with such individuals. When disability is recognized it is often treated with the same patronizing and humiliating tone that is common throughout Western society, according to the 'norms' expected of disabled people. A letter to *The Pink Paper* (Staples, 1996: 10) highlights this point.

> I am collecting used postcards and used postage stamps in aid of the Guide Dogs for the Blind Association. This would go towards helping gay and lesbian blind people *who have very little in life* [emphasis added].

Crossing the divide and entering gay space involves a recognition of identity and can be a big step for any individual (Valentine 1993a). If the welcome is less than supportive due to ableism the experience can be all the more traumatic. Shakespeare *et al.* (1996) list many examples of ableism in the gay 'scene' collated from their interviews with disabled people. Examples involved: a man with a learning disability, wearing a gay rights T-shirt, being questioned as to whether he realized he was entering a gay bar; security staff at gay clubs repeatedly making excuses on the grounds of 'safety' for a disabled person to be barred from entering; people repeatedly being patronized or used as a tokenistic disabled friend at parties.

Invisible impairments may at first be considered less problematic, but false assumptions about the 'norms' of 'ability' can lead to further misunderstandings and marginalization. For example, if an impairment is revealed in an intimate social interaction the individual often suffers rejection and is aware of a rapid withdrawal by formerly interested parties (Shakespeare *et al.* 1996). Simple problems of an assumed understanding of communication through body language can cause a disabled person difficulties. The inability to make eye contact or stand up with ease can mean that finding a partner is no easy feat.

> Disabled people may . . . find it difficult to initiate contacts in pubs or at parties. To take the initiative and take a seat close to someone who is attractive may be very difficult for someone in a wheelchair, and for visually impaired people it may be impossible. (Oliver 1983: 72)

The inability to respond to another's body language when they 'take the initiative' may appear rude or give inaccurate suggestions that the individual is not interested. These are problems which disabled LGBs are aware of and which can make them feel as uncomfortable and isolated in gay space as many LGBs do in heterosexual space. This does not, however, mean that access to gay spaces are not still of great potential value.

Access to the 'scene'

The impact of the 'norms' expected of disabled bodies affect not only the social structures and hence reactions disabled LGBs receive from other LGBs directly, but also the more tangible infrastructures of the gay 'scene'. As with all areas of life the movements of disabled people in the gay 'scene' are often limited by the physical structuring of the built environment (Field 1993, Shakespeare *et al.* 1996). Shakespeare (1996: 199) suggests that at venues 'where sex is on the agenda', the assumed asexuality of disabled people as well as the repulsion of any idea of them as sexual beings, results in the failure to plan for disabled access to such spaces. This can be a self-perpetuating circumstance as inaccessible environments reduce the visibility of disabled people still further and any apparent need for the financial outlay to improve the situation.

While it may be one of the most obvious, planning and building design are not the only ways in which the structure of the environment causes disabled LGBs problems. Due to the pressures of conformity and normalization, 'in Britain, it is possible to be gay (only) in specific places and spaces', as discussed above (Bristow 1989: 749). Availability of information in order to access such spaces is vital, but requires the possession of social and cultural, as well as material, capital. The importance of 'passing' to avoid homophobic abuse makes the ability to conceal one's sexuality a desirable skill. Flexibility in an individual's sexual image is advantageous at different times and in different places (Valentine 1993b). As a result, the ability to identify a homosexual individual in heterosexual space is not often an easy task (Valentine 1993a). 'Dyke spotting' is an acquired skill (Munt 1995). Learning to recognize the clues takes time for someone new to the 'community'. There are subtleties of dress which are employed to produce mutual recognition. Knowing looks, eye contact and other body language between LGBs, and subtleties of architecture, layout and decor in gay pubs and clubs all help to keep the 'scene' secret from the heterosexual world (Weightman 1980, Bell 1991). They need not be discussed in great depth here. Suffice to say that they exist, but that their significance relies heavily on an understanding of their visual symbolism and, therefore, the ability to see. Equally the ability to express them relies on bodily control.

Word of mouth is another important way in to the gay 'scene' (Bell 1991, Valentine 1993a). Subtle references to homosexuality may be dropped into conversation to test others reactions in an attempt to make contact with other LGBs in heterosexual space (Valentine 1993a). However, a prior knowledge of the significance of given venues' names and other topics of conversation, as well as the ability to hear or lip read, are of great importance. It quickly becomes apparent how impaired individuals can be left isolated from such information sources and their rewards. Switchboards and support centers are also an important means of access to the gay scene. Bell and Valentine (1995b) point out the importance of anonymous, accessible telephone services in the development of support networks between isolated individuals in rural communities. These services in urban areas are likewise of value. The gay press is also of significance (Bell 1991). Advertisements for clubs, events or in the personal columns all have their obvious purpose if an individual has access to the relevant literature, television and radio outlets. However, these services often fail to cater for the needs of disabled people, particularly those with sensory impairments.

As with planning issues, the invisibility of the disabled LGB population reinforces the lack of information in a suitable format for them. More publications in Braille and on tape for visually impaired individuals and more minicom systems on telephone helplines for deaf

234 The Moral and Medical Regulation of Sex, Sexualities and Gender

individuals are just two examples of what is needed. The lack of resources in the form of newspapers, books and other literature for isolated rural LGBs (Bell and Valentine 1995b) mirrors the lack of information available to disabled people and limits the awareness of social and political advances among both populations. As Bell (1991) notes, gay bars and clubs open and close with high frequency and low profiles; up-to-date information about their whereabouts is essential for access.

It should of course be recognized at this point that it is not only ableism within the gay 'community' that creates these restrictions on disabled LGBs lives. Homophobia in the disabled community, as well as both ableism and homophobia in society in general, all play their parts. For example, at a national level the situation has been exacerbated by Section 28 of the Local Government Act restricting the promotion of homosexuality. At a more micro-level, a major problem in the lives of disabled LGBs is that a third party is often needed to gain access to information, people and places. As Shakespeare (1996) points out, 'professionals' may be prejudiced and insensitive over service provisions. So called 'professional' care workers, as well as parents and guardians, are as susceptible to homophobia and ableist attitudes towards disabled people's sexuality as any other member of society. To find personal assistants willing to support an individual in their desired lifestyle, especially if intimate assistance is needed before sex, is no easy task (Shakespeare 1996). The essential role played by 'matriarchal', 'network brokers' in lesbian friendship networks (Valentine 1993a) equally relies on them being open to the idea of disabled people as sexual beings. The individual's rights to recognize and express their sexual identity are often denied.

Over protective parents and close family members often cause the most serious problem of invaded privacy and restricted freedom of expression for disabled people.

> Parents of disabled youngsters are sometimes over protective and reluctant to allow their children to take the usual teenage risks. Furthermore, disabled teenagers may find it difficult to do things that perhaps they should not (when they go out they probably have to be transported by their parents). They therefore can't lie to their parents about where they have been or who they have been with. (Oliver 1983: 72)

This is a problem for heterosexual disabled youths, but homophobia among parents and carers adds another dimension to the difficulties of

LGB disabled youths. LGBs with AIDS returning to the family home in rural areas may have to face the homophobia that caused them to move to the anonymity of the city in the first place (Bell and Valentine 1995b). Carers, especially in cases of severe and or mental impairments, can control who the disabled person has contact with, at times restricting the access of long-term partners (Shakespeare *et al.* 1996). Coming out of genuine concern, carers' intentions in this way may be good, however, they are often misguided by the pressures they feel to introduce the same practices of compliance with social 'norms' in the lives of those they care for as they do in their own. The restrictions these actions bring with them mean that their love can be suffocating.

Strategies of resistance to categorization

While acknowledging the difficulties ableism, impairments and homophobia can cause, it is not the intention of this chapter to paint a picture of doom and despair. It should be noted that both the society and category level 'norms' expected of people and which they may strive to attain are not constant, but are rather 'constructed and reconstructed over time and space' (Valentine 1993b: 239). Peoples ideas of what is 'normal' and acceptable change as they interact with others from different social categories and exposure to various media outlets. Change may be slow, but it can be positive.

It should be noted that most interviewees in Shakespeare's (1996) study of disabled people's sexuality accept their appearance and feel positive about their looks most of the time. Feminists' work on women's issues has drawn attention to their circumstances and aided their struggle to change those circumstances. Much disability research, however, even working within a feminist framework, has not empowered the disabled population in the same way, but passively illuminated a sorry state of affairs (Morris 1996). This is not the aim of this chapter. It would be inaccurate and politically dangerous to suggest that disabled people are either helpless or unresourceful. It must equally be remembered that a degree of initiative is needed by any individual attempting to access the gay 'scene' (Valentine 1993a). Fear of homophobic abuse, a lack of knowledge about or dislike for a venue, or restricted access in terms of transport can put limitations on any LGBs freedom of expression (Valentine 1993a). Disability must not be accepted automatically as either the sole or dominant cause of an individual's problems. It is not productive to consider being gay and disabled – a 'double disadvantage' – as one does not inevitably and continually compound the experiences, negative or positive, of the other. However, the images disabled LGBs and others have of them do have to be addressed. To cope with social interactions, the expectations others have of them and in turn their views of themselves, as discussed above, it is necessary either for them to put on an act accepting their expected role in society or publicly fight the expectations others have of them. Whatever their decision tensions will occur. It is difficult in homophobic, ableist space for a disabled LGB to display their true sexual and physical identity at any given time. The more commonly practised act of 'passing', equally comes at a price.

The negative stigmatism and marginalized status of the categories of LGBs, and the homophobic abuse which can occur, can result in individuals attempting to hide their identity and 'pass' as more socially 'normal', heterosexual, in spaces outside the security of the gay scene or behind the closed doors of the lesbian or gay household (Egerton 1990, Valentine 1993a, 1993b, Bell *et al.* 1994, Bell and Valentine 1995b, Johnston and Valentine 1995). The negative images of weakness, stupidity, incompetence and dependence linked to the category of disability means the act of 'passing' has also been recognized by disabled people, regardless of their sexual orientation. Corbett (1994: 344) writes: '. . . closeted gays pay too high a psychological price for passing', a contention that Abberley (1987) and Morris (1991) apply to disabled people. 'While there may be little truth in others' assumptions about disabled LGBs, they can strongly affect their public identity, marginalized position in society and when internalized their self image' (Shakespeare 1996). 'Stigma, once established, is perpetuated and fuelled by internal oppression' (Corbett 1994: 345). To deny the existence of a person's sexuality restricts their ability to explore their identity and express themselves fully as already stated (Morris 1989). However, 'passing' as able bodied, can allow some individuals to express their sexual desires and still be taken as 'normal' at least some of the time, in gay space. For LGBs who cannot hide their impairments, the 'norms' expected of the category of disabled people can have their advantages. For example, few people will think twice about an individual carrying a white stick taking hold of the arm of a person of the same gender. One interviewee in Morris' (1989) survey of women's experiences of paralysis notes how the assumption of asexuality placed upon her has removed the pressure on her to marry, take the role of a wife and mother and made it easier for her to live her life as a lesbian.

On a further beneficial note Shakespeare (1996) notes how sexual relationships involving a disabled person can put less pressure on both parties to 'perform'. He suggests that with the need to experiment, the emphasis can be moved away from Western society's obsessions with penetration and on to other parts of the body, the sense of touch and so on. As well as offering 'safe' sex this in turn results in a more equal power balance in the relationship. The nature of their impairment may mean disabled people have to take more responsibility for their sexuality and articulate what they want and need more effectively, thus leading to a better sexual relationship. It is possible to argue that disabled people may be more attuned to their bodies and feelings than able bodied individuals.

Despite these positive factors for some there are times when complying to others 'norms' of behaviour and appearance is unacceptable and they choose to fight the images and expectations of them in a stronger manner, most obviously by attending pride festivals, proudly declaring their identities as 'Queer Crips'. A growing literature on disability and homosexuality of both an academic and more accessible nature equally has its political purpose (see for example Polio 1994, O'Toole 1996, Shakespeare *et al.* 1996, Tremain 1996). This type of more direct action has started to promote new images of disabled LGBs. They challenge both their categories marginalization from society 'norms' and the more specific and narrow range of characteristics considered as their category 'norms' with which they are stigmatized. It has begun to draw the gay community's attention to the realities of disability. Role models are beginning to appear for other disabled LGBs. Such actions play their part in social education, integration and changing attitudes, offering hope to both disabled people and able bodied partners who, it should not be forgotten, also bear the stigma of disability, as they are often depicted as gold diggers, saints, insecure, inadequate individuals, or quite simply desperate (Morris 1989, 1991).

The problems facing disabled LGBs are being eased by general improvements in telecommunication, email, gay helplines and mainstream media services for the LGB population as a whole. It is equally true that like-minded disabled people are learning to help themselves. Organizations such as GEMMA (a disabled lesbians organization), REGARD (a disabled lesbian and gay group), VIGG (the Visually Impaired Gay Group) and LANGUID (Lesbians And Gays United In Disability) have been established to offer support and help between disabled LGBs. It should be noted that these support services are predominantly London based at present, but that their size, numbers and geographical dispersion are increasing. There is still, arguably, a lack of recognition of the differing experiences and needs of individuals with different impairments, social, economic and political circumstances, but disabled LGBs are, like other minorities before them, beginning to recognize their oppression and learning to fight back. The nature and implications of that fight back are the issues to which researchers and activists alike must now turn their attentions.

Conclusions: a different future?

> Work must move away from emphasis on select 'gay Mecca', and researchers should be aware that findings are not fully transferable across space, time, gender, lifestyle. The 'gay community' must thus be seen in its full diversity, with studies focusing on single groups, or on certain spaces: there are different gay geographies of living, working and relaxing. (Bell 1991: 328)

These words are equally true of the disabled population, ethnic minorities, members of religious orders and a host of other populations. As outlined in this chapter, literature has recognized how society functions around a series of 'norms', related first to the society as a whole and second to individual categories within it. However, in much past research each category has been considered to be mutually exclusive from all others. Research on the gay community, for example, has failed to recognize its disabled members and vice versa. Future research may possibly show that society level 'norms' encourage categories of people to distance themselves from others which they feel more marginal than their own, in some kind of struggle for acceptance. Whatever the causes, however, the costs of the discrimination that members of more than one category can face can be dear. The lack of recognition of diversity within a single category and the silencing of voices from debate limits our understanding of society and the effectiveness of the social policies that are sought and introduced. The limited provision of services for disabled LGBs discussed above are mirrored for other members of mixed minorities, such as black LGBs or black disabled people.

   The significance of, and value associated with a united front within a particular category of people has been connected to a belief in political strength in numbers and the old adage that 'together we stand, divided we fall'. While essentialists and constructionists may disagree as to whether biological characteristics have any inherent meanings in an individuals' embodied experiences, what remains common to both arguments is their support of a single unified identity of any particular oppressed population. Recognition of differences within and between the disabled and LGB populations has resulted in the proposal of policies of strategic essentialism (Gibson-Graham 1996). While recognizing that one would ideally want to challenge simplistic dichotomies, Barrett (1991: 166) argues that 'political silencing can follow from rejecting these categories altogether'; division and the loss of a group identity is apparently too costly. However, the difficulties facing disabled LGBs illustrated in this chapter make clear that until difference is recognized the range of needs and services required to meet their and other marginalized groups' needs will not be acknowledged or provided. The pain of marginalization and exclusion will continue to be reality for LGB disabled people in the LGB and disabled 'communities', but does this need to be the future they face?

A Foucauldian perspective suggests that power is everywhere inscribed. From this standpoint Gibson-Graham (1996) argues that all work has a theoretical and political stance, or entry point. One is not less political because it promotes difference. The politics of group identity is not the only viable political form. The modernist concept that knowledge and theory are separate and prior to change, and politics must surely be a fallacy as knowledge and its production is in itself a political process. There is no single knowledge which everyone sees and agrees with, a single political aim for change. Difference in this context is a political weapon which will be used either for or against social movements. Failure to recognize individual experiences as needs will itself result in division and disunity. Members of the populations that political voices seek to represent feel misrepresented, if represented at all, and more distant observers, whom the movements seek to influence, will be aware of its short falls from personal observation. What is more, if implemented the policies they strive for will be of little use to those at the grassroots level, whose needs have been ignored, but will delay the passing of further more practical legislation. If the roots of discrimination are ever to be fully understood and met with practical solutions, the future must surely be one of difference.

Acknowledgements

I would like to thank Hester Parr, an anonymous referee, and, especially Gill Valentine, for their helpful and thoughtful comments on earlier drafts of this chapter. Thanks also to Kathryn Backett-Milburn for her patience with my disregard for deadlines.

Notes

1. The following definitions of disability and impairment will be used through-out this paper. Impairment: lacking all or part of a limb, or having a defec-tive limb, organism or mechanism of the body. Disability: the disadvantage or restriction of activity caused by a contemporary social organization which takes no or little account of people who have physical [or mental] impair-ments and thus exclude them from the mainstream of social activities (UPIAS 1976).
2. It is acknowledged that the term 'community' is one of the most elusive and vague terms in the social sciences. It has many different meanings to many different individuals. In this paper I use it loosely to refer to the population of lesbians, gay men and bisexual individuals (LGBs) who have a broad sym-pathetic association, living not necessarily in the same area.
3. LGBs is used throughout this paper as an abbreviation for lesbian, gay men and bisexual individuals, due to the limited space available. However, it is stressed that these people are individuals and not a homogeneic unit as the abbreviation may regretfully infer.
4. The term 'scene' is used to refer to spaces and places (physical or other spaces of communication, such as cyber space) where LGBs can be out and express their sexuality freely, for example gay pubs and clubs, homosexual house-holds, support groups, helplines and so on.
5. Homosexuality has, like disability, been considered by some to be a medical condition rather than a social label. Some believe that there is a gay gene, others that it is a psychiatric condition. Many individuals have been forced to endure electric shock treatments and/or psychiatric counselling after the referral and/or diagnosis of their 'conditions' by medical practitioners.

Bibliography

ABBERELY, P. (1987) 'The concept of oppression and the development of a social theory of disability', *Disaility, Handicap and Society* 2:5–20.
BAKER, N.C. (1984) *The Beauty Trap.* London: Piatkus.
BARNES, C. (1991) *Disabled People in Britain and Discrimination.* London: Hurst.
BARRETT, M. (1991) *The Politics of Truth: From Marx to Foucault.* Cambridge: Polity Press.
BELL, D. (1991) 'Insignificant others: lesbian and gay geographies', *Area* 23:323–9.
BELL, D. and G. VALENTINE (eds) (1995a) *Mapping Desire: Geographies of Sexualities.* London: Routledge.
BELL, D. and G. VALENTINE (eds) (1995b) 'Queer country: rural lesbian and gay lives', *Journal of Rural Studies* 11, 2:113–22.
BELL, D., J. BINNIE, J. CREAM and G. VALENTINE (1994) 'All hyped up and no place to go', *Gender, Place and Culture* 1:31–47.
BRISTOW, J. (1989) 'Being gay: politics, identity, pleasure', *New Formations* 9:61–81.
BUTLER, R. (1998) 'Rehabilitating the images of disabled youths', in T. Skelton and G. Valentine (eds) *Cool Places: geographies of youth culture.* London: Routledge.

BUTLER, R. and S. BOWLBY (1997) 'Bodies and spaces: an exploration of disabled people's use of public space.' *Environment and Planning D: Society and Space.* 15(4):411–33.

CAMPBELL, J. (1995) 'Disabled People International', in *UK Coalition of People Living with HIV and AIDS newsletter.* 7th edn.

CORBETT, J. (1994) 'A proud label: exploring the relationship between disability politics and gay pride', *Disability and Society.* 9, 3:343–57.

D'AUGELLI, A. and M. HART (1987) 'Gay women, men and families in rural settings: toward the development of helping communities', *American Journal of Community Psychology* 15:79–93.

Disability Now (1995) 'Why should I be proud of my disability?' June:26.

EGERTON, J. (1990) 'Out but not down: lesbians' experiences of housing', *Feminist Review* 36:75–88.

FIELD, J. (1993) 'Coming out of two closets', *Canadian Woman Studies* 13, 4:18–19.

FINGER, A. (1992) 'Forbidden Fruit', *New Internationalist.* 233:8–10.

FOUCAULT, M. (1977) *Discipline and Punish.* London: Allen Lane.

GIBSON-GRAHAM, J.K. (1996) 'Reflections on postmodern feminist social research', in N. Duncan (ed.) *Body Space.* London, Routledge.

GOFFMAN, E. (1963) *Stigma.* Englewood Cliffs, NJ: Prentice Hall.

GREENGROSS, W. (1976) *Entitled to love: the sexual and emotional needs of the handicapped.* London: Malaby Press.

HEARN, K. (1991) 'Disabled lesbians and gays are here to stay!', in T. Kaufmann and P. Lincoln (eds) *High risk lives.* Bridport: Prism Press.

JENNESS, V. (1992) 'Coming out: lesbian identities and the categorization problem', in K. Plummer (ed.) *Modern homosexualities: fragments of lesbian and gay experience.* London: Routledge.

JOHNSTON, L. and G. VALENTINE (1995) 'Wherever I lay my girlfriend, that's my home: the performance and surveillance of lesbian identities in domestic environments', in D. Bell and G. Valentine (eds) *Mapping Desire: Geographies of sexualities.* London: Routledge.

MCDOWELL, L. (1995) 'Body work: heterosexual gender performances in city workplaces', in D. Bell and G. Valentine (eds) *Mapping Desire: Geographies of sexualities.* London: Routledge.

MORRIS, J. (ed.) (1989) *Able lives.* London: The Women's Press.

MORRIS, J. (ed.) (1991) *Pride against prejudice.* London: The Women's Press.

MORRIS, J. (ed.) (1996) *Encounters with strangers: feminism and disability.* London: The Women's Press.

MUNT, S. (1995) 'The lesbian Flâneur', in D. Bell and G. Valentine (eds) *Mapping desire: geographies of sexualities.* London: Routledge.

NORMAN, L. (1996) 'We have sex too', *Guardian. The Week.* 30 November: 6.

OLIVER, M. (1983) *Social Work with Disabled People,* London: Macmillan Press – now Palgrave.

O'TOOLE, C.J. (1996) 'Disabled lesbians: challenging monocultural constructs' *Sexuality and Disability.*, 14, 3:221–36.

POLIO, S. (1994) 'Being Sam's mum', in L. Keith (ed.) *Mustn't Grumble.* London: The Women's Press.

SHAKESPEARE, T. (1994a) 'Disabled by prejudice', *The Pink Paper.* 1 April:13.

SHAKESPEARE, T. (1994b) 'Cultural representations of disabled people: dustbins for disavowal' *Disability and Society*, 9, 3:249–66.

SHAKESPEARE, T. (1996) 'Power and prejudice: issues of gender, sexuality and disability,' in L. Barton (ed.) *Disability and society: emerging issues and insights*, Harlow: Longman.

SHAKESPEARE, T., K. GILLESPIE-SELLS and D. DAVIES (1996) *The sexual politics of disability*. London: Cassell.

SIBLEY, D. (1995) *Geographies of Exclusion*. London: Routledge.

STAPLES, D. (1996) 'Helping hand for the blind', *The Pink Paper* 17 May:10.

TREMAIN, S. (1996) *Pushing the limits: disabled dykes produce culture*. Toronto: Women's Press.

UPIAS (1976) *Fundamental Principles of Disability*. London: Union of the Physically Impaired Against Segregation.

VALENTINE, G. (1993a) 'Desperately seeking Susan: a geography of lesbian friendships', *Area*. 25, 2:109–16.

VALENTINE, G. (1993b) 'Negotiating and managing multiple sexual identities: lesbian time-space strategies', *Transactions of the Institute of British Geographers*. 18:237–48.

VALENTINE, G. (1995) 'Out and about: geographies of lesbian landscapes' *International Journal of Urban and Regional Research*. 19, 1:96–111.

WEIGHTMAN, B.A. (1980) 'Gay bars as private places', *Landscape*. 24:9–16.

YOUNG, I.M. (1990) 'Throwing like a girl: a phenomenology of feminine body comportment, motility and spatiality' in *Throwing Like a Girl and other essays in Feminist Philosophy and Social Theory*. Bloomington: University of Indiana Press.

Index

244   *Index*